MOTHER PIOUS LADY

One of India's best-known social commentators and advertising and marketing professionals, Santosh Desai is a columnist with several prominent publications. He writes extensively on media, popular culture, consumer markets and everyday life. He heads Future Brands, a branding services and consulting company, and was earlier the president of McCann Erickson India. Desai is a graduate in economics, and a postgraduate in management from the Indian Institute of Management, Ahmedabad.

Praise for Mother Pious Lady

Reviews

'Desai is a brilliant commentator... For all its laughter and its sense of detachment, it is a book that cares... one of the outstanding books of the year...'

—Shiv Visvanathan, *Mail Today*

'The pieces are... thoughtfully written and cut to the very core of our existence as Indians... a must-read...'

—*Deccan Herald*

'*Mother Pious Lady*... does not have the arrogance of a single view, and to that extent, comes closest to the idea of India.'

—*Ahmedabad Mirror*

'Santosh Desai's book... is like India's much-loved pickle — so much of stimulating analysis packed in a few hundred pages.'

—*Bangalore Mirror*

'Desai is the nearest thing to a R.K. Laxman in prose – a chronicler of middle-class India.'

—Raja Menon, *Outlook*

'If you want to get a fresh perspective on India through the familiar, this is the book for you. Once you get engaged, it's hard to put down.'

—*Business Today*

'Desai's annotations are in the best tradition of cultural studies – he has an eye for rich details, the smarts to get beyond the obvious and a heart more inclined to empathy than scorn.'

—*Financial Express*

Advance praise

'This is a rare and captivating book, wise and witty, on the inner lives of middle class Indians. Desai both enlightens and entertains through his insight, elegant writing and disarming humour.'

—Sudhir Kakar, psychoanalyst

'Delicious and full of brilliant and insightful observations. This is a fine and enjoyable study of the Indian middle class!'

—Nandan Nilekani, chairman, Unique Identification Authority of India and former CEO and MD of Infosys

'Santosh Desai writes with wit and wisdom – a rare combination. He shines the torch on ourselves, making us laugh, agonize and shudder, but all with a delightfully light touch. It is remarkable how Desai is able to draw profundity from the simplest everyday observation. This is surely a gift.'

—Dipankar Gupta, sociologist

'This book puts together the seemingly insignificant details that collectively help explain the enigma called India, in a manner that only Santosh Desai could. His observations and insights are erudite, entertaining and magically real. This book is total paisa vasool and much more.'

—Kishore Biyani, Group CEO, Future Group

'This book is charming, thorough, funny and thoughtful. No aspect of new India's popular culture escapes its scrutiny. It isn't just for newcomers to India, but also for all Indians who want to make sense of the bewildering sea of change that we are in the middle of.'

—Rama Bijapurkar, author of *We Are Like That Only – Understanding the Logic of Consumer India*

MOTHER PIOUS LADY

Making Sense *of* Everyday India

SANTOSH DESAI

HarperCollins Publishers India

a joint venture with

New Delhi

First published in India in 2010 by
HarperCollins *Publishers* India
a joint venture with
The India Today Group

Copyright © Santosh Desai 2010

ISBN: 978-81-7223-864-3

6 8 10 9 7

Santosh Desai asserts the moral right to be identified
as the author of this book.

Grateful acknowledgement is made to the *Times of India*,
where most of the material first appeared, albeit in a different form.

HarperCollins *Publishers*
A-53, Sector 57, NOIDA, Uttar Pradesh – 201301, India
77-85 Fulham Palace Road, London W6 8JB, United Kingdom
Hazelton Lanes, 55 Avenue Road, Suite 2900, Toronto, Ontario M5R 3L2
and 1995 Markham Road, Scarborough, Ontario M1B 5M8, Canada
25 Ryde Road, Pymble, Sydney, NSW 2073, Australia
31 View Road, Glenfield, Auckland 10, New Zealand
10 East 53rd Street, New York NY 10022, USA

Typeset in 10.5/15 Sabon
Jojy Philip New Delhi 110 015

Printed and bound at
Thomson Press (India) Ltd.

In memory of my mother, Japasvini Ramesh Desai.

To my father, Ramesh Narendrarai Desai, who is the source of it all.

CONTENTS

Contents

SECTION THREE
DILEMMAS OF CHANGE

ACKNOWLEDGEMENTS

This book has grown out of the various bits of writing I have done, most notably the weekly column that I write for the *Times of India*. In my column, *City City Bang Bang*, I look at everyday life and write about what it says about who we are as a people.

I would not have been writing at all but for Vikram Doctor of the *Economic Times*, who heard me speak at a seminar and suggested I write an occasional column documenting cultural changes in India for the *Brand Equity* supplement of the paper. *City City Bang Bang* came about thanks to the belief that Rahul Kansal, now chief marketing officer at Bennett, Coleman & Company (publishers of the *Times of India*) and my boss on two occasions and frequent philosopher and guide, had in the usefulness of what I had to say. I must express my thanks to the *Times of India* for allowing me the use of the material that first appeared in its pages.

My gratitude to Rama Bijapurkar for early encouragement and frequent challenge, which have helped shape my world view. Thanks are due also to the entire Strategic Planning team at McCann Erickson, conversations with whom were very helpful. My gratitude in particular to Anirban Mukherjee, Arvind Mohan and Ameen Haque for many stimulating discussions. The book has been designed by the supremely talented Naved Akhtar and his tireless team at Shop Advertising, for which I am deeply grateful.

For the last couple of years, I have been fortunate enough to have interacted with Kishore Biyani at close quarters and his ability to think about India without any preconceived notions has been revelatory.

I need to acknowledge the input of those who have influenced me through their writing. And while they are in no way responsible for the shortcomings that might be present in my use of their work, it has helped shape my world view and hence this book. The writings of Sudhir Kakar, Ashish Nandy, V. S. Naipaul, Arjun Appadurai, Veena Das, Dipankar Gupta, Satish Deshpande and Shiv Vishwanathan need to be mentioned in particular.

This book is the result of the untiring championship by Amit Agarwal of HarperCollins, who pushed me in his gently persuasive way for almost five years, and whose understated but penetrating comments have played a vital role in shaping the book that you hold in your hands.

To say that this book wouldn't have been possible without the help of my family is to say little. My father has been a constant source of encouragement and feedback. An accomplished writer himself, he thinks nothing of shooting off ten-page handwritten rejoinders to an 800-word submission of mine. My brother, Ashesh, went through an early draft and provided valuable perspective. I know I am not allowed to say anything embarrassing, but I have to mention my daughters, Pallavi and Ketaki, and my wife, Vibha. They know what they did.

INTRODUCTION

Everything in India is capitalized. Ours is without doubt the land of the swollen cliché. We live in Grinding Poverty with which we cope with a sense of Cosmic Fortitude. We are on Our Way to Reclaiming Our Rightful Position in the World but are frequently undone by our Slumdog status. People travel to India not to find a country but to find themselves. We are a Timeless Civilization and an Impatient Uncaged Tiger. India is the receptacle of all extremes and accommodates in its commodious canopy every adjective invented.

The India that I grew up in was all of these things, but it has always seemed to me that most things written about India have tended to focus on the extremes. We have either the India that decants its deep wisdom on unsuspecting passers-by in surprising ways, or we have the India that asks you to look inside its wretchedness to find some glimmer of a universal truth. We have also had enquiries into Middle Class India, but most of these have been efforts that look inside from a safe and indeed superior perch outside. These are critiques of the middle class by people who are both fascinated and deeply repelled by it.

My effort in this book has been to examine Middle India from within. I have grown up in a middle class family; my father worked as a civil engineer in a public sector company, an occupation that ensured that we travelled from town to town, arriving when there was nothing there and leaving as things began to get comfortable. I studied in nine schools in all, across seven towns, and went to college in three different places. To me, the essence of growing up as an Indian, if there is such an essence, is really in understanding what it takes to actually experience India in all its trivial everydayness.

What follows is an analysis of changing India as seen through its daily life. The truth about things is often locked in the smallest actions it engenders. It is what we do without conscious and deliberate thought; it is when we behave naturally and with reflex that we give away who we really are. We have been shaped by the small things that made up our past – the silly jokes that made us laugh, the knowing winks that we shared, the places we scratched and the footwear we left outside the door. The pleasure of the second ice gola, the white sheets reserved for the men of the family, the railway reservation form that could accommodate only six names at a time, the agony of knowing that it was the fifth song in *Chitrahaar*, the cool touch of mandir steps, the dolorous singing of Mukesh songs, the resoling of Bata shoes, ducking under a chain to enter a bank, getting photographed in Himachali costumes on Mall Road. What do all these things mean? How do they sit together in developing an Indian way, this not being the Grand Indian Way but the way that we lived India?

The symbols of yesterday are being replaced with a whole new range today. We have the remix song and Vegetable Manchurian; apartments with names like Ridgewood Greens and Chancellor Hills, designer bindis, reality bahus and nighties that are worn daylong, computer horoscopes and arranged love marriages. Modern India has its own artefacts that help us excavate the present even as it unfolds.

Instead of seeing these signs only as amusing and heart-warming symbols of middle class life, what if we were to discern the underlying pattern that they reveal? In doing so, we look at

India not as an abstract noun but as a verb. We look at what lies behind our doing the things we do.

The idea of this book is thus to piece together a story about changing middle class urban India through small fragments of its everyday life both yesterday and today. The result is a patchwork quilt of sorts where individual essays are knitted together to provide a larger picture which, while it holds together as a single piece, makes no bones about the fact that it is composed of little scraps of observations that have been sewn together. And since I am writing through the filter of my own experiences, the book carries with it in-built biases.

The book makes liberal use of the word 'we' when describing middle class India. Now, I am acutely aware that there are many Indias and that the diversity of India cannot be collapsed into a single undifferentiated 'we'. Instead of describing the Indian middle class as such, I have chosen to use the first person, because this book has been written from the inside

Understanding India is an occupation of considerable complexity. Especially today, when a new India is visibly emerging from within the folds of its many pasts. This new India needs to be seen with new eyes, free from the baggage of yesterday's characterizations. As it is, we live in a world of instant judgements. I am not here to criticize or commend a class or group. Indeed, I think that statements like 'the middle class needs to understand its responsibilities' or that the 'educated need to display more gender sensitivity' are the kind of utterly useless bromides we can do without. I am not here to change the world or, for that matter, offer a way in which India can make the next century its own. There are abler minds pursuing this question; my purpose here is to understand what is happening.

The book is organized in three sections – we begin our journey in the not-too-distant past in pre-liberalization India, moving then to examine the changes we see around us before posing some questions about the dilemmas of change. The chapters within each section are loosely arrayed around broad themes, the purpose being to provide some structure for the reader while leaving enough freedom for the book to be read in a non-linear fashion.

SECTION ONE

WHERE DO WE COME FROM?

CHAPTER 1

OUR *CHITRAHAAR* SELVES

The idea of the middle class, as the name suggests, is one sandwiched between other labels. To be part of the middle class in India was not really to be in the middle, for there were too many people at the bottom, but to be caught between competing goals. Middle class India negotiated ceaselessly with itself, other classes, the government, and above all, with circumstances. Balancing responsibility with indulgence, the need for external display and internal comfort, the family and self, anxieties and aspirations, desires and duties, self-respect and pragmatism, these were all quests of an unheroic, everyday kind that made the Indian middle class what it was. Coping with dignity in ways gainly and ungainly was its lot. Understanding the middle class calls for an understanding of these trivial negotiations that we have been carrying out.

THE DHANIA FACTOR

Paisa vasool. The ultimate Indian idea of good value; not to be confused with miserliness. Paisa vasool means that the purchased item is worth its price. It indicates a satisfaction in extracting every drop of consumption liquid from each paisa. When you wring the act of consumption dry, and leave no discernible residue, it is then that you feel the warm after-glow of paisa vasool. Consumption thus is not about the act of purchase, but instead about the use value of the object in question. It occurs over a period of time, the longer the better, and the nature of use often morphs into something quite unimagined at the time of purchase.

Our compulsive need to recycle things is a pointer to this need. Long before eco-trendism placed the idea of recycling on its current pedestal, the Indian has recycled. The first stage of recycling is in extending the life of any possession. So shoes were resoled, shirts recollared and disposable lighters refilled with a syringe. A common sight in smaller towns even today is a handkerchief worn to protect the collar, as is the ubiquitous 'purane kapdon ka doctor', who specializes in coaxing a few more years of life from a recalcitrant garment flagging in spirits. Extending the life of things meant acting proactively: most of us have grown up wearing clothes two sizes too large till 'we grew into them', and of course, all trousers had 'margins' that could accommodate the unreasonable growth young children were capable of.

Then, if one could not coax any life out of things, they were put to new, altogether more innovative uses. Old sarees were stitched into very comfortable quilts while old toothbrushes cajoled naadas through pyjamas.

Finally, of course, one could always sell one's old stuff to the raddiwallas who came to every doorstep every week. Selling raddi was an art form with the price, as well as getting the raddiwalla to weigh accurately, being high skills. Old clothes were – and still are – exchanged for utensils, with old Scotch bottles commanding a wholly explainable premium.

Given the stubborn residue of consumption utility in objects, which one couldn't quite exhaust, it is easy to see why throwing things away was – and still is for many of us – so difficult. Lift any mattress inside any home in India and you will see a proud collection of plastic bags lovingly gathered over a period of time. We hoard plastic spoons, grow plants in ice-cream tubs and buy insatiably large quantities of Pet jars in promotions. When we buy a TV set, we are actually buying a TV set, the shrink wrapping, the thermocole that it comes packed in, the outer carton and any miscellaneous clips or pins or plastic pouches that accompany it. And all these precious odds and ends lie tucked away in some forgotten corner waiting no doubt for that fateful day in 2058 when finding thermocole will be a matter of life and death.

Coping with scarcity meant that one needed to run a very tight ship. The household budget was minutely detailed, and every deviation recorded with a heart-stopping sense of foreboding. Indulgences needed to be planned; impulse was the biggest enemy that had to be kept at bay. In a larger sense, we feared our senses and their ability to lead us astray. Growing up in middle class India was an elaborate exercise in learning to detach action from one's senses. We did not eat ice cream because we felt like it, but on occasions when celebrations had been planned. We did not just buy new clothes but did so with ceremony at key festivals, ensuring that we stepped out in starchy, crackling finery.

Festivals were the safety valves in our otherwise restrained lives; they gave us sanction to experience little atolls of freedom.

Because spending was controlled so tightly, on the occasions that we did, we needed to get full value for the expense. A necessary skill for every housewife was – and continues to be even now – that of bargaining. For that ability is the most tangible way in which she converts her almost visceral need for value into everyday reality. Through hard bargaining, she ekes out value, rupee by rupee. (Husbands across the country have blanched at the effrontery while their wives begin their negotiations of something priced Rs 100 at Rs 10. Shopping with mothers and aunts was always a painful experience since for every plastic clip, a dozen shops would be scoured and about twice that many rounds of negotiations entered into.) This results in her unique ability to have saved up that crucial little while having tended to her family's needs with very little to start with. The skill lies in economizing on the right thing and displaying largesse on a few critical occasions.

The idea of 'paisa vasool' is not always about finding new ways to economize; it refers to the feeling of satiation at having extracted full value from a thing or service. So a good masala film, with the right mix of ingredients, is deemed a paisa vasool film. No one grudges the extravagant spending that we lavish on marriages for here the return on money is not economic but social. Families deny themselves the most basic pleasures for years but will spend ruinously on weddings in the family, often ending up in debt.

It can be argued that this picture is changing as middle class India moves towards greater affluence. While this is true to some extent, it is important to recognize that the mindset governing consumption is not changing all that much. Take the example of the way housewives buy vegetables. Regardless of whether she stays in an affluent neighbourhood or in crowded flats, she must get her dhania and hari mirch free. It has nothing to do with affordability; it is about sneaking in additional value to make the transaction fulfilling.

Eventually, getting the right value then becomes an issue of fairness: of being asked for the 'theek daam', of knowing that one has not been taken for a ride. And of feeling reassured that no consumption juice remains in the discarded object.

This ability to see utility in all its dimensions in any object and to not rest till every ounce of it is exhausted, has perhaps more to do with the ingrained cultural memory of scarcity, than with a real need for economy. Finally, it is not about how much we spend, but how 'vasool' is the paisa we have parted with.

THE GREAT INDIAN JOURNEY

Just a two-line postcard telling us you have reached safely – that's all' – how many of us have grown up with that urgent pleading directive every time we travelled away from home? This, in spite of a whole gaggle of relatives having been present to 'see you off' at an unearthly hour, waving goodbye till well after your train had crossed into the next state. Add to this the ritual of checking out an auspicious day, the teeka on the head, the genuflecting nod to all presiding deities, gods included, and you have a good picture of the extreme disquiet evoked by the very idea of travel; more precisely, the idea of leaving home.

The fear spilled over into the way we travelled. The double locking of the metal coffins we called luggage, the strings that held the beddings together, the compacted currency notes in the watchpocket of our trousers, the smug hiding of money in unlikely places in our bags, the plump diving into the blouse for the clasped money bag, the chain lock available on platforms, the stories of educated, well-dressed, 'people like us' who chat up the naive, only to make off with the luggage after drugging the food.

We counted the pieces of luggage innumerable times, managing each time to come up with a different number. Journeys were managed with the importance of war and the incompetence of politics. Men fretted and barked random orders of authority, women clucked, children wailed in a blur of scattered disorder. Relief disentangled itself slowly from the chaos as the train pulled out of the platform, the youngest males of the 'seers-off' stepping off the moving train last in a show of macho bravado.

As the journey progressed, the tightness slackened, the protective elbows guarding our seats softened, we surrendered to the culinary charms of various aunties, some of whom insisted on being called Mummy, and as always, We Adjusted. But we continued to count the bags periodically, looked suspiciously at newcomers and spent moments in ashen agony when Papa got down on platforms to fill up the water bottles.

Travelling was always an experience giddy with fear. Unused to tearing ourselves away from our larger selves, journeys made us aware of our solitary status as individuals. Travel made us alone even as we met strangers and experienced new sights, sounds and smells. We carried our identity in the many potlis we carried, aware at all times of the straying from our umbilical moorings. Our luggage was the tangible manifestation of our selves, our anchor in a sea of turbulent strangeness and we held it close to us at all times – the fear of loss being not of our possessions alone, but somehow of ourselves as we ventured out of the familiarity of home. Everything was personal, everything we carried belonged to one's cavernous, secret inner world. An involuntary oozing of one's cultural self manifested itself in these small bundles, in the parathas, papads and pickles we had to have, in the quaint accessories without which one's sense of self got violated.

The fear of separation from one's roots runs deep in our way of life. From the recurring motif of exile in our great epics, the tearful ritual of the daughter's bidaai, to the many renditions of the lost-and-found theme in our cinema, it is clear that the idea of being abandoned in an unfamiliar world is a central fear that we keep trying to deal with. Conversely, re-unions crackle with emotional electricity and the idea of becoming whole again after being fragmented is an intensely pleasurable one.

At a certain level, journeys evoke a universal feeling of dread.

Think of the number of Hollywood films that end at airports or railway stations. The 'big finish' happens with the man trying something epic to keep the girl from leaving town, instead of taking the next flight himself to pursue her. There is something final about a train pulling out of a platform, something symbolically irreversible about a person leaving on a trip. As audiences, we understand that sometimes, leaving is forever.

As the world becomes a smaller place and we travel increasingly for pleasure, the fear of travel is giving way to an ability to deal with it more matter-of-factly. But even now, you can spot a flight to India at any international airport a mile away. The un-geometric milling of anxious passengers, carrying a staggering number of bags which we want to carry on board is a dead giveaway. We never travel alone – we travel with our entire way of life and sometimes that has trouble fitting into an airline cabin.

STAINLESS STEEL MEMORIES

The middle class' love affair with the modern took wing with stainless steel. Growing up, I remember the passion it generated as women collected one utensil after another, sometimes on a special occasion, often through gifts, by exchanging old clothes for new utensils, and always on Dhanteras. There was something about stainless steel that mirrored our obsession with gold, so fervid and uninhibited was the desire for it.

Every utensil bought was the triumphant product of a heroic campaign waged over days involving several shops and some very hard bargaining. Every utensil came engraved with memory – who bought it, when and for what reason was etched on its side in fine print for posterity. Material progress in a household was measured one utensil at a time. It was the most accessible unit of accretion; durables were bought once in a few years while utensils, even stainless steel ones, could be afforded more regularly. One could never go wrong with stainless steel; in a world where all that was material was suspect, where the fabric we bought shrunk inexplicably to half, and the milk we bought was half water, we could trust stainless steel to be all that it promised. It was an assurance of permanence, a rare guarantee that the material too could be credible.

Most fascinatingly, stainless steel managed to meet deeply traditional needs by being incontrovertibly modern. It was seen as pure and indestructible, the two virtues that give it pride of place in a kitchen. And yet, unlike gold, which is interwoven into custom and the ritual role of which is well established, stainless steel had no past in India. Dubbed as 'ever-silver' in the early phases of its introduction, it was clearly a modern substance, glinting with metallic hardness. It replaced brass and strode over aluminum; the former being too cumbersome as time started being a scarce commodity, and the latter too flimsy. Aluminum reinforced all our fears about modernity by demonstrating a quick descent from being sparklingly light when new to being yellowed, battered and tinny when older. Stainless steel dulled gracefully with age while aluminum carried the yellow pallor of death.

Perhaps the power of stainless steel came from its magical combination of heft, clunk and glint. It felt reassuringly substantial, sounded resoundingly but firmly metallic and shone with a radiant bliss that seemed to come from within. The stainless steel shine was not an imposition but a sign of the essential goodness of its internal properties. It was akin to a face radiating health – to an extent where we could see ourselves in it. The combination of the utilitarian with the aesthetic, where the latter could not merely be read as an accomplice of the former but as its result, helped stainless steel reach its pre-eminent position.

In doing so, it created a kind of modernity that middle class India could comfortably aspire to. It was a sign that worked in both directions – outward to the world, signifying prosperous modernity, and inwards to the family, connoting rooted adhesion. The family ate in stainless-steel thalis and used stainless-steel tumblers; guests were served in glass and those regarded as help in utensils made of 'lesser' substances – maybe plastic or aluminum.

As middle class India has found new signs of modernity, stainless steel, while still continuing as the backbone of the kitchen, is no longer as potent a sign as it used to be. To be sure, it has found new sites of expression – we see it more in the living rooms as an aesthetic object than we did in the past, but middle class India doesn't need it quite as much. It is perhaps the first sign of modernity as a cycle with yesterday's modernity becoming today's tradition.

Even the kitchen now sees much more plastic, 'non-stick' ware, bone china and glass. But for those who grew up in pre-reform India, there is something about stainless steel and the meaning it provided that will never lose lustre. It might dull a bit, but the shine still remains. I have a steel tumbler in front of me where the engraving tells me that it was gifted in 1952 by a relative I cannot place now. Try that with a glass sometime.

THE POSTCARD REMEMBERED

A ny letters? The first inevitable question on reaching home.
Then the careful sorting of mail with the most significant
letter being kept for the last. Letters were never private; they
were always to be read out, while stumbling over the near
indecipherable handwriting of some aunts. Every new listener
would mean that everyone else got to hear it again. Letters were
read to family, friends, neighbours and anyone who was not
a rank stranger. The first post used to come at 11 am and the
second at 4 pm. If one was at home, one eye would always be out
for the postman who on some days would trundle by without
stopping, to the intense disappointment of those following his
every step.

The postcard was the most basic unit of communication – one
was expected to 'send a postcard' for the most trivial of reasons.
The inland letter came next in the hierarchy, followed by the
envelope. The telegram was a reason for high panic, unless it was
about the arrival or departure of some relatives. The trunk call
was the ultimate investment, in time, money and lung capacity,
as one practically shouted oneself into the ear of the listener.

It is interesting how a sense of being close-knit was achieved
with such little actual communication. A letter of a hundred words
took two weeks to reach; the reply took a correspondingly long
time. The closeness was achieved by virtue of the amount spent
in thinking about and anticipating a response. The period when
the letter was in transit was when most of the communication

actually took place, not in reality but in the conversations we had in our minds.

And, of course, the brevity of the communication itself was multiplied many times over by the intensity with which it was consumed. It was as if by squeezing out every drop of communication, one could convert the infinitesimal into the infinite. Every re-reading of the letter revealed just that little bit more, and added to the satisfaction. Like P.C. Sorcar's Water of India trick, where the liquid in the magic glass never seems to finish but is equally never more than a trickle, the postcard dripped communication long after it was read. And, of course, nobody threw away the letters they received. In our house they were mounted on the makeshift wire that passed for a billfold, and many a pleasant afternoon were spent discovering ancient missives from the bottom.

We are a much better communicated society today. With free e-mails, messengers, sms and mobile phones, communication today is easily accessible, cheap and instant. No more waiting for hours to get a trunk call through, no waiting for two weeks to find out that one's son had 'reached safely'. And yet, at the risk of being nostalgic about inefficiency, there is something that is missing. A vital emotion surrounding communication has been lost.

At one level, this is simply the problem of plenty. In a world of scarce communication, every line on a postcard was steeped in the ink of remembrance. Now that we can pick up the phone any time, communication has become extremely accessible and thus commonplace. Also, regular mail has become the preserve of leaflets, bills and birthday greetings from overzealous customer relationship programmes. For the first time today, we can throw away letters unopened, something unthinkable a few years back.

At a deeper level, there is something about the form of paper and ink that creates a feeling of personal intimacy. The postcard is an individual and personal act of communication. The communication intent has an independent corporeal existence that carries the personal signature of the sender and can be read, re-read, crumpled and torn. The electronic screen is not home – it is like a terminus for all communication. The screen does not discriminate between different kinds of communication. E-mails do not reek of the author; as communication pieces they are stillborn on the screen; their existence can be comprehended but not savoured.

In the same way that a digital photograph on the screen, or even printed out, is not really a photograph – if anything, it is the photographic intent of the photograph – the electronic letter is nothing but the intention of writing a letter. Communication becomes industrialized; the letter is reproduced instead of being mailed. It serves the purpose of the original without ever being that.

What we are seeing thus is a reordering of the notion of communication. The new technology brings with it new possibilities. Today we can be one with our loved ones through a webcast and maintain a form of umbilical-mumble through sms. But there was something about ripping open an inland letter that we will miss. The sense of being thought about, being remembered and being missed needs the tactile immediacy of a letter.

Our need to stay connected continues unabated. Perhaps our gleeful embrace of the mobile phone as a technology is a sign of how important this aspect of our lives is to us. However, with a mobile phone, we reach individuals, not a collective; conversations in this case have been privatized. The postcard lived in an era of publicly-owned conversations. We lived not only our own lives, but those of everyone around us. Joy multiplied as did sorrow and the postcard helped bind us together.

SHARING SCARCITY

The property dispute has been a venerable Indian institution that challenges all claims that can be made about the collective nature of Indian society. Closely knit families seem to fall apart and fight acrimonious battles which, thanks to the Indian legal system, last decades. It is quite likely that in this period, the dramatis personae change owing to forces of natural decay, but the battle is fought to the bitter end, till someone earns what can often be a Pyrrhic victory. Indian courts are clogged with such family disputes, and it is worth asking as to how one can reconcile a culture that values family togetherness so much with this behaviour which smacks of burning personal greed. And this is an issue that does not belong to today, when it would be easier to understand the emphasis on the material, but in fact it thrived in times when we thought of ourselves as a society that valued family ties over all things material. At one level, the focus on inheritance reveals an implicit belief that wealth could have been generated only in the past and hence the desperation to hold on to it. But even so, the bitter nature of feuding that accompanies this division deserves greater scrutiny.

The irony, of course, is that property disputes grew at a time when the dominant theme was one of seamless sharing. The idea of personal ownership of things was not particularly well developed and was restricted to very few objects. Space, for instance, was rarely marked out as personal, and the home did not assign any domain rights to particular individuals. Rooms were shared, ten people slept on six mattresses, joint families running into tens of people found no trouble in sharing one toilet. Conflicts arose, but rarely assumed intractable proportions.

Food was a collective idea. In most parts of India, food units are rarely individual. The portions are collective and one is served from this collective pot by solicitous women of the household, who take care to make sure you have enough and equally, that you don't have too much. Guests who dropped by had to be asked for a meal, and the rest of the family magically re-calibrated its hunger around this addition. Resentment was extremely rare, and a way was found to distribute a little over a lot.

Clothes too, while seen as being more personal, were up for grabs. Sarees were exchanged, cousins wore each other's shirts and, of course, hand-me-downs were the norm. One passed through shoes rather than owned them, and given that with repeated resoling the life of a shoe took on elephantine proportions, a whole brood of brothers may have ended up wearing a single pair of shoes while growing up.

In a larger sense, the family was a highly elastic notion. People belonged to your family by meeting very relaxed qualification criteria. One was expected to do favours for someone from the same caste or village as a matter of course. Even within a family, children were quasi-community property, and the distinction between cousins was not sharply demarcated. Everyone brought everyone else up, so to speak.

The sharing was not limited to families. The right to ask for dahi 'jaman', the small portion of curd used to 'set' more curd, was a universal one. Neighbours freely helped themselves to cups of sugar, utensils, mattresses and quilts when there were guests at home and some were happy to read newspapers by borrowing them from neighbours all their lives. Magazines too were circulated in offices, with one having to await one's turn to read *Stardust* as per hierarchy. Growing up, one got to read magazines a couple of months late – they came with an official-looking distribution list stuck on one of the pages carrying designations in terse officialese. Circulating libraries were the other product of this era, where one could borrow books and magazines on a daily basis by paying a monthly fee.

Of course, there was no shame in trooping across to a neighbour or a very distant acquaintance to watch the HFF, the Hindi feature film, or even the Wednesday *Chitrahaar*, on their television set. I remember inflicting myself with clockwork regularity on people who I did not really know then nor now, without feeling the least bit embarrassed. It was common for a TV-owning household to host a few dozen random people from the neighbourhood every evening.

It is interesting that sharing came automatically in an environment of scarcity. The absence of a sense of entitlement to things allowed for a loose convention of sharing to develop. There was an implicit mutuality at work for who knew what one would need from the other person tomorrow. Within a family, this sense was even stronger, and helped paper over the inevitable undercurrent of tensions that develop in closed groups.

The trouble perhaps arose when the idea of ownership had to be confronted not as a social convention but as a legal fact. The implicit flexibility in the system broke down when faced with the need to spell out who got what. The system of primogeniture was challenged by new laws, which gave all siblings, including daughters, equal rights over the property. Forced to think of property in a personal way, which, if one didn't get it, someone else did, the ability to accommodate the other collapsed.

The division of families was one of the central anxieties in an earlier era. Cinema is full of films that document the tragedy that befalls a family when it gets broken up, either through chance or through the machinations of some 'external' vested interests, before reuniting at the end with a vast shudder of relief. The united family had its own share of undercurrents but it found a way of making do with little. It seemed as if families in India were more comfortable sharing things when they didn't own much rather than when they did.

The property dispute brought into sharp relief the simmering issues that resided for years under the surface between siblings and within families. Without an arena of conflict, these hairline fractures continued for years without causing much pain, but the moment property ownership became a legitimate battleground, the faultlines exerted themselves with dramatic ferocity. Families moved from seeming harmonious and close-knit to being bitterly divided in no time at all.

As we move into a time when affluence is a promise rather than a legacy, perhaps we will see fewer disputes of this kind. But the change is likely to be a slow one. Ask Mukesh and Anil Ambani.

REMEMBERING THE SUMMER HOLIDAYS

Do children really need such long summer breaks, was a question posed by some experts recently. Apparently, such a long break disrupts their development and comes in the way of their learning process. Let's get the tykes back to their books, is perhaps the expert view, if not in so many words. One would have thought that children were doing too much during their vacations and not too little, given the plethora of courses, classes, camps and workshops involving swimming, art, personality development, music, computers and the like that seem to cram their calendar. Even the trips taken in the name of holidays seem laden with exotic destinations and customized experiences packed into a short period of time. We can 'do' Europe in ten days and Australia in a week and come back armed with digital memories and overflowing suitcases. Holidays are, in some ways, no longer a break but an intensified search for experiences not normally encountered in everyday life.

It is a far cry from summer holidays one experienced growing up. For holidays every year meant one thing and one thing alone – you went back to your 'native place', logging in with the emotional headquarters of your extended family and spent two months with a gaggle of uncles, aunts and 'first and second' cousins. The happiest memories of childhood of a whole generation seem to be centred around this annual ritual of homecoming and of affirmation. We tendered tacit apologies for the separateness entailed in being individuals even as we scurried back into the cauldron of community and continuity represented by the family. Summer vacation was a time sticky with oneness, as who we were and what we owned oozed out from our individual selves into a collective pot.

Looking back, it seems clear that we did very little. Barring the rationed hedonism of a Hindi movie every fortnight (converted with much abject wheedling into a weekly frequency) and the exuberant, if inexpensive, forays into street foods of all descriptions, the two months were spent doing small things with inordinate pleasure. Idiotic invented games with cousins, pillow fights, gossip sessions extending late into the night, midnight snacks, card games where everyone felt duty bound to cheat, raucous attempts at 'antakashari' were all ways we found of rescuing pleasure out of the trivial. And even then, much of the summer was spent with damp backs that felt fleeting relief when the fan creaked back into placid action once the power came back. Boredom yawned frequently, and stretched languidly even more often. Complaints about boredom to one's parents resulted in the ultimate punishment – being carted to sundry relatives whose claim to any kinship tie was extremely tenuous: 'he is your first cousin's father-in-law and his younger brother was our neighbour in Bandikui twenty years ago' seemed to be a good enough reason. Of course, the more obscure the relative, the greater the chances of encountering the dreaded 'do-you-remember-who-I-am' question that always ended in incoherent mumbles.

Looking back, one is struck by how little material was used in creating such a rich and satisfying experience. Scarcity, when pooled, seemed to transform magically into an abiding sense of plenty. Pleasure derived from a resource grew in inverse proportion to its availability. So if seven people were crammed into a rickshaw, it was somehow more fun than if three travelled by it. Five beds on a terrace accommodated eight and there was no passing thought of any discomfort that I remember. There was little concept of the personal, and virtually no conception of privacy. No doors were ever locked and one now wonders at the plight of the conjugally challenged uncles and aunts who found themselves marooned in a Platonic wilderness.

Come to think of it, summer was not really a break, but a joint. It was the bridge used to reaffirm one's connectedness with one's larger community. One did not travel, one returned. It was not an attempt to experience the new and the extraordinary but one that emphatically underlined the power of the old and the ordinary. As times change, what we seek from our summer breaks too has changed in a fundamental way. Today, we are attached much more to the work we do and summer helps us temporarily detach from this new source of identity. We refuel our individual selves now; and do so with much more material than we did in the past. But for those who grew up in different times, summer was the best time of their lives.

MERE PAAS MA HAI

The Indian mother has changed. Or to put it more precisely, how she gets represented in cinema and advertising has changed. The mother of today is an effervescent, dynamic cheerleader who propels her children forward by feeding them a variety of healthy things, taking care of their and her own appearance and breaking into a jig with them when required. She is the mother you can take to school, and confide in about your crushes. A friend, an aggressively alert monitor, a fun playmate and an ambitious cheerleader, all rolled into one. And while this is a fantasized depiction of mothers, it does point to what is expected of mothers today.

It is a far cry from the India of an earlier time. The mother then was experienced, imagined and represented quite differently. 'Mere paas ma hai.' Four words that establish what really mattered, what could not be bought or achieved, merely earned. The woman may be discriminated against from birth, seen as a burdensome liability in her youth, be treated unfairly and badly by the husband, actively harassed by her in-laws, but somehow when it came to her role as a mother, particularly of a male child, her power and influence knew no bounds. To the Indian imagination, the mother represents the source of all things.

In more than a few ways, Indian society conspired to make the woman most comfortable in her role as mother. In every other role, she was frequently evaluated, circumscribed and diminished. But as a mother, she faced no censure and no limits.

It was alright for her to lavish indulgence on her offspring, she could pamper them without any restraint and stand up for them against other people. To be acting in the interests of her children was the ultimate cloak of legitimacy.

The Indian mother was a giant ball of affection. Her love was infinite and her lap inexhaustible. She wore old saris and smelled of wet atta. Her sari chheda (end) was her most versatile instrument. It wiped faces and dried tears and in an emergency became a bandage. She came last in everything and first in everything else, she put herself after everybody else but was always there before anyone else. Her fingers were forever lined with deep furrows that came from slicing vegetables and her ankles were scuffed from overuse. She was ageless and eternal. A mother was never absent, never too ill to look after others, never bored, never just tired. Her presence was liquid, seeping into everything and oozing out of everywhere. She was invisible and omnipresent. To a mother, there was no problem that could not be solved with food. She had a limited armoury of answers, but they were surprisingly effective. She asked small questions endlessly but never any big ones. On the really big issues, the mother was one's loyal ally, entreating, browbeating or just beating the father down with ceaseless wheedling on your behalf.

Her husband was someone she loved in a way that preceded language and feared in a way that did not preclude action. She knew his buttons, and his moods. She controlled him through an intricate language of eyes, which she used with extraordinary dexterity, particularly when with others. She would agree to being steamrollered when it came to herself but rarely gave in when the child was involved, never without putting a really good fight, which included all means fair, foul and devastatingly devious.

The Indian man in particular owes much to the mother. Brought up in an environment where he could do no wrong and where every whim of his was somehow catered to, at least in part, he finds the sticky bonds of maternal love very difficult to extricate himself from. The mother is an eternal presence in the son's life, certainly for my generation, and in this relationship the son is always Munna, Pappu or Bittoo who is still seven years old and needs to be rocked to sleep. The mother infantilizes the child, who never quite outgrows that role.

The battle with the daughter-in-law was thus a foregone conclusion. The son was her possession, her creation, her magnum opus. She had constructed him in her own likeness and was not about to let go of her prized creation. If the daughter-in-law had sex on her side, the mother had smell. The boy who had grown closeted in her vaporous fragrant bosom, did not know how to let go. 'Mere paas ma hai' is in some ways a tautological statement, for there was no way the mother would have let go. She might strategically have withheld her affections and thereby inflict the greatest punishment known to an Indian man – to be, in the words of Sudhir Kakar, 'banished from the Eden of your mother's affection', but she could not be purged from his consciousness. But otherwise the mother was blind in her love and all forgiving. The son could do no wrong.

To the daughter, the mother was a more ambivalent figure, sending conflicting messages of love and indifference. The mother knew that she could never own her daughter, that she was a responsibility who would never be able to give anything back in return. The daughter received love tinged with the knowledge that comes early to women in India. The mother's role was to turn her little girl into a knowing woman as soon as possible and to keep her son a little boy for the rest of his life.

For most children then, the mother was the most absolute experience in their lives. To be able to rely so unquestioningly and so completely on someone else created a sense of stability that was extremely resistant to change. With one's mother, one was safe. Life was never a mystery, and bliss was a laddoo away.

THE DIGNITY OF ULTRAMARINE

Remember ultramarine? The blue powder we used to make our once-white-now-grey-with-use shirts carry off an impersonation of white? White clothes were flogged, boiled and then blued in an attempt to get them looking something approaching white. In fact, they ended up looking like colourless clothes streaked with telltale blue lines. By a vast conspiracy of silence, this was accepted by all of us as the closest the clothes would come to being white. I have never thought of colours as having a life, but the white that we managed had the pallor of last week's death – it was as if we were not maintaining old clothes but embalming them and then proceeding to pretend that they were alive and well.

Growing up in scarce times meant that we stretched everything, and clothes were by no means an exception. Turning collars so that they looked new, wearing socks with holes and without elastic till one day they crumbled and disappeared are two of the many devices we used to make a little go a long way. But the need for ultramarine points to another kind of need altogether. The whiteness of clothes was a sign – of a belief in things simple and pure, of an inner resolve to stand apart from the corrupting power of time and circumstance. To wear white was to wear simplicity like an ornament and assert victory over the base, the impure and the expedient. The desire for white was a sign of our desire to turn back the inevitable decomposition that nature brings to all things it touches. Whiteness became a sign precisely because it was so difficult to maintain – it soaked up effort and resources and indicated that the pursuit was important enough for the wearer. Ultramarine never really made clothes white, but it showed that one cared enough to continue to try.

What we called middle class values were in reality nothing more than the whole protocol of actions we developed to deal with insufficiency with dignity and grace. Middle class insufficiency was the poverty of the full stomach – one was cursed with the ability to have whatever one really, truly needed, but virtually nothing of what one wanted. A comrade of our needs, and an enemy of our desires, this 'tightness of hand' was accompanied by a value system that sought to minimize the acknowledgement of the role that desire played in our lives. It featured as its protagonists the father who did not take a cycle rickshaw to office because he 'liked walking' and the mother who insisted that leftovers were tastier. Call it the poignancy of pretence or the heroism of self-limiting restraint, the idea that less could be ennobling was a part of the ethic that middle class India grew up on. Ultramarine was in one sense then a thin film of culture, a sheen that glowed with the pride one felt in one's chosen way of life.

This is what makes the relative affluence seen by the urban middle class in recent times so sweet. Nothing is more liberating than the feeling of not having to worry about money before any and every expense. Today, for a section of society, it is possible to give in to a small indulgence without a second thought. Children get pampered because we relive our childhood through them, enjoying vicariously our ability to deny them nothing. Hindi film blockbusters help us relive our nostalgia by populating the happiness of yesterday's large families with the energy of today's affluence. We watch a prosperity-propelled version of our own past, made all the more romantic through the hazy filter of time. As more sons get starting salaries that are fatter than their father's salary at retirement time, we begin to see an unprecedented sense of well-being well up around us. Yesterday's heroic self-denial legitimizes today's consumerism.

Interestingly, today ultramarine itself is no longer the force it once was. It has been replaced by liquid dye-based whiteners that fulfil the same purpose but in an entirely different way. They dye the clothes violet and this makes the clothes look white. In keeping with the times, this method is cheaper and more expedient. It sees our desire to keep our clothes white as a pragmatic need, and offers a practical solution. So what if a little optical artifice is being used? If ultramarine reflects the values of a generation brought up in brahminical propriety, the dye evokes the impatient energy of an emerging class, eager to acquire the sheen required to make a mark in today's world. Like an English-medium education for our children, the new whiteners promise an upgradation in class driven purely by external signifiers.

So as we move ahead in a world where scarcity is no longer a given for some of us, what happens to the ability to find virtue in insufficiency? That ability was our defiant match in a stormy night. Now that the night is no longer as stormy, will the light too go out?

THE CIVILIZING CREASE IN OUR TROUSERS

Growing up in the discreet constraints of middle class India, one learnt to make do without a lot of things. One or two 'good' shirts for special occasions, loads of hand-me-downs from assorted cousins, clothes that were always engineered for some mythical time in the future when one will grow to be 6'4", trousers with the prominent V at the back that comes from the 'margin' being opened up, learning not to ask for second helpings (if there's enough, you will be served, otherwise make do) and finding ways to enjoy leftovers from yesterday's meal. In the midst of all this 'making do', it is curious that the one thing that we did not compromise on was in wearing well-ironed clothes.

The trousers may carry the petulant shine that comes from overuse, they may be darned in a place or two, but by god they would be ironed before being worn. They would go to that ubiquitous epitome of human fertility, the neighbourhood dhoban, if one could afford that, or one would slave over the clothes trying to coax the straight-as-a-dye crease from the flagging spirits of the soggy terrycot. In extreme cases, one would slip the pant under a mattress and sleep heavily on it to get something approaching a line from them.

Why should the crease in our clothes be so important to us? What are we really confirming, what are we really seeking when we insist on a line appearing through the middle of our garments? Surely there is nothing intrinsic, nothing natural about this desire. Look around you on the streets – you will find people living in really constrained circumstances spending money to get this mark of order on their clothes. When there are so many needs that compete for their money, why does this become a priority?

In some ways, ironing clothes is part of our effort to affirm the supremacy of the human spirit. We rise above our circumstances when we imprint our will on them. The crease in our clothes is the insignia of civilization; a sign of the discipline we are able to bring to bear on the inanimate world that we rule. To not iron one's clothes is to surrender to the chaos of nature and submit to its vagaries.

Another similar ritual we follow is that of combing our hair. Driving down the streets of Mumbai the other day, I saw a homeless mother applying hair-oil on her ten-year-old daughter's head and tying her hair in neat plaits. To oil one's hair in the midst of squalor and despair is for hope to keep its head above the swirling, muddy waters of circumstance; it is a sign that the belief in one's ability to shape one's future still survives. It is to reaffirm that the human spirit by itself is of value and is worth preserving and displaying.

In a larger sense, we communicate our faith in the ways of our world when we opt for order. Scruffiness is a sign of rebellion, of someone unwilling to become part of the social mosaic we have so carefully constructed. Parents spend an inordinate time fussing over the combing of their children's hair – to the abiding mystification of children, who cannot figure out why it is so important.

It is interesting that in both cases, what communicates the triumph of human-ness is the straight line. If the trouser has its crease so does our hair. We spend some time making sure that the hair is parted along a straight line – the task is incomplete till then. The straight line might well be the most significant contribution human beings have made to this world. Look at our buildings, our highways, the way modern cities are laid out and you will see how critical linearity has been to us. The straight line is a journey in human resoluteness – it connects two points and then there is no stopping it; thereafter, it needs no guidance and heeds no circumstances. It is arbitrary and absolute – think of borders drawn as straight lines on maps and you will know what I mean. The straight line border cuts up territories without regard to natural landmarks, cultures or languages – it is an impostion of arbitrary order.

In a similar sense, when we crease our shirts and comb our hair, we impose on ourselves a discipline; we reaffirm that we belong to a group and that we abide by its rules. By doing so, we hope that the system will in turn abide by us. This, of course, does not always happen, but as long as we believe, hope lives.

THE DYING WINDOW

Once upon a time, we lived our lives out of windows. Sitting by a window, hour after dreamy hour droned by, as we saw the world whirl around, lost in its own torpid rhythm. The window was our access to the action outside, our personal vantage point through which we saw our unique version of reality. The idea of sitting and watching – of being the perpetual spectator, of enjoying being in the presence of action, was a big part of life in urban India.

The need to be close to centres of activity was, and continues to be, a big part of our lives. We like our markets to be crowded; our temples to be teeming and even our hill stations must stay away from solitude-inspired bliss and focus on chana-bhatura-fuelled raunak instead. In each of these instances, we are comforted by the act of being near activity – it does not translate into a need for doing very much oneself.

We were safe as spectators, preferring to be comforted by signs of life around us. We never really saw ourselves as key players and in truth even the people we watched were not engaged in anything significant. We contrived to find significance in their activity when we could but, for the most part, we were hypnotized by activity itself. Motion was entertainment enough.

In many ways, the window was the theatre of our imagination. We sat there, eyes sighing with dreams just out of reach. It bred insatiable curiosity in the lives of others, and bound us all in a community of eyes. Everyone watched everyone else in a neighbourhood – no event went unnoticed, no transgression unpunished. Windows, and their elder cousins, the balconies, allowed the lovelorn to lead a rich life filled with imagined romance. Just a fleeting meeting of glances with the object of one's fervid affections was an occasion calling for celebration. The idea of 'nazar' as surrogate action made the act of watching the world more or less the same as playing an active role in it. As exciting as watching the world from a window was to look inside another one. The Girl at the Window, occasionally visible and rarely accessible, represented a tantalizing glimpse of the possible. In a world where reality was almost always drabber than imagination, the window became a conduit to an alternative, altogether richer life.

Of course, in a world where everyone sat at the window or on the front porch, we wound up watching each other watch each other. Multiplying stasis did not somehow increase boredom, or if it did, it didn't really matter. Sight itself was an activity, an achievement, especially when purposefully directed. If nothing else, continuous sight consumed time; as we directed our unblinking stare at the world outside, time ticked and tocked away.

In the last few years, the role of the window has changed. It is no longer the perch from which we consume the world outside. It continues to be a device that lets light and air inside but is equally likely to be a source of leakage to the world ouside. It is likelier to be grilled, wire-meshed and curtained. The outside world is beginning to look unattractive – the action is too erratic, too unpackaged to hold our interest. Motion by itself no longer holds that much promise. The window of yesterday has been replaced with the TV of today. We allow ourselves to be sucked into a world of electronic simulation where reality comes to us in entertaining bite-sized pieces. Boredom is our number one enemy and the idea of luxuriating in it while leaning out of a window is a distasteful one. The window needed the world to be slow enough for the eye to follow and it was the mind that filled in the details that added depth to what was being seen. The TV draws us in completely and excludes imagination – everything is explained; all stories are processed for our enjoyment. In TV, every minute must hold our attention because otherwise the channel will be switched.

The notion of neighbourhood too has changed. In a world where, as an anthropologist put it, aerials have replaced roots, the urban community is much more impersonal and inward-looking. The window serves a much more limited purpose today. Yesterday it sat at the threshold of many things – the outside and the inside, action and inaction, reality and imagination. Today, it serves a more functional purpose. The 'view' is still important to us but our gaze has changed. We are no longer happy just to participate in the world – we want to own it.

IN PRAISE OF THE
UNANNOUNCED VISIT

Every time we heard the sound of an autorickshaw entering our lane, the conversation would trail off till either it passed or stopped short of our house. In the event that it stopped in front of our house, then of course the conversation was over as we all rushed out to see who it was. Every time the front gate creaked, we expected some new visitor, someone dropping in unannounced. Doorbells ringing at odd hours contained the possibility of a delightful surprise, of some uncle or cousin dropping in for the night en route somewhere else. Growing up in middle class India meant that one was firmly enclasped in the bosom of a large family with very blurred and decidedly elastic boundaries, and this sense of kinship was kept alive by the institution of the Unannounced Visit.

You dropped in on people without warning and usually without purpose. The thought popped into your head that you hadn't seen someone in a while and that was enough for you to make the trek using the bus, cycle or train and land up unannounced at the doorstep of the remembered one. If it was morning, you got a cup of tea, if it was meal time, you were quickly accommodated and served. No questions were asked about your purpose and, in a few cases, no real conversation was expected either. I remember a granduncle who for years dropped in for a visit and never said a word; he spent the day with us and left before it got dark.

We lived in a time of an extraordinary elasticity of accommodation. For all the middle class tightfistedness that one grew up with, there was never any problem accommodating four surprise guests who decided to 'drop in' for a fortnight. There was a mysterious limitlessness of food that I find difficult to explain today, looking back. Along with the tightness, there existed an ability to stretch what you had quite seamlessly. So even when obscure relatives and relatives of relatives dropped by, there was rarely any resentment at being put upon by these visits.

Of course, this also meant that you did the same, and as a child the idea of landing up at some distant relative's house and having to spend hours listening to tales of even more distant relatives was an act of colossal boredom. But at that time boredom had no currency; it was bereft of the exchange value it has today.

In fact, relationships were based on the draining out of visible purpose and came without the expectation of any immediate or tangible reciprocity. They necessarily involved large tracts of barren time; it was as if the land was kept fallow so as to underline the fact that it was the land that was important, the crop was transient and would follow. Relationships were built on the rock solid foundation of boredom. Time was a communal property as was space, to a large extent. You could not intrude on someone's 'private' time or trespass on their 'personal' space because these didn't really exist. Individuals were the form in which the collective manifested itself and were treated as such.

As the individual becomes more important, we mark out the spaces around us more definitively. Everyone comes equipped with a radius of aloneness and we need to stand outside at the perimeter and knock before entering. We become aware of our own separateness as that of others, and we learn that we need to prepare ourselves for allowing people into the hallowed ring we call our private space.

Technology today has been a key force in enabling this conception. Technology individualizes us by offering us the ability to stay connected on our terms. It legitimizes the radius of aloneness by creating virtual bridges between people. The telephone, particularly the mobile phone, offers us the possibility of endless, continuous connection and in doing so frees us from purposelessness. We can call anyone we want but more often than not, we do so only when we need to. We now call people before landing up, which gives them the opportunity to determine a 'good time' for the visit, which in turn makes us more circumspect as to whether they are merely being polite. The relationship becomes ordered, it takes on the contours of our mutual expectations. We are in control of the relationship and mould it as we see fit.

As a result, last night when the doorbell rang at 11, I didn't bother thinking who it might be. I knew it would be no one I would be surprised to see.

MOTHER PIOUS LADY

Sunita was born in a status KKB family and was fortunate enough to be throughout convented while being non-manglik. By the time she was 25/160, and completing her CA, her status family started thinking about her early decent marriage to a teetotaller NRI from another status business family. Her wheatish complexion was a problem, but then she was slim and homely, apart from being from a status family, and hence received many proposals upon sending her BHP. Her marriage to a Bisa boy 27/170 with income in five figures (Mother pious lady) was brief and unfortunate and she returned 27/160, an innocent divorcee seeking another status match, this time caste no bar.

The matrimonial ad has invented a language and a culture that is uniquely its own. It is a mathematical composition of terse eloquence; it speaks in guttural acronyms and reveals as much in what it is silent on as in what it says. It converts something as personal and intimate as marriage into a transaction between two different social units. The language of the matrimonial ad is matter-of-fact and businesslike. No discomfort is felt at converting such an intimate relationship into an unabashed transaction.

A person becomes a bundle of saleable attributes encrypted into matrimonial jargon. To the insider, its code is obviously not difficult to crack. VB means very beautiful and BHP stands for birth horoscope and photograph. Decent marriage means openness to dowry and uses contact lens means someone who wears thick glasses. The language used has its own pitfalls – in a world where everyone is fair and beautiful, we begin to see people being VV Fair or Really Beautiful. Of course, this is also the reason why Photograph (Returnable) has become de rigueur. The emphasis on all marketable attributes sometimes results in descriptions that are occasionally mystifying. It is not entirely clear how 'Brother settled in the US' is an advantage. Even more mystifying is 'Mother pious lady', a description that is perhaps meant to connote a mother-in-law concerned more with burning incense sticks than daughters-in-law. The matrimonial ad takes twenty-five words to abbreviate a person into marketability and like the thirty-second commercial, makes its user a master of compressing meaning. It becomes a fascinating snapshot of our society as it deals with a central concern – marriage – and the ensuing continuity of our way of life.

The matrimonial ad tells us that marriage in India has historically been a social transaction between families, consummated through the almost incidental device of the boy and girl. When the Hindi movie mother asked her son for a bahu, she meant it literally. The household was making an acquisition of a new daughter-in-law; the boy was useful but only a part-time owner of his spouse's time and attention. The matrimonial ads are always brought out by the parents; this is not a decision that the boy and girl are grown up enough to make on their own. The nomenclature of 'boy' and 'girl' is by itself revealing – the individuals involved are miniaturized into pliability. You can be forty-four, look like a hirsute tractor when you walk, but in the marriage market you are still a boy.

In a study I was involved in a few years ago, we analysed matrimonial ads across thirty years to examine what had changed, and found some very interesting things. The biggest change, expectedly, was in the importance given to appearance. Adjectives describing this aspect had increased sharply, with a new premium on being tall and slim. Fairness as an articulated quality went up sharply in this period, a trend that even a cursory glance at the current matrimonial ads will tell us, has only intensified. Boys were evaluated on their income and their family, and girls on their appearance, qualifications and family. Boys articulated their expectations from girls using more words than did the girl's side. Interestingly, the proportion of ads that mentioned the caste origins of the candidates remained constant.

However, while the individual is now more important and expresses his or her need with greater specificity, the essential nature of the system has not changed. Even today, matrimonial ads barely make any mention of any personality traits of the individuals involved. The individuals are summed up entirely by their background, appearance and occupation. The underlying mental model is still that of marriage as a relationship between stations in life and not individuals.

What has changed a little more is perhaps the process that follows the ad. In the earlier days, the boy and girl barely saw each other out of the shyness imposed by being in the midst of two armies of relatives watching them like hawks while tucking into large quantities of food. If they were lucky, they could expect to be given ten minutes in a symbolic corner where they could exchange 'views'. Today, these ten minutes can stretch up to two or three meetings in some cases and chaperoning too is becoming optional.

One would expect that with the rise of individualism, the first change would be seen in how we as a society find mates for ourselves. The arranged marriage should have been, by all rights, an early casualty. After all it depended on the middleman who got families together and offered the security of a personal guarantee. However, the matrimonial ad, in spite of its impersonalness, has turned out to be a viable alternative to the earlier system of middlemen thanks to its ability to establish a clear set of conventions that all of us are able to decode.

In his book, *Blink*, Malcolm Gladwell talks about the power of thin-slicing, by which he means the ability of taking big decisions based on fleeting input. There can be no better advertisement for thin-slicing than the Indian arranged marriage. The matrimonial ad is a very thin slice that goes a very long way. Sunita 27/160 need not despair; Shekhar 29/175 issueless divorcee is just cutting out her ad.

AN ODE TO THE SCOOTER

If the Indian middle class man were to be reborn as a product, chances are it would be as a Bajaj scooter. Squat, a belly going to pot, wearing a grey safari suit, undistinguished but resourceful. With a wife perched uncomfortably at the back, Gudiya squeezed between the two and Cheeku standing up front. No product comes close to capturing the essence of middle class India as well as the scooter. For decades the scooter was both literally and metaphorically at the heart of the Indian middle class consciousness, imparting its own unique flavour to how we lived our lives. Today, with the motorcycle having all but erased the scooter from our hearts and minds, it is worth examining what made the scooter the force it was and asking what the transition from the scooter to the bike says about the Indian man today.

The scooter carries with it an aura of safety (over its macho cousin, the motorcycle) that its engineering does not quite merit. Its smaller wheelsize actually makes it a less stable vehicle than the motorcycle but the air of safety that it so convincingly carried had more to do with images that surrounded it. It had a stepney, which provided a welcome safety net on independent-minded Indian roads. It had space to squeeze in a full family, a place to carry vegetables, a dickey to store sundry needs of the family – in short, it seemed safe because it catered to all those stable, worldly things that made a man a 'responsible' person. Most importantly, the scooter hid the machine from view. Unlike the bike, which revels in displaying its muscular architecture, the scooter covers up the beast within with rotund blandness. The rounded soft shape of the scooter helps it be seen as a domesticated beast of burden, anonymously performing the duties asked of it. Overall, the scooter is middle class and safe because it goes out of its way to advertise its lack of masculine ambition; it wears its unprepossessing modesty on its sleeve, by eschewing any heroics.

This is evident in the manner in which the scooter negotiates the road. If the bike sees the road as a woman to make love to, the scooter prefers instead to haggle with her. The bike hugs the curves of the road, melting the rider onto the tar; the scooter maintains an awkward distance, unconvinced that continuous mobility is a natural human condition. If the bike purrs, the scooter stammers; where the bike is a gushing river, the scooter a spluttering tap; if the bike is an untamed stallion, the scooter a recalcitrant mule. The bike's pillion rider fuses into the driver – dropping a girl home on a bike is a rake's pleasure, on a scooter it's a 'cousin brother's' duty. If John Abraham is the poster boy for bikes, Amol Palekar on his way to the ration shop is the abiding scooter role model. 'Heroes' on bikes wear bubble helmets and boots, on scooters they chew paan and give signals with their feet.

The scooter celebrates the functionality of motorized mobility, not its recreational energy. At a time when we coped with scarcity with heartbreaking dignity, the scooter was our imperfect solution. It needed to be kicked incessantly, first aggressively and then pleadingly, at times it needed to be tilted at an impossible angle for the fuel to start flowing and its spark plugs needed more cleaning than Bihar politics, but it blended in perfectly with how we lived and what we believed in. Restrained, repressed, modest, versatile in an unassuming way, the scooter spoke for us and our way of life like nothing else. No wonder the Hamara Bajaj campaign rung so true – for once advertising made us look into a mirror and told us a truth we all recognized.

The transition to the bike too tells a story. In the era of the
scooter, the bike was a Yezdi, Rajdoot or Bullet, all belonging
to the hirsute world of grown-up men. The bikes that actually
did well in India were the colourful 100 cc bikes that offered
the tamer, less intimidating version of the real thing, with fuel
efficiency to boot. This allowed us to move gradually from the
stolid functionality of the scooter to the plastic seduction of the
bike in baby steps.

The bike today speaks of the emerging India that is driven
more by outward appearances and is not afraid of the motive
force of change. It is an eloquent symbol, but it cannot sum
up who are we in quite the same way as a scooter could. Now
that Bajaj has decided to stop manufacturing scooters, we have
lost a vital part of our connection with our sense of our middle
classness. Something has changed, decisively.

DECODING THE AUTORICKSHAW

There is something about Indian roads that seems to defy order of any kind. The Indian road is indeed a barely functioning anarchy. And at its heart, playing a key role, is the autorickshaw (called variously a scooter, a three-wheeler or simply an auto). Why does the autorickshaw seem so naturally and effortlessly Indian?

The auto is the urban rat: a wily, crafty creature that wriggles its way through the urban sewer. The auto deals with the road on a second-by-second basis, recognizing that the Indian town is the abode of the Constantly Changing Circumstance. Twisting and turning constantly, the auto dribbles its way through traffic, mankind and chaos in no particular order. Every inch of territory is fought for using not courage but guile. The auto defies the idea that the road is a straight line but sees it as a chessboard, contemplating the next move as if a world of options is open to it.

In many ways, the auto is perfectly at home with twisty by-lanes, gullies and mohallas and mimics their lack of linearity. In fact, even on a straight road, the auto contrives somehow to avoid linearity as it zigzags its way out of sheer habit. The auto, like so many other things in India, almost actively seeks to subvert order by insinuating itself wherever it can. It brings to us a vastly enhanced sense of sub-atomic distances by intruding so close into the vehicle just ahead that distance becomes a state of mind rather than a state of being.

The auto is also the one vehicle that moves in three-dimensional space, spending as much time off the road as it does on it. This it owes to the nature of Indian roads as much to its own design. This results in a unique ability to transfer the topography of the road into the passengers' innards, converting road bumps into digestive experience.

The key to understanding the auto is to understand its design. The principle governing its design is perhaps a world view that celebrates compromise not as a 'lesser choice' but as an 'inevitable, and eventually, the only sustainable choice'.

Take, for instance, the speed the auto is capable of travelling at. It is significantly faster than a cycle and much slower than a car but looked at from the reality of Indian roads, it travels at the ideal speed. Any slower and cycles would zip past, any faster is not possible given the nature of the traffic and the quality of the roads. Its suspension too is self-limiting, being designed for its speed; the moment the auto begins to travel faster, one's insides mimic those of a food processor's. The auto represents the idea of personal transportation, but barely so. It is a shanty-on-wheels, offering just about adequate protection against the elements, which it more-or-less keeps out, without offering any real guarantees. The technology that goes into its construction speaks in a pidgin dialect, and reeks of the mechanical era when rivets were bolted into blocks of machinery by grunting human hands. It splutters into a clumsy start when a human hand yanks at a lever, often more than once. There is nothing silken about the autorickshaw, nothing comes easily in this world but somehow, things do keep moving, in however rudimentary a fashion.

The auto driver belongs to the nowhere land of rootless urban dwellers. Exuding an air of sullen displacement, he, along with the railway coolie, is the master of the prolonged argument. Like the auto, which consistently negotiates with circumstances, an auto ride begins with a reluctant acceptance of the passenger and ends with a resentful rejection of the fare offered. The auto driver works without transparency when it comes to the fare. The meter rarely works and if it does, it does so in a blatantly suspicious way, blurting out miles when kilometres should have been whispered and when the passenger protests, the driver embarks on an argument that always seems to end in muttered resentful dissatisfaction. His world view finds reflection in the brooding self-pity that marks the 'shairi' found inscribed at the back of the vehicle.

The auto's appeal comes from its ability to provide a real luxury; it offers us the power of individualized motorized transport. In doing so, it allows those of us used all our lives to being one of the 'masses' to rise above this collective status. When one hires an auto, one is placing value on one's own time. Rather than wait for public transport, an auto is hailed and one's precise destination is reached. The autorickshaw's implicit deal with us is that while it gives this wonderful luxury, in return it strips everything else in the experience that could remotely reek of luxury. Everything else just about works, because of which it is as affordable as it is.

In a larger sense, the auto captures the hybrid mongrel nature of towns in India. It is both dissatisfying and deeply comforting. It captures the variable and uneven nature of life in an India that is not too poor to have no choices in life and not so affluent that it can take life for granted. The autorickshaw makes life easy in a miserly way. It reaffirms and gives substance to the Indian belief that life may be hard but that there is always a way. And you can always trust an auto to take you there. Sort of.

THE APPLIANCE AS
INSTALLATION

I was never allowed to touch the stereo. It was something children had to be kept away from for mere touch would somehow ruin the intricate insides of this temperamental and magical device that emitted glorious sound. There were people who 'maintained' their appliances well, which really meant that they obsessively guarded access to their prized possessions, tending to them as if they were tender sprigs of some exotic plant that emerged only for a few weeks in September. The handling of appliances was a ritual of grave masculine import, bristling with a deportment that verged on the baritone. No wonder there was a premium for 'single-owner-maintained cars' and perhaps more curiously, for 'owned by army officer', which somehow connoted that the said vehicle had been fussed over, maintained and buffed till it shone white, or maybe grey, even as it crossed its twentieth birthday.

Every appliance was a battle won with circumstance. You did not merely buy one of these things, you agonized, sweated blood and tears before actually going out to a dozen shops over a few months before settling on your latest acquisition. Once it arrived, it was promptly swathed in plastic or in some variant of a tablecloth and admired copiously for several weeks. It was used sparingly and in order of patriarchal family hierarchy. To buy a durable was an act of home building. Each appliance was a floor in the imagined mansion called home. A household unit was known by the appliances it had managed to accumulate, for each acquisition marked a stage in progressing towards reaching a state of man-made civilization. Appliances were part of the act of 'ghar basana', the setting up of home, and thus homes were deemed incomplete without a full complement of appliances.

Of course, this was a time when a full complement comprised of not very much. A radio, a mixie, a sewing machine, a fridge, a B&W TV, a tape recorder, a stereo, if lucky, and a scooter pretty much completed the list. It didn't take much for an appliance to be coveted; a Sumeet mixie was among the most prized of possessions, and even implements like a flour mill and a water purifier were considered massive acquisitions. Why, even the pressure cooker was an acquisition of note, with Prestige, India's most popular brand, being advertised as being a sign that husbands loved their wives and cared enough to buy them a Prestige! Every time a new appliance graced a home, it was an occasion of celebration, with some minor religious ceremonies involved. Repairs were a nightmare, and every time a gadget failed to work, it was as if the elements had conspired against one.

Every appliance differed a little in its character. The refrigerator was all about sophistication; I remember crunching ice for many weeks after we got our first one. It took us time to figure out that food could be stored there – for the first few weeks the magic of cold water was enough. The television was the ultimate purchase, for it ushered in a world of untold entertainment for at least an hour a day. We had, by that time, *Chitrahaar* twice a week. Of course, the television was no mere gadget, it was an installation of considerable importance. It came in flourishing wood cabinets, which could be unlocked using sophisticated aluminium keys that looked like metallic strips. It had knobs that leaped out from its body, and it needed considerable physical coaxing, sometimes by way of adjusting the voltage in the stabilizer, on other occasions by willing the vertical hold to stop its vertical perambulations, and at most other times by banging on its side till magically the desired effect was produced.

The transistor was the truly modern appliance, in that it was used freely and it ordered every day with its mellifluous offerings. It revolutionized the very idea of entertainment by making it mobile, it allowed us to make our lives fragrant with music, wherever we might be, whatever we might be doing. Students, farmers, housewives, shopkeepers, all carried transistors wherever they went, the Indian answer to the boombox. The tape recorder, when it first came, was used less for listening to songs and more for the sheer exhilaration of recording and listening to the voices of our near and dear ones. Hours, sorry minutes (tapes were expensive as sin) were spent recording what, in retrospect, sounds like thinly veiled garbage in each other's voices, as we discovered our own importance through the act of recording something we ourselves created.

Owning a scooter, after the requisite homage to the enormity of the act by way of waiting for eight years before one could get one's Bajaj Chetak (Priya or Super, if less lucky), was a sign of one's arrival into the upper middle class. Cars were for those in the stratosphere, and when my father committed the karmic folly of buying a second hand car (Fiat 1961 vintage bought in 1976, a mere stripling), we spent many pleasant months pushing it up and down what seemed like very hilly roads. We did spend a few minutes inside the car too and it was fun. It was just punishment for trying to reach a station that was clearly above ours. Air conditioners were sinful, and were outside the bounds of fantasy, even. Those with ACs were another breed, an exalted race that one could never hope to know, let alone rub shoulders with.

Today, as DVDs explode in sales, and the television market saturates, as non-AC cars start looking like anachronisms and homes have music systems in every room, appliances no longer carry the magic they once did. Why, we even discard them ever so often by exchanging them for something better. Of course, we are perhaps defined even more by what we own, but not with the same intensity of feeling that accompanied every small step we took in our desire to make something of ourselves and our homes.

THE DOCTOR IN FILMS

Inhein dawa nahi, dua ki zaroorat hai, says the man in a white coat with depressing finality. With these words, the doctor in a Hindi film is handing over the baton to his immediate superior, God. The doctor is otherwise a bastion of the absolute knowledge that is the gift of modernity; all his opinions are pronouncements as he rushes from one Operation Theatre with a flashing red light to another. Even when his prescription is as dodgy as asking for a change in 'hawa-pani', in other words allowing Sunita ('Thank You, Dadddeeee') and her friends to frolic in some hill station in lavender slacks, his tone is funereal and quite, quite final.

The doctor as a character in Hindi films, especially of the sixties and seventies, makes for fascinating study for in his persona lie embedded many popular notions about the idea of fate, health and its differential impact on people. For the doctor has a very different role to play depending on whose life he makes an appearance in.

To the poor, he was the voice of doom that circled their lives, intoning matter-of-factly about the cost of some vital operation without which either the mother would die or the sister's blindness would stay. The doctor spelled out God's miserable plan for the poor, and served to squeeze out whatever limited options that existed. Often, a life of crime was the result; the obstinate contrariness of ill health turned the poor into the justifiably immoral. The doctor represented the unreasonable unfairness of fate; his knowledge was immovable in the face of the entreaties of the unfortunate.

For the rich, he was shown as the voice of the well-trained conscience that knew the limits of truth it was supposed to tell. The idea of the rich man's health was that of a finely tuned instrument that needed equilibrium rather than intervention. Rich men had heart attacks and needed rest and, above all, a complete absence of any stress or 'sadma'. Their health was an enabler; it allowed them to enforce their will. They were protected from any bad news or any actions that they might not like lest it upset their fragile constitution. The rich were nursed back by the devoted 'seva' of their close ones; this normally meant late nights punctuated by glasses of milk, accompanied by medicines. The rich man made others dance to his needs even on his deathbed. In the world of the rich, ill health magnified the power of their wealth; they either had their way or went off to Shimla to recuperate and meet Shekhar and fall in love just before the interval. Fate as seen through the lens of health was manipulable for the rich and was represented by the ill propped up in fluffy beds, while for the poor it was an as-yet suspended sentence represented by incessant sounds of retching in a dingy hovel.

The doctor character appeared as a part of the storyline quite often; his role, apart from playing the rich man's nag, was to function as a white-collar relative of some kind, occupying a grey area between friend, employee and relative. The idea of Doctor Chacha who was sort of always around to handle the health problems of the well off, is one seen in many films. Sometimes, advantage would be taken of his liminal position by making his character a Muslim, as in films like *Dulhan Wahi Jo Piya Man Bhaye*, or, in *Hum Aapke Hain Kaun*, where he straddled the line between the outside and the inside.

The doctor as protagonist tended to be depicted as one carrying the heroic burden of knowledge. In our conception, the doctor was one who was closest to answering questions that only God had answers to. This God-like burden was the calling card of Dr Bhaskar of *Anand* played by Amitabh Bachchan, surely one of the most memorable doctor characters in cinema. His expertise drowned out his ability to experience life, be it in terms of expressing his own romantic feelings or in accepting that being God-like was not quite like being God. Even as Anand lay dying, he was off looking for an 'injection' that could forestall the inevitable. The idea of the difference between life as seen in medical terms and life as it can be lived is explored in *Munnabhai MBBS* more recently.

The doctor in films was really a representative of our feelings about fate and its finality. As God's first cousin, he offered us the view from the vantage point of mortality. Of course, today the need for such an arbiter of fate is perhaps less pronounced – we feel more in control of our lives now – and hence the doctor is not the stock character he once was.

CHAPTER 2

VEHICLES OF ESCAPE

In a world otherwise populated by arbitrary rules and heroic restraint, there were enough carefully constructed patches of green that allowed for extracting a lot of pleasure from life without paying a corresponding price. The ability to find extraordinary joy in the ordinary, to sip noisily at the last drop of anything remotely enjoyable made the little go a long way. To separate enjoyment from expense, to use scarcity to multiply rather than to diminish was an innovation that helped grease the creaking wheels of life. Of course, the extraction of pleasure existed against a backdrop of inarticulate desire and hence found expression in unusual and interesting ways. The devices found were many; we tooted merrily in our chosen vehicles of escape.

OF PITHTHOO, RUMMY AND ANTAKSHARI

In the age before television, we farmed the arid wilderness called time with some very special games. These games served to maximize pleasure for the largest number of people for long periods of time with minimal equipment. The national indoor sport, especially for large groups, in India has to be Antakshari. As the name suggests, this sport consists of one team starting a song with the syllable that the other has ended with, and for some reason it has managed to engage us for decades. The film song is the great equalizer in India and most group events, if successful, have a tendency to dissolve into some form of communal singing. Antakshari represented the organized sector in this part of our lives, ordering our desire to sing sad songs full of morbid self-pity around a rudimentary structure.

There were many co-conspirators working together silently behind the scenes to make this so. We had Vividh Bharati, which catered to popular taste, something that AIR otherwise seemed loath to do, ensuring in the process that we knew songs that we didn't know we knew, so burned they were into our collective unconscious. We had the transistor that allowed the radio to become a mobile accessory, indispensable in every bicycle basket. And finally, this wouldn't have been possible if Indian languages were not phonetic in character. Because the alphabet name is the same as the sound it makes, we can instantly think of songs that begin with syllables. In English, this is much tougher because the sound 'ma' is conjured up by the alphabet M, which produces an 'em' rather than a 'ma' sound. Also, the correspond between alphabet and sound is a tenuous one in English; for instance, the 'cha' sound needs the collaboration of two different alphabets c and h in its production.

Antakshari allowed us immersion in shared moments of joy and needed no money of any kind to be spent. Hours were spent in the raucous butchering of beautiful songs as the teams (boys versus girls, front 5 rows versus the back 5 rows in a bus, adults versus children) unleashed one song after another at each other. There were songs that were sung only at Antaksharis ('Na, na, na, na meri beri se ber mat todo' comes to mind as does 'Hum kale hain to kya hua dilwale hain'), songs that were prized because they began with rare alphabets ('Thandi thandi hawa mein dil lalchaye', 'Dum dum diga diga') and there were the Antakshari experts who seemed to know every song ever sung. Arguments over whether a song had been sung previously or over its correct beginning were common. Antakshari reduced everyone to an infantile level of simplicity and we were all happier for it.

In fact, most games one grew up playing were all cheap pleasures. Cards were the staple of most families with Rummy, Kotpees and Black Queen (Hearts on the Windows roster) being the games of choice. Childhoods were dotted with Stapoo (hopscotch), Oonch Neech and Piththoo, again games with at best marginal investment in equipment. Flying kites required some gear but relied essentially on the motive force provided by nature.

These were the games families huddled around, games that bound us tightly even as they provided low levels of stimulation. Families revelled in being together; no deep conversation took place, no secrets were exchanged; it was understood that it was enough for us to play together in order to build something deep and unstated. These games were thinly disguised arenas of kinship building, where a common handle of belonging was proffered to each member of the group. We not only were family, but we acted like one when we played cards together. We broke bread together by mutilating songs together. In the India we have come from, the middle class in particular was glued together in the way we led our Small Lives – the street food we ate, the games we played, the festivals we got together for. It was in the way we distracted ourselves from boredom that we came together the most. In a world where money was hard to come by, we found ways to make sure that joy wasn't.

THE PLEASURES OF
VIVIDH BHARTI

Where would we have been without Vividh Bharati? Starting out as a grudging concession made to the baser side of Indian listeners, Vividh Bharati became a vivid presence in our lives, ordering our day with its programmes. The opening strains of AIR, called Akashvani, an inspired choice of name, ushered in a new day with the solemnity of a dawn breaking. The arrival of the transistor allowed us, for the first time, to be entertained wherever we might be, and whenever we chose to do so. The transistor was a surrogate friend, an occasional lover and a confidante; one crooned into it, clung to it and swung it around in exultation. The personal nature of the transistor allowed a more intimate relationship to develop between the listener and the world it transported her to. Words in songs took on special meanings and yearnings that most of us did not really understand or have a way of articulating, got expressed with this vicarious device.

The legions of requests from all over the country, including the famous Jhumri Talaiya, from where 'Bittu, Bablu, Guddi, Pinky aur unke bahut se saathi' wrote in, were testimony to the depth of penetration of this medium. The format was more or less uniform throughout the day – listeners wrote in with their request which the host played amidst some florid descriptions. One was drawn in by the unpredictable nature of the fare for one had no idea of what song was to come next. The special 'Fauji bhaiyon ke liye' *Jaimala*, hosted by famous personalities, was the high point every week and I remember some of those programmes to this day. Teenagers were widely accused of being ruined because of their obsession with Vividh Bharati, which had to be switched off when one was studying in earnest.

If Vividh Bharati brought some entertainment in our lives, Radio Ceylon was the elusive seductress. Hiding out on 25 metre band, and available once in a while on 31, tuning in to *Binaca Geetmala* meant that you dropped everything and concentrated with safe-cracker like tenacity on turning the knob of the transistor, and sometimes the transistor itself, with the greatest delicateness, till you could hear Ameen Sayani do his bhaiyon-aur-beheno number, especially when you glued your ear to the speaker. The weekly countdown show was our first introduction to the idea of consumerism, where popularity made a song most desirable. The idea of ranking songs created a hierarchy of value, albeit of a non-monetized kind.

If one was drawn into the radio, one was transfixed by television. The moving image was hypnotic in its power even in poor-quality black and white, where the picture kept moving every time the voltage fluctuated. If Vividh Bharati was bountiful in its entertainment, if not particularly discriminating, television was neither. It eked out anything pleasurable through gritted teeth, deigning to screen a feature film once every week and *Chitrahaar* twice (only if you were lucky and lived in the right town). The fourth song of *Chitrahaar* was always accompanied with a sinking feeling in the stomach, and on the occasion when a sixth song was squeezed in, much joy prevailed. There was no pattern to the songs shown, and they were picked with bureaucratic inscrutableness. But we didn't complain, as we sat unified across the country by those six songs for that half an hour. Television began to be a real part of our lives only with the advent of the serials. *Ramayana, Hum Log, Mahabharata, Buniyaad* began a new kind of relationship with the medium. Television became a universe in which we found our own place. Our acceptance of what television offered was absolute and unconditional. If radio transported us into our own world of fantasy and gave symbolic voice to repressed desires, television arrested us into its world and helped create new kinds of desires.

Of course, the big daddy of entertainment has always been cinema. Our fascination with films has been deep and abiding. I grew up at a time when the world seemed to be full of people who saw films twenty-six times. There were fans who were crazy about their favourites; people who saw every Dev Anand film a few dozen times, people who had shrines in their house devoted to Mukesh, and people who came to blows discussing the relative merits of Dilip Kumar and Raj Kapoor. The act of going to see films had its own well-developed culture. One looked at the listings in the newspapers, took a bus and stood in a queue to get advance reservation and took a bus again to go and see the film in question. The joy of sitting in a theatre anticipating the beginning of a film, the pleasure of sitting through ads and trailers, the eating of copious quantities of food, most of which had been carried from home, and the squeezing of the last drop of enjoyment by discussing the film afterwards and describing, in great detail, the story to those not fortunate enough to have seen the film, were all essential parts of the pleasure of watching movies. As a child, one watched the opening credits with an eagle eye, rejoicing when one caught a glimpse of the name of a comedian, with the best news, of course, being the presence of a fight master, which indicated that the film had its share of 'dhishoom dhishoom'.

We were really never only consumers of cinema; we were always consumed by it. Cinema was a form of mass therapy, packed as it was with ideas of licentious escape. We were infantilized by movies, for they spoke to the child in us, soothing us, cosseting us, titillating us with delicious brushes with adulthood. We did not go to the movies for anything new but to be comforted by all that was familiar. We wanted to re-hear the same stories and relive the same fantasies.

The idea of entertainment was central for it provided release from the onslaught of reality in our everyday lives. We squeezed out disproportionate pleasure from the small and surrendered at the altar of big pleasures like cinema.

HOW MANY TIMES HAVE YOU SEEN *CHUPKE CHUPKE*?

My score is 157. Or maybe twice that, who knows. And every time I am as involved, as enchanted and as fulfilled. Normally, on repeat viewing, one tends to pick up nuances that you lost earlier, but I am past that. I do not watch *Chupke Chupke* for any other reason but that I enjoy watching it. Over and over and over again. Just as I enjoy watching *Bawarchi, Gol Maal, Chhoti Si Baat, Khubsoorat, Naram Garam...* you can complete the list yourself. The Middle Class Family Entertainer (MCFE) was a genre of its time, but manages to retain a peculiar resonance even today.

There is something about this genre of films that connects with us in a unique way. The films are evenly paced, eschew intensity (that becomes difficult to watch over and over again) and are exceedingly good-natured. With time they have shrunk into a scale that works splendidly for television, given the sensory hyper-amplification that has got coded into our cinema now. But there is a deeper reason why they appeal to us so much after such a long time. For these films are the best advertisements for what we see as our 'middle class values'. Each of these films evokes a world that we long to be part of – a world of warm kinship unsettled by an odd idiosyncrasy that gets comfortably corrected, so that all is well again.

They manage to do this in many different ways. The characters are a far cry from the Eastmancolored Hyper-heroes with Biceps and Mother; they usually live in small houses and take the bus. The dramatic tension usually comes from constraints imposed by human whimsies. In *Gol Maal*, we have an Utpal Dutt who insists on his employees sporting moustaches and in *Naram Garam* he is driven by astrology. In *Khubsoorat*, we have a matriarch who is fixated on discipline and in *Guddi* a young girl is obsessed with movie stars. Regardless of whether or not the protagonists live in scarce circumstances, their problem rarely arises out of their poverty. The minor flaw in an otherwise perfect world is usually corrected by taking recourse to harmless subterfuges that create mayhem, before things settle down at a higher level of equilibrium.

Unlike other mainstream Hindi films, which were arrayed around some key axes of conflict, the primary among them being the battle of an individual to get some freedom, enacted of course with much melodrama, the MCFEs left enough room for the individual; the characters here were more than the Vicky Malhotras that dominated the screen otherwise.

In doing so, they re-established the importance of family, underlined the roles across gender and class, and maintained good-natured order. In *Khubsoorat* the 'wild' Rekha displays her responsible side to gain acceptance. In *Guddi* an 'immature' Jaya Bhaduri learns to appreciate the sterling qualities of her man. In *Chitchor* the carefree Zarina Wahab learns the pleasures of domesticity as she moves from her child companion to an adult one. In *Bawarchi*, the natural patrilineal order is restored and age regains the respect due to it.

It is interesting that these films fulfil the same purpose that another genre, the family social, strives to do. However, unlike the family social, which usually depicts an ideal family breaking up and reuniting after a lot of cravenness and tears, the breezy comedy does so in a more sophisticated way. Lessons are gentle, and rarely overt. If the family social is a blunt moral fable, the comedy is a warm advertisement. It works by bathing the idea of the family in a warm glow and makes us want to be a part of the world shown.

A big reason for the continued appeal of these films is that they tell us that happiness is independent of money. It is not that all these films depict people in constrained circumstances, but merely that money is not germane to the story. It is instructive to look at the differences between *Bawarchi* and its remake-of-sorts, *Hero No. 1*, made more recently. In both the films the protagonist is the impostor do-gooding servant who brings peace to a disintegrating family. However, if in *Bawarchi* the instruments employed for the reconciliation are good food, classical dance and music, and an occasional wink at a drink, in *Hero No. 1* it is the power of money and influence. Rajesh Khanna wins people over by his numerous abilities in cooking, singing, dancing and mathematics, Govinda by his physical prowess in saving the daughter of the house from being raped and by the power vested in his father's money. *Hero No. 1* is a chronicle of our times, making us nostalgic about the purity of the value system depicted in *Bawarchi*, however romanticized that depiction might have been.

As the world becomes more monetized, and as our pleasures becomes more loaded with sensory excess, the nostalgia for yesterday's simplicity is likely to grow. A *Chupke Chupke* tells us that there is always a way to be happy and that the answer lies within our existing way of life. Change is gently neutered as we all chuckle at its foolishness.

OF TAKIRA, CRAZY BOYS
AND OSIBISSA

I saw it again yesterday. An Indian wedding baraat, dancing to the tune of Takira, aka Tequila. With a beat-up sound system, fashioned no doubt out of a few megaphones, the unmistakable strains of the melody were squeezed out by the band, punctuated now and then by a voice that said Takira in funereal tones at the appropriate places. Since the beginning of time as I know it, Indian weddings have played this song and really, there is no reason on earth why this should be so. Why should an obscure instrumental of the sixties occupy such a permanent place in a traditional Indian wedding custom?

But then the topography of our memory is dotted with such strange monuments to the once-modern. Remember a series of films going under the banner of *Crazy Boys* that were all the rage in the seventies? These were a bunch of morons who went from one setting to another doing such idiotic things that they made *The Three Stooges* look like post-modern philosophers. I remember following every one of their escapades with unconcealed glee. Similarly, there was a series of spaghetti Westerns starring Terence Hill and Bud Spencer that I thought of as cinema classics. *Trinity Is Still My Name*, *My Name Is Nobody* and *All the Way Boys* are some titles that have cemented their place in my mind. And then there was a film called *The Gypsy Camp Vanishes into the Blue*, apparently an art film, which was yearningly seen over and over again by those lucky enough to be eighteen or look it (I was neither), because of a 'hot' scene.

And, of course, who can forget Osibissa, who were the closest we came to anything resembling international stars.

Our exposure to the world 'out there' was conditioned by the cultural material we had access to. We grew up reading Commando comics full of racist stereotypes and revelled in the Banzais, Achtungs and 'take that, you lousy Krauts' emitted by the noble British soldiers. We read about Billy Bunter and Biggles, and imagined England to be a place teeming with potted meat sandwiches and hot buttered scones. P.G. Wodehouse was our reigning writer-deity and we chuckled over every deliciously convoluted phrase that he wheedled out of the English language.

Growing up in India, one's access to the rest of the world was mediated largely by chance. We saw the movies NFDC decided to import and developed a taste for movies, books and music that were all our own. Our sense of the outside world was formed by these random scraps of influence that came our way. Outside influences came in by chance, were stranded in our environment and some, like Tequila, grew an alternative life far removed from their origins.

Our skewed grasp of the modern also shaped our depiction of it. The double-laddered mansion of all Hindi films, the rich man signified by the silk gown and pipe, bands in night clubs with six guitarists, the piano in the living room into whose keys all heroes decanted their heartbreak, the Vat 69 drunk in sinful looking goblets, were all products in some indirect way of our fragmented exposure to the world.

In a time when everything was available to us in small doses, we proceeded to take what came our way and built an imagined world around it. As we pull back with the benefit of both time and a fuller perspective, we can see how disjointed our picture of the world was. But then this is only natural. This is something that we see across the world. India was till recently associated with Raj Kapoor and *Awaara* in many parts of the world. Britain consumes huge quantities of Indian food never heard of in India. We construct nostalgic memories not necessarily because they are real but because they fulfil some need of ours. Dancing to a western tune that was easy to grasp and had only one word that we could mispronounce made us feel modern. Nothing wrong with that. A shot of takira, please, to celebrate.

THE GREAT INDIAN HONEYMOON

The other day I had the dubious pleasure of having to go through the honeymoon pictures of a newly married couple that I know only vaguely. The couple in question is a reasonably conservative one; their marriage was an arranged one, but the photographs they thrust upon me with practised flair would have given Mallika Sherawat and fellow frolicker something to think about. They were not at all uncomfortable sharing some very private moments with a near stranger; it was as if the honeymoon and one's action therein were exempt from the usual social codes that we are otherwise so bound by. The honeymoon not only gave them licence to act uninhibitedly but also the courage to harass innocent bystanders with a richly detailed pictorial account of their amorous activities. One was perhaps expected to look over the picture, carefully avoid articulating the thoughts that came to mind, taking particular care not to correlate the people in the pictures with those sitting opposite oneself, and instead very casually say something like, 'So, did you get a good deal on the hotel?'

But then in many ways the honeymoon in India is a strange custom. For starters, it has become an Indian custom in spite of its cultural strangeness. Since the early days, when the word honeymoon was a hot whisper of salacious promise, it has today become an almost boringly prosaic idea, yet another 'event' that needs to be organized in the ever expanding Indian wedding celebration. In a social framework where any form of sexual expressiveness is frowned upon, the idea of importing an alien custom that celebrates precisely that is, at first glance, somewhat confounding.

In some ways, the honeymoon is merely an extension of the notion of the 'suhaag raat', again another Indian ritual that celebrates sex with a robustness that borders on the broad. The first night is clearly about sex; the relationship between marriage and sex is underlined by celebrating in marriage what was proscribed outside it. The decorations, the milk and badam, the bawdy whispers that precede the event and the artificially constructed amphitheatre of privacy where a million eyes and ears are present by being absent are all part of the wedding night ritual. In celebrating the sexual union of the newly weds, a personal moment between two individuals gets socialized; the two are merely enacting their roles as husband wife in full public hiding.

The acceptance of the honeymoon as a legitimate ritual acknowledges that the traditional Indian marriage must create more space for individuals. It permits a once-in-a-lifetime window of privacy where the two individuals, armed with a roseate vision of each other, enact exaggerated rituals of affection towards each other. The honeymoon happens in a place that is the opposite of their everyday reality and allows room for personal expression and discovery. In an arranged marriage the honeymoon is really the period of wooing, for love most often happens only after marriage. The man and the woman treat each other with the exaggerated respect we accord to a new car, careful not to scratch the bumper and wiping it clean just for pleasure.

For most people who grew up in an atmosphere of sexual denial, the honeymoon allows a legitimate period of unbridled freedom where the pursuit of pleasure is socially decreed. So whether it was the young couple who showed me photographs of their callisthenic adventures or this young man I saw in

Manali who was walking down the street using his new wife as
a squeaky toy, the honeymoon does allow us our brief moment
with public improprieties. The honeymoon is a good illustration
of our understanding that we can hang on to our way of life only
when enough safety valves are built into what historian Sunil
Khilnani calls a 'self-coercing and self-disciplining' social system.
Be it the bawdiness of the wedding songs or the rough physicality
of Holi, we keep order and continuity by building small alcoves
of freedom that come with clearly defined boundaries.

Of course, for most the honeymoon marks a transition into
the all-too-real world of responsibilities into which we 'settle
down' with a resounding thud. There is nothing to do but to
bring out those honeymoon photographs once in a while and
marvel at the wonderful foolishnesses we were once capable of.

THE POWER OF STREET FOOD

There is something about street food that induces unconcealed lust. Personally, my street food of choice is the matar-chana with kulcha that you get out of brass pots all over Delhi. Every time I pass one of these small bicycle vendors, I tingle with frank desire. I indulge only once in a while thanks to the wholly unnecessary modern fad for hygiene, but I tingle always. Growing up for the most part in Delhi, one remembers all kinds of chaat, especially the aloo chaat; add to this the greasy irresistibility of the chana bhaturas, and the Delhi aloo tikkis, which are to die for. Holidays in Baroda meant ragda-patties, bhel-puri, pav-bhaji and, of course, the epitome of Gujarati sinfulness, the aamlet. One's childhood was peppered with kulfis, baraf-ka-golas, banta-soda, jaljeera, bhuttas and, of course, that now nearly extinct ambrosial liquid, sugarcane juice. A visit to the market was strategically dotted with one or the other of these inducements. Every scrap was licked off, juice from lime was squeezed till one saw blood and extra masala on the bhutta was invariably wheedled out of an exasperated vendor.

Street food exists for the tongue. Having avoided being classified as serious food with its attendant responsibilities, it is free to explore the nuances of our palate without worrying about wholesomeness. It is often greasy, spicy, and unhygienic and we love it. It harnesses all that is excitable about food, gathering all taste notes that chortle with impish delight to give us an experience that is rarely sinful but almost always dirty. Street food is a performance of gastric misdemeanour, an indecorous act of biological defiance. It speaks to our baser selves; we cannot help but respond. As the Pied Piper of our taste buds, it draws us irresistibly out of our civilized selves to itself.

Eating out when growing up meant literally that. Eating out on the streets. The idea of going to restaurants was a very distant one, reserved for special occasions that always ended with hushed force-field of silence around the bill accompanied by brave smiles of pretend nonchalance all around. The occasion was more important, not the food, and the pressure of using the fork and knife in any case made eating an exercise in mechanical dexterity rather than epicurean enjoyment. The act of ordering skirted the fine line between temptation and restraint as our eyes danced between the left side of the menu and the altogether more oppressive right side, and everyone carefully articulated their lack of hunger or their preference for dishes with the least heart-attack-inducing price tags. And meals were never complete without someone commenting as to how home food was so much better in any case, something that made the expense incurred on eating out all the more Pyrrhic.

On the other hand, eating at home was all about order of another kind. Home food was wholesome, nutritious and predictable. It came accompanied by its own set of rules: no wasting, finishing leftovers before eating the fresh food and eating everything, including the disgusting lauki-tori kind of gourds. Being made to eat tasteless mush was considered good for the soul, with many lectures on their alleged goodness.

Between the comfortable order of home and the ill-fitting pretence of restaurants lay the street. The food here was wickedly delicious and fiendishly compelling. The dish was always prepared in front of one; there was always a magical coming together of ingredients put together with an artisanal flourish. Most street food uses everyday ingredients but in a completely new way. You simply could not replicate street food at home; even the ordinary masala that you got with the guava was available only in the street.

It is as if street food comes out of some shared mysterious collective knowledge about who we are and what we respond to. It is a powerful collective of the palate that marks the idea of cities as communities. We step outside our caste and regional culinary pasts and participate in a shared celebration of the lowest common denominator in taste. We mix and match, garnish and spice till we are able to tune into the invisible wavelength of the tongue. Street food captures the essence of a place in terms of what it really responds to. That's why a chana bhatura in Mumbai can never taste like it does in Delhi and a jhal-muri in Bangalore is like a fax copy of the original. One can think of street food as a moving map of a city's culture. It translates culture into the language of the tongue on a continuous basis. As a city collects its inhabitants from a wide range of migrants, street food gradually alters its character to reflect the tastes of its residents. It is a testament of both the city as it was and as it is becoming.

To lose touch with street food is to detach oneself from one's past in a very real sense. Street food is popular culture updated to this very minute. All changes in our tongue have been accounted for. To move away from street food is thus to move into a world where one is on one's own. Going by the evidence of the popularity of Hadiram's and its ilk, the purveyors of street food in a sanitized form, it seems as if we are in little danger of that. More importantly, we see a slew of programmes on television that are going back to, and glorifying, the irresistible truth that seems to lie coiled in every morsel of food that comes out of streets all over India. The street is not going anywhere anytime soon. Burp.

THE SONG OF THE
INARTICULATE HEART

Every few months, our national anthem changes. Some Hindi film song captures our collective imagination and becomes a collective addiction, used to express all emotions. For instance, for a brief period we were inundated with the phrase 'Chak De', followed shortly by 'Dard-e-Disco' only to be replaced by 'Singh is Kingg', which became a mandatory headline in every medium. It is clear that hit film songs give us an easy currency of language to express ourselves in. And then there is the additional advantage of being able to dance to these slogans-in-song.

Our relationship with the Hindi film song is a long and deep one. We have sighed, spun, moped, hummed, waltzed, wept and whooped to the strains of songs for over sixty years now. They have allowed us to express different facets of ourselves across a wide range of situations. In the tradition of 'playback' singing, they become the background articulation of our inner feelings. They magnify and mould, beautify and breathe passion into our yearnings.

At some point in their lives, everyone has heard a Mukesh song in self-pity. We grew up in an India where millions of young men and women (particularly the former) turned to the comfort of a 'Mere toote hue dile se' or 'Dost dost na raha' when suffering from an imagined heartbreak caused by the imagined infidelity of one's imagined lover. The Hindi film song was the anthem of the inarticulate as it put in eloquent lyricism feelings that were trapped inside the hearts of so many but had no way of being expressed or realized. They were baubles of expressiveness that adorned us briefly before the business of living our more mundane lives exerted its authority. They remained as tiny sparks of freedom that caught fire occasionally either in times of stress or under the influence of alcohol. Liquor was the quickest way to descend into a maudlin bout of singing, with ghazals in the seventies and the eighties being the favoured vehicles of descent.

The Hindi film song made our emotions poetic; it rarefied our feelings into something fine and epic. There was no place for the grittiness of real life; this was a world full of refined allusions and subtle sign-language. Longing was expressed metaphorically and physical attraction through externalizing the idea of beauty. Songs were replete with references to the moon, the sea, the dawn and dusk.

Of course, there are many genres of Hindi film songs. We have Holi songs, Rakhi songs (almost all of which are drippy with extra sag), Janamashtami songs, patriotic songs, dosti songs (particularly in the seventies and eighties, when men sang more about other men than about women, something one must have some sympathy for given that leading heroines included the likes of Padmini Kolhapure and Reena Roy), picnic songs, bidaai songs, bhajans, qawwalis (used very often with the hero putting on a beard and singing a song on husn and ishq right in front of the police commissioner), happy birthday (to Sunita) songs, cabaret songs, wedding songs (who can forget the execrable 'Aaj mere yaar ki shaadi hai'), tawaif songs, sad versions of happy songs and so on.

We used all of these and more when we sat down to play antakshari every time we were in large groups and bored. Most parties would end in song, either in drunken incoherence or in embarrassed deference to someone singing 'Ghoonghroo ki tarah bajta hi raha hoon main' in earnest self-flagellation.

Our romance with the Hindi film song continues; one has

only to look at the number of film titles spawned by old songs (*Laga Chunari Mein Daag, Hum Hain Rahi Pyar Ke, Dil Hai Ki Manta Nahin, Kabhi Alvida Na Kehna, Kabhi Khushi Kabhi Gham, Tara Rum Pum Pum*). Of course, we now use the film song a little differently. Having become a little more articulate in everyday life, and not being so repressed about expressing our emotions, our need from the Hindi film song has changed. We don't need it as much to be a ventriloquist to our dummy but to amplify and underline what we wish to say. Our preference today is increasingly to use words of a song as footholds to get a dancing grip on. Lyrics no longer stammer with pent-up feelings, and in not doing so, lose some of their beauty. Which is why we have songs that are more contextless, with meaningless phrases ('Hamma hamma', 'Shaava Shaava', 'It's Rocking', 'Nach Baliye') becoming pivots on which the songs whirl.

Of course, the quest for meaning through songs continues. One has only to look at the songs of films like *Omkara, Rang De Basanti, Parineeta*, to name but a few, to see how we still need the poetic imagination of film songs to say things we would like to, but do not have the words for.

DECONSTRUCTING THE HINDI FILM HERO

When someone wants to be become a Hindi film hero and is unlucky enough not to have a father, mother or uncle in the industry, he needs to go in for some formal training. Not in acting, but in dancing and fighting. Although, truth be told, even that is not really necessary. All you need is to look like a hero, which means that you must be able to preen with excessive narcissism and make extravagant gestures when you speak. This will not necessarily make you a successful hero, but you will become a hero nevertheless.

For the classic Hindi film hero that we have grown up seeing is an archetype that stands above and beyond the character he happens to portray. He is first and foremost The Hero. The Hero is signified in many ways – he is usually fair or made to appear so; his hair is usually puffed relentlessly using a diet of blow-driers and yeast; his face glows with the made-up pride of the bread-pakoda handsome. He displays plumage instead of merely wearing clothes, and has the unique ability of making his attire strut with vain-glorious shrillness. The effect is achieved with a combination of luridly improbable colours, an impossible tightness of fit that has him forever panting in a shirt open till the chest hair runs out (or so we hope) and a jacket with its sleeves pulled up. He resembles a macaw in heat squawking out mating cries across valleys in sundry hill stations. The most important weapon in the Hero's arsenal is the Exaggerated Gesture. He flings his head back, throws his arms wide open, runs his fingers through his considerable mane and runs in slow motion (ask a certain Ms Sherawat about the effect this can have). While Rajnikant may represent the pinnacle of the Extravagantly Gestured Hero archetype, every hero worth anything was a master of the deliberate gesture.

In many ways the classic Indian Hero is the opposite of cool, some exceptions notwithstanding. Everything about him boils over in an orgy of 70 mm excess. Heroes constantly refer to themselves as 'shers' to the villain's 'geedads', 'baaps' to the others' 'betas' and are always fulsome about their own masculinity. Pumped up with a lifetime supply of 'maa ka doodh', the Hindi film Hero revels in onanistic bombast with Raj Kumar and Shatrughan Sinha being the posters boys of this trait. The traditional Hindi posters too were coded with this sensibility and were resplendent with purple faces and red eyes. The cut-outs in the South extended this notion in space and made the desired magnification that much more real.

The Hindi film Hero was then this cauldron of masculinity boiling over with an enormous regard for himself. He was the centre of every group, the absolute 'tara' in the mother's 'ankh'. He wooed his woman by first harassing her with the abrasive tumescence of his manliness and then using it to protect her from other practitioners of the same craft. He was always an archetype, never a real person, and his role was to protect our way of life unquestioningly. His name was generic North Indian – Ravi Varma, Raj Malhotra and the like – as was his belief system. Fathers must always be respected, if not always obeyed, mothers must be surrendered slaveringly to, women must be tamed and then contained, and bad guys must feel the wrath of one's righteous rage. The Hero rarely conversed; his job was to act and to be seen to be acting. Every word he uttered was either in defence of something or a diatribe against what he saw as wrong.

Everything about the Hero was a counterpoint to the institutional self-restraint imposed by the brahminical order. In a time when one took care not to stand out and sought to limit one's desires so that they were never likely to rock the boat, the Hindi film Hero was our animal opposite. He was what we wanted to be, but could never admit to, except in the bad dream called cinema. He was the child with chest hair who raged with infantile yearning for attention and the belief that he was legitimately the centre of the universe. He aggrandized himself in space and time, throwing his voice across vast valleys and decimating evil in slow motion. He made us live out the repressed side of our yearnings in a way that we never could aspire to nor could completely deride.

If the kind of masculinity that the Hero has to display is indeed an index of our unfulfilled needs as a society, then we have a lot to think about. For all problems in this world are resolved with the help of masculine force. A staggering number of romances in movies begin with an act of protecting the woman against rape; it is as if the only door to a woman's heart is through another man's lust.

The Hero of today is changing, albeit slowly. His clothes are more normal and he woos his woman less roughly, but in many other ways he is the same. As a society we still need our Heroes to do six impossible things before the first song in Switzerland. He must not appear ordinary, for we still have too much of that commodity going around in our own lives.

CHAPTER 3

RULES OF HIERARCHY

As a society we have converted inequality into an art form. Everything has its place, by which one means that there are other things both above and below it, and we all know the pecking order. Hierarchy in India serves many purposes, one of which is to act as a substitute for motion. By having many rungs on our ladders, we might well be trying to create a sense of movement.

HIERARCHIES UNLIMITED

For the world's largest democracy, we take an extraordinary interest in hierarchy. So much in India is arrayed on a hierarchical axis; and everyone knows who stands where. Caste, of course, is the most fundamental of hierarchies with its intricate and refined modes of discrimination. Fine distinctions are drawn on the basis of caste, sub-caste, the place of origin of the sub-caste and so on. The government has its own caste system with the IAS being the super-Brahmins followed by the lesser Brahmins, which are the other services, followed by the state administrative services. Then, of course, we have the designations that are accompanied with differential levels of entitlements; the kind of quarter one gets to live being a prime advertisement for one's station in life. Official cars are standardized, only the Ambassador has to suffice, but rare is the high official who does not festoon the automobile with flags, sirens, and if all else fails, designations on the number plate.

Our love of hierarchy is not restricted to officialdom alone. Take an area like education. To the Indian mind, the world of knowledge is divided into three broad categories: Science, Commerce and Arts. In the intricate algebra of educational options, Science is the undisputed leader, towering above nondescript Commerce and cowering Arts. Nobody questions this absurd practice; it is also unclear as to what forms the basis of this hierarchy. It is not entirely based on the likelihood of a successful career; it would be difficult to argue that a BSc

(Botany) has dramatically better career prospects than a BA of any description. It is not entirely based on the difficulty of the subject matter; try going through some text on Sociology or Anthropology on a Sunday afternoon and you will know what I mean.

The divisions run even finer. One can confidently walk up to a student doing Civil Engineering and commiserate with him about not getting mechanical, for everyone knows that had he done so, BE (Mechanical) is what his qualifications would read.

And then, of course, we have the institution of the VVIP, a uniquely Indian invention. The VIP is a charlatan, a mere pretender who needs to be paid obeisance to only in the absence of the real McCoy, the VVIP. Nothing illustrates our understanding of hierarchy better than the board one sees when one passes through security screening at airports. Outlining the people who are exempt from frisking, it lists governors of states and goes on parenthetically, 'not of Union Territories', the latter being clearly not of the same fine fibre that the former are made of. That such a board exists is, of course, revealing; it was no doubt put up to avoid arguments with other self-important people, including spiritual leaders of various hues, who believe they are demeaned by frisking.

This trait gets taken to truly absurd levels near toll booths on our shiny new highways. At one place I counted four massive hoardings, constructed no doubt at a very high cost, that merely list down the people exempt from paying the lousy twenty rupees to cross the bridge!

The reverence for hierarchy and the delicate questions it raises is underlined in the controversies that routinely surround dignitaries like the service chiefs, such as the one about their having to undergo frisking while sundry politicians did not, and the subsequent decision to exempt them from the procedure. The plaintive question raised was whether the people we trusted with saving our country were to be suspected of being hijackers or terrorists. It seems a fair enough question but it misses the point.

For it argues about who should get exemption rather than ask as to why anyone should. From a security standpoint, any person entering an aircraft could be the witting or unwitting carrier of a weapon and hence needs to be frisked. There can be no absolute a priori assessment of who is likelier to be a greater risk and hence no one should claim exemption. In most societies, politicians, in particular, might well insist that they be treated exactly as others are merely to underline, at no great personal cost, their egalitarianism.

Not so in India. For the desire not to be frisked in India has nothing to do with one's trustworthiness. It is a sign of hierarchy, plain and simple. The Union Territory governor is of a lower rank and hence cannot enjoy this privilege. If service chiefs were to be given this 'honour', then all the sundry bureaucrats who are of the same rank must be similarly accommodated.

At its heart, democracy is an impostor in India. Instinctively, we feel little need for equality. It is easy to blame politicians for this but that is to miss the point. Power of all kinds needs to carried as an immunizing halo around us; one's importance must be auratic. So we have the spectacle of senior military officers being 'received' by a gaggle of less senior officers as if they would otherwise have been lost in transit. Even the very same journalists and editors who rail about this in newspapers have no problem in having an airline minion carry their tiny briefcase up to the plane with them. Magistrates and even minor district officials carry their designations on their car registration plate and sirens of course are everywhere.

The 'do-you-know-who-I-am' question so often asked by the allegedly important needs to be understood fully. The emphasis is on the first part of the statement – do you know? For what use is my power if it doesn't keep you at awed distance? What use is my importance if a 'lowly' airport security guard can put his grubby hands all over me in full public view? Power is real only when the weaker person is aware of his relative status. The siren is such a powerful symbol of power because it converts an abstract noun into an insistent compelling whining verb. It flashes neon urgency and snappy impatience; we are put in our place with its relentless importance. I have always wondered what it would be like going through life travelling in a shrieking car but obviously to the politicians it is just the comforting drone that accompanies their success.

Equality is a sterile idea that is scrubbed into us. We need to strip ourselves of all that we possess and all that we have become in order to be equal. In a country where historically any success has been very hard to come by, we are in no hurry to become equal. We can rave and rant and shake ineffectual fists at the power hungriness of our rulers but the truth is that given a chance most of us will switch on that siren the moment we can.

We need hierarchy because it helps simplify our world by making it deterministic. Science is better than commerce so why tax your mind about what to choose? It standardizes the world on a single linear dimension and helps you know your place without any ambiguity. The individual and her desires are extracted from the equation; we study what we deserve rather than what we want. In a world with few choices, hierarchy offers the comfortable sense of certainty. What we are seeing today is large-scale economic and social mobility for virtually the first time in recent history. It is terribly important for the world to notice who we are and so we advertise our climb up the grease pole of hierarchy, be it through a siren on our car or a larger flashier car itself.

We are already seeing a movement from hierarchies embedded in birth to those that get created by human exertions. But even now, our mental model is of slotting people by virtue of who they are rather than what they have done. A designation converts achievement into a defined rung on a ladder; the individual gets located in a social framework.

As we are able to express our achievements in more and more diverse ways, the idea of a single linear hierarchy will perhaps recede. Till then we live in a world where a western potty makes me a better man than someone on his haunches on an Indian one. Oh! the subtle hierarchies of evacuation!

THE DRIVER'S MOLL

Every bus driver has a muse. Or so it seemed to me growing up in Delhi travelling in DTC buses. While the rest of us would smother in each other's vapours and claw our way to the exit two bus stops after it had passed, some woman would always be allowed to sit in the seat opposite the driver. This is a phenomenon you can see in many parts of the country and extends even to the chartered buses that have become so popular today. The bus would wait for her arrival if it needed to and the crowd would part to allow her to sit in the seat reserved for her. The relationship with the driver was never remotely improper; there was rarely any conversation or even any overt acknowledgement; it remained an unspoken pact between the driver and his muse. He basked in the glow of a fixed feminine presence and she in the reflected power of his authority.

And then were those men who had the privilege of nonchalantly plonking themselves on the bonnet of the engine next to the driver. This was an act of extreme familiarity open only to those who had the equivalent of a VIP pass in the bus (and a backside made of specially toughened leather), and was looked upon by the other passengers with much envy. Both the driver's muse and the driver's buddy were instances of otherwise ordinary people hitting air pockets of minor power, and emerging briefly from an undistinguished crowd. In both cases the beneficiaries glowed with the importance of those who have been set apart and the onlookers with the wistful envy of those who have not.

Another great example of this towering sense of achievement comes in the form of the extreme pride some of us feel when we park our scooters a little distance from our regular paan-wallah, nod imperiously in his direction and he brings us our paan exactly the way we like it – with its arcane bio-chemistry of banarasi patta, geeli supari, katha, chuna and chatni. We glow with the dazzling brilliance of our own significance and cannot stop ourselves from turning to our companion and pointing out with careful nonchalance how the paan-wallah does not need to be told what kind of paan we want; he knows. The need for us to be a 'sahib' for somebody is a critical one.

The cheapest hotels in India, the lodges around railway stations and bus depots too do not scrimp on the facility of room service. It is as if the idea of a hotel becomes invalid in the absence of someone being at one's beck and call. The dhaba boy will always be called 'chhotu' or something equivalent to emphasize our relative superiority. For us, the idea of service cannot really be separated from that of seeing some visible signs of servility; witness how frequently and easily we use the call button on airplanes to summon the air hostess for any and every need the moment it arises.

In a world where the 'common man' is nameless and anonymous, we look for whatever means we can find to stand out and be recognized as people of some significance. The city imposes anonymity on its denizens in a variety of ways. We live in a house that goes by a name like Type 2A 14B/43, Phase 1, and which looks remarkably like the one that is Type 2B, except for the extra balcony. We travel in buses and trains, and are referred to as being the 'masses'. It is easy to see why we yearn to be seen as individuals in our own right and why we use any means available to us to partake of this feeling. The current crop of reality shows tap into this need for significance. The reason why so much emotional investment is made in these attempts is because the underlying need for feeling important is so great.

On the other side of this desire runs an undercurrent of anger. Facelessness makes us touchy about being acknowledged as important. It manifests itself in diverse ways – from insisting on marks of respect like the 'salaam' to the eruption of mob anger that feeds on the accumulated frustration of the overlooked. As we become more aware of our individuality, our need for marks of respect will only grow. And we will continue to find these in our everyday lives, in ways small and large. And if this includes being able to sit on a burning bonnet of a bus engine as a sign of privilege, so be it.

THE MEANING OF THE SLAP

In Hollywood, angry men punch each other. In Bollywood angry people slap each other – mothers-in-law slap errant bahus, husbands slap sacrificing wives, parents slap children only to be remorseful later, honest police officers slap villains bearing bribes and so on. A road brawl starts with a slap, an altercation with the neighbours ends with one. The climax of a social film often has the slapee slapping the slapper to complete the cycle of revenge.

What explains this deep-rooted fascination for the slap as the preferred mode of meting out physical punishment? What does the slap signify that allows it to hold such a prominent part in our everyday lives?

The slap imprints humiliation on the face, the part of the body where our identity resides. We are our face, more or less. We hide our face in shame, worry about 'with what face can I go back to the people I may have shamed'. The slap connects the hand, the site of action, with the face, the seat of identity. The slap is a corrective lesson in social hierarchy, and is aimed less at the body than at our sense of who we are. It aims at taking us down a peg or three, at symbolically dwarfing us in the eyes of the people watching.

It is interesting that the slap is used to reinforce traditional lines of authority – fathers slap children, the rich master slaps the servant, and husbands slap wives. The intention is to keep status quo intact, to discourage the recipient from rising above his or her appointed station in life. It is no accident that the slap in Hindi films is so often accompanied by the word 'aukat', which captures the feudal spirit behind the slap. Know your place and do not attempt to rise above it, says the slap.

The punch, on the other hand, is an act of war. It opens hostilities, and relies on the masculine force backing this initiation. The punch aims to knock down the other guy, to flatten him physically. The punch asks for a counter-punch, and is reminiscent of all male jousting, aiming to establish who the cock of the walk really is. The punch is an index of physical strength, not social power.

Our unfamiliarity with the punch is obvious from the way our cinema depicted it. The 'dishoom-dishoom' sound so embedded in our memory (interspersed with the giddier 'e-bhishoom') is a patent contrivance. In earlier films, when men punched each other, it was obvious that we were seeing an enactment of violence, a choreographed necessity that preceded the happy ending. We needed to manufacture the sound of the punch, in order to make it appear tangible. The slap needs no such artificial support – it resounds unmistakably, supplementing its visual imprinting with ringing aural authority. It is also secure in its cultural moorings; for a society that is so intricate in its hierarchy, the slap is a vital device that keeps social order intact in our everyday lives.

The slap is an act of symbolic violence – its role is to magnify the intent behind the punishment and to render it exemplary. The slap rarely receives a counter-slap; unlike the punch, it does not set in motion a physical contest. It is designed as a one-way message – it may provoke a response later but at that point in time it usually proves definitive.

The idea of shaming that is such an important part of the slap is usually a part of most childhood punishments. Standing on the desk or outside the class are punishments of shaming by exclusion. The child feels debased by being singled out;

he is separated from the security of belonging to a group and advertised as someone unworthy of society. The punishment is an exercise in power – the child suffers the symbolic violence that is handed down to him by those in authority. The slap too converts its recipient into child-like helplessness by its symbolic power.

As an index of social change, perhaps we should follow the popularity of the slap as some sort of measure of our belief in social hierarchy. The slap carries with it all the accumulated power of the past; it uses an entire social class as its accompanying army. As we relate to each other as individuals not necessarily embedded in our respective hierarchies, perhaps we will punch each other more frequently. In some truly ironic way, that might be good news.

THE DYNASTIC URGE

We love dynasties. For all the breast beating that we indulge in about the stranglehold of the Nehru-Gandhi family on the ruling party, the truth is that this is a phenomenon not restricted to the first family in the country alone. Take Bollywood, where dynasties rule the roost, and where people like Shah Rukh Khan and Aishwarya Rai are sterling exceptions in a sea of dynastic names like Hrithik Roshan, Aamir Khan, Salman Khan, Farhan Akhtar, Sanjay Dutt and Abhishek Bachchan, to name only a few. Of course, the list should also incude less illustrious presences like Fardeen Khan, Raj Babbar's son and daughter, Mithun Chakraborty's son, and several other such star aspirants who have come and gone, or are in the process of fading away.

And why Bollywood, politics too bristles with genetic material in Nehru topis. Across the party spectrum (with the single exception of the Left), sons and daughters are striving to inherit the legacies of their parents. Spanning the regional parties, the BJP, the Shiv Sena, the Samajwadi Party, the idea of the dynasty is alive and well. The difference is only that in the Congress, the dynasty is more successful.

The underlying notion is of power as a possession whose ownership can be transferred. One's achievements become one's estate, a jagir which can then be passed down generations. At a deeper level, we seem to find it difficult to separate role from identity, which is why we embrace power not as a transient condition but as an ingrown trait. We become transformed into the powerful; our children behave as the progeny of the strong. A corporator's son too begins to believe in his inherent specialness. Perhaps it has something to do with seeing the world in terms of caste; power and success create a new caste, which provides a set of exclusive privileges to those belonging to it.

The really interesting part of the dynastic urge is its easy acceptance by most of us. We really see nothing wrong in Tushaar Kapoor trying to become a star; on the contrary, there is always some curiosity about a star child. Nepotism to us is a responsibility more than a misdemeanour. As parents, many of us would probably do the same. We acknowledge the right of parents to make their own present a starting point for their children's future. The individual is singular but never alone; he is part of a continuum that draws from the past and contributes to the future. We do not see the child and the parent as two completely separated people; in our minds they blur into each other, allowing us to accept the younger as a version of the original.

What this means is that the second generation gets a free pass, but only up to a point. It is easy to accept the son or daughter being the front for the parent. The second generation can exercise power on behalf of the older but finds it much more difficult to be taken seriously on its own strength. There, the rules of performance come into play. Whether it is Indira Gandhi in politics or Abhishek Bachchan in cinema, the successful transfer of legacy involves the hammering out of a new personal agenda while basking in the goodwill of the past.

As we move forward, we are seeing a change in the source of our identity. We define ourselves less by where we come from and more by where we are going. But even as we do this, we do not yet see ourselves as being sharply differentiated from our personal pasts – the present is seen as a continuing version of the past. Till that happens, we might occasionally crib about the children of the powerful but eventually we might come around to asking ourselves, as the press has begun to do, Why not Rahul Gandhi?

THE BADGE OF DISORDER

Consider this piece an ode to the badge. I am talking about the one sported by all 'organizers' of events in India, the round orange-purple-and-yellow satiny thing with two flaps, that is a kind of magic passport at such events. Be it a ladies club function or a durga puja pandal, a Lions Club felicitation or a variety entertainment programme organized by the Residents' Welfare Association, the venue is always awash with worried looking people sporting these proclamations of importance. These badges are a public acknowledgement of hierarchy, separating those who matter from everyone else.

What makes them interesting is that over time, we seem to have arrived at a tacit understanding of what these badges should look like, and across the length and breadth of the country they look pretty much the same. They represent a common currency of extra-official officiousness, a kind of civilian honour that we keep bestowing on ourselves. The badge is a quasi-uniform converting disconnected people into a cadre. The badge converts a lower division clerk into an officer bristling with disappointment at the proceedings around him, and a housewife into a despot with untrammelled powers.

In a society where hierarchy was embedded and social and economic mobility was low, the avenues for feeling significant were few. Most people lived out a predictable existence, with few opportunities to feel important. Which is why we are able to invest an astonishing amount of emotional energy in the pursuit of feeling important. Witness the kind of politicking that takes place in the smallest of elections – office welfare associations, the housing society or at mahila mandals. Observe the kind of designations that proliferate, the deal-making that surrounds these elections, the effortless ability to fragment into cliques, factions, splinter groups and blocs and, of course, the existence of the perennially disgruntled, who periodically throw a tantrum-coated spanner into any consensus that might be emerging.

Over time we have invented many devices that help fulfil this need that we so obviously feel. The Lions Club (which refers to its small-town luminaries as Lion-so-and-so), the Rotary, the Jaycees and so on elevate our otherwise ordinary lives into something more significant. The garlanding by everybody of everybody else keeps us in a state of floral bliss. Meetings of the most mundane kind are minuted with exaggerated care and we love the idea of proposing, seconding, referring and passing resolutions whenever we can get our hands on them.

The other distinguishing sign of importance is disorder. Anything important is by its very nature chaotic. Erratic motion is the Indian shorthand for the important; the prize distribution after a cricket match in India is a case in point. The podium is always spilling over with officals of visible importance but no visible duties. The stage at a political rally is another study in calculated chaos, with an incredible amount of trivial activity occurring all the time. From the Olympics Torch ceremony to the local jagran, the story is the same. People move around wringing their hands, feverishly muttering instructions to each other, huddle conspiratorially or just mill around advertising their own importance. And of course, they wear these badges. Those round, orange-purple-and-yellow satiny things.

CHAPTER 4

DISCLAIMER INDICA

It happens only in India. We are like this only. These are but two ways of articulating what is a widely used disclaimer, the Disclaimer Indica – forgive us, we are Indian and sometimes we behave in ways that would seem very strange to you. But there is an implicit logic, or at least some sort of an explanation that might render these Indianisms more comprehensible. The most interesting examples of this peculiarity lie in everyday life and exploring these can give us a glimmer of understanding about India.

THE STOMACH HAS ITS REASONS

In the gastro-centric view of the universe that we subscribe to, the stomach is without doubt the organ around which our world revolves. It is a finely tuned instrument that is somehow forever imbalanced and needs a high degree of tending on a daily basis. As a people, we are always deeply aware of the stomach, its machinations and its temperamental needs, and spare no efforts in keeping it in fine running condition (pun definitely not intended).

For most of us, the stomach has an independent consciousness and we refer to it as a separate being that resides in us. My stomach is giving trouble again, we confide to our neighbours several times during a day, as if it were another teenage child with an attitude problem. We measure our health through the stomach – all problems originate there and no matter how distant or seemingly unrelated the site of affliction, make no mistake, the stomach is somehow involved. Consequently, there is no problem that a purging cannot solve. This was accomplished in the past with a tablespoon of castor oil in one's tea, an act that established two things in one go – that there was something viler tasting than boiled cabbage and that a tablespoon contained much much more liquid than a teaspoon.

The obsession with the stomach and its constant friskiness did not translate into any frugality when it came to food. Balance was sought by adding things to one's diet rather than by cutting out anything. Restrictions pertained to avoiding certain combinations (milk and besan being one, if memory serves right, although why anyone would want that combination is not immediately clear) and specific foods at specific times of day. Fasting was another mode of discipline, although it was carried out in the pursuit of things more lofty and less pressing than the state of one's stomach. Otherwise, the idea of food itself was, by definition, a good one, and the more of it we had, the better it was.

The stomach was a barometer of our lives. It was the crucible where civilization played itself out. Cause and effect were palpable – the sixth kachori you had was clearly responsible for the uncomfortable night that followed. Every food item had its own unique force field – the role of the stomach was to mediate between all the diverse influences and retain its balance. The stomach was the Diwan-i-am of our bodies, where complaints were heard and justice delivered. After everything was said and done, and all the pluses and minuses accounted for, the only question that remained was – how was your stomach feeling?

And the stomach could feel an almost impossible array of things. We have a rich vocabulary to describe the stomach and its many consequent products. We become truly lyrical when the subject turns to that of bowel movement and we express ourselves freely, frankly, fearlessly and it must be said, fully. No detail is small enough and we make sure that the run of events is described in its true sequence. We initiate a broad ranging discussion on this subject and we cover the entire gamut of detail encompassing colour, texture, viscosity and frequency. We may be reticent when talking about what goes on inside our minds but this clearly does not extend to what is happening inside our stomachs.

This comes partly from the comfort we feel with the body and its many functions. A good meal calls for a good burp and why stop there. We express ourselves on this subject from many parts of the body. Perhaps it is in the ingredients or in the way we cook or indeed in the way we eat, but every now and then our inflatable bodies explode in small paroxysms of gassy relief.

With the advent of self-consciousness and the regrettable advances that grooming has made, the favoured technique today is that of the Silent Bum-lifting, which consists of a look of intense concentration on the face, a marginal lifting that creates a pathway and a silent release. It is possible to do this in company and get away unnoticed.

You can still get away, but hardly unnoticed, when you are face to face with the Hissing Stinkbomber. This is a silent but deadly emission that gets everyone around scurrying to proclaim their individual innocence by looking accusingly at everyone else.

In the earlier days, however, there was none of this pussyfooting around. There existed a proud generation that believed in the art of rhythmic punctuation. One expressed oneself as one carried out one's daily activities and declined to give too much attention to one's stuttering rear end. This practice was elevated to an art form by old aunts who, blessed with wall-to-wall hips, went room to room in unbroken self-expression.

If on the outside I am my face, on the inside I am without doubt my stomach, is the implicit belief at work here. The mind, and the higher body in general, focus on the intangible, rarefied stuff, and the lower body is caught up in our baser instincts that we do not really understand. It is in the middle body where all things are tangible and within grasp. The stomach is the real seat of accessible knowledge; everything finally boils down to things digestive.

When food was the centre of our existence, the stomach was the seat of our soul. Today, a small section of India is beginning to get infected with the food-as-poison discourse that originates in the US. For the first time, we are beginning to challenge the notion that food is, by definition, good. This does not come from any great concern about one's health but is influenced more by a desire to look good. However, our hearts are really not in this new-found fad, and whatever little exercise we have begun to subject ourselves to, is undergone so that we can have that extra samosa or a second helping of dessert. The reign of the stomach continues, for now.

THE MEANING OF THE THALI

I hate sit-down meals of the Western kind. They are interminable, they come in dribs and drabs, you eat too much without feeling satiated and you always get to sit next to two of God's Most Boring Creations on Earth. Also, one doesn't know if one should hold back for the next course, which might be better than the sawdust you are eating, or thank your lucky stars that you have found something edible at all. I guess part of this problem comes from having grown up on the thali.

The thali is an interesting way to eat. The idea here is to eat the entire meal all at once. No waiting, no guessing about what lies ahead. The thali is a wardrobe full of food; one gets to feast one's eyes and tongue on all that one eats simultaneously. To be sure, the hot chapati does keep arriving to replenish the overflowing thali, but that is merely a replacement for the previous one. The hot chapati serves to animate the rest of the thali; it brings tidings of freshly minted joy and carries off the accompanying vegetables and lentils in its wake.

Little else can beat the rampaging joy with which we eat our rice in our thalis. Heap the rice, drown it in daal, shovel in the vegetables, drag in the pickle, slide the chutney across, mix in some curd or raita, crush some papad on the lot and if you are unpolluted by modern fads about health, pour in some ghee. Stir, mix, knead all of this into a slurry and enjoy. The pleasure lies in the symphony of discordance that different food types, tastes, textures, flavours and colours create when they

collide seamlessly. The collisions in taste are of several kinds
– the blandness of the rice, the fiery tanginess of the pickle, the
acid sweetness of the chutney, the crackling crunchiness of the
papad, the serene cooling of the curd, all come together to create
a truly satiating experience. This is a complete meal that makes
one complete.

The thali is little India for in many ways it captures the joy we
are able to extract from our untidy and chaotic pluralism. The
thali preserves the individual integrity of each food item before
combining it. In that sense, the thali is not a composite meal, a
dish with its individual, separate identity. Most common Western
food comes as a dish which is structured as a core preparation
accompanied by some select embellishments. A steak comes
with some veggies on the side and a sauce of some kind. The
thali is instead a conglomeration of independent food republics
that chooses to come together.

The thali accommodates everything; nothing can lie outside
its pale. The rice we eat is assimilitative; I know of many people
who mix unspeakable things in their rice – Horlicks being one
such example. The thali moves from order to chaos and in doing
so, generates pleasure. In many parts of India, the food in the
thali is ritually positioned – there is a set place for everything and
even the order in which food gets served is pre-determined. Once
this order is established, however, it is then wilfully destroyed.
What we get is a 'rainbow of chaos', to use Chagall's words
utterly out of context.

The Western meal structure is a linear one; we move from
one course to another in a sequential and orderly fashion. It is
as if one set of taste buds is serviced before attention is turned
to the next. This neat progression ends in a crescendo called
the dessert. The thali, on the other hand, is utterly non-linear.
It revels in untidy collisions. Structurally, the thali is very much
like the Hindi film – all the ingredients are present in all films. A
murder mystery will have a comedy track involving the sidekicks,

an ailing mother will wheeze tirelessly and heroines will slither in Switzerland.

Perhaps it is a function of historical scarcity that we like to see all the food we intend to eat sitting together in front of us. The thali brims over with abundance, and our eyes join our tongues in the feasting. Certainly in the thali lies a story about the Indian ability to create harmony out of discordance and to find pleasure in chaos.

THE PICKLE AS CULTURAL DISTILLATE

It was the end of a long international trip and I was waiting to get to my next destination in some desultory German airport. The air of thickened boredom that is usual on such occasions had set in and I was addled into a state of indifference when my senses awoke with a start. I could smell the quite unmistakable smell of Bedekar's mango pickle. An Indian family had fished out a packet of wafers and was consuming it with the pickle with slow, painstaking and very obvious relish. I watched in burning envy as they demolished the packet, carefully wrapped the pickle bottle in some polythene and returned it to the inner recesses of their improbably shaped bag. I was not alone; all the Indians in the vicinity watched them as intently and with as much naked greed. For those not-so-brief moments, we had all been transported back to our cultural origins, thanks to the very distinctive sensory stimulus provided by the pickle.

The pickle exists to transform the dullness of other items on the plate with its own concentrated brilliance. It is stuffed with taste; and delivers more sensory thrills per square inch than almost any other food item. A little bit of it that one delicately bites into with the front of one's teeth is usually sufficient to make the taste buds squeal with delight. The pickle is the item number in the food platter that heightens the taste notes into a crescendo of pleasure.

To pickle something is to preserve something in its most

interesting form. Usually what one pickles is interesting enough to begin with; raw mangoes, green chillies, lime, garlic are all foods that are packed densely with taste. However, this is not a given and one can pickle virtually anything, with meat, chicken and radishes being the blander tastes that often get pickled. The end result, however, is almost always the same – an intensely interesting taste experience packed in very little quantity. This is a trait shared by its cousins, the chutneys, which perform the same role as the pickle, with even greater economy of ingredients.

It is easy to see why the pickle is so central to our diet. It is an inexpensive way to suffuse our food with taste; it allows taste to reside in one small corner of our plates and travel to every morsel that we eat. It isn't as if our diet is otherwise bland but the pickle ensures that we will never be wanting in that direction. A dry chapati with one vegetable, some raw onion and one spectacular pickle can be quite a gourmet meal! In a larger sense, the pickle points to the democracy that exists with respect to tasty food in our society. Cheap food may compromise on many things but not on taste. Even today, it is difficult to eat bad food on any street in India. In fact, there might even be an inverse relationship between price and taste – try eating chaat or bhelpuri at an expensive restaurant! It is interesting that in the food hierarchy in India, what becomes inaccessible to the poor are sweets and 'rich' food; delicious food is accessible to all.

In many ways, the pickle is the ultimate cultural distillate. Every community and region puts something of itself in the way that it makes its pickle. The pickle transforms something known and generic into the specific and cultural. The pickle carries within it the trace memories of the past and evokes with unerring precision a familiarity with our own cultural selves. We recognize ourselves when we eat a familiar pickle; it binds us tighter to our moorings. It is perhaps true that nothing defines our way of life as our food and as a corollary nothing defines 'our' food as sharply as our pickles and chutneys. The individual is important, how my mother made the mango pickle might differ a little from how my aunt made it, but in both cases what the pickle evokes is something larger and collective.

Which is why the pickle is nothing but culture packed in a bottle. Time, tradition, palate, lineage all get captured in the glass bottles that we carry around and protect so jealously. As with all things, today fewer families make their own pickle; it is so much easier to buy them off the shelf. And while these bottles may not carry as much authentic history as those earthen jars where we once stored our pickle, they are good enough to fulfil the essential function that pickle must perform. Take any food and infuse it with spicy excitement in an unmistakably Indian way. And evoke a reassuring sense of familiar belonging that identifies who we are to ourselves.

RIGHT, NO?

Isn't it a typical Indianism to end questions in a negative? Right, no? Hai na? In our everyday language, we use the negative ending to a question all the time in an unconscious way. As a mannerism of language that we employ routinely, it is useful in pointing towards an underlying cultural characteristic. The negative in the question prevents an opinion or a suggestion from being an assertion. It includes the person being spoken to, allowing for his or her input. In some ways the person is unconsciously apologizing for having an individual opinion and is appeasing the other person by attaching a note of self-doubt at the end. The doubt is dangled for the purposes of etiquette, and gives the speaker an escape route if the listener were to disagree.

The dangling negative inquisitor, to make it sound official and inevitable, is a sign of a culture that was uncomfortable with prickly individualism and helped turn individual inquiry into collective assent. It was like draping a verbal arm around the shoulder of the listener, making the act of saying something an act of confiding instead.

Interestingly, when used in a normal sentence, the no-ending communicates an urgent request as in usages like 'aao na', 'baitho na', 'bolo na' (say something, no!) etc. Here the negative underlines the positive instead of diluting it, and becomes an entreaty. The assertive suggestion is softened and what could have been a command becomes an endearing plea. The power shifts to the person replying even though the action is suggested strongly by the speaker. The demand becomes a need, and it is for the listener to now satisfy it. Language subtly creates a win-win for both parties and no one loses face.

The effacement of individuality and individual achievement is a cultural trait that we saw often in many other areas, particularly in the past. The 'aap ki dua se' syndrome, or the prefacing of some good news with an acknowledgement of the role played by others' blessing, is a way in which achievement becomes a communal rather than personal property. The prefacing ensures that the credit to others registers before any self-congratulation. The ritual reference to oneself as the insignificant 'nacheez', or one's abode as 'gareebkhana', are part of this larger desire to minimize the sense of an individual rising through his achievements or possessions beyond the ranks of the collective. Even the rich went through exaggerated displays of modesty; typically when asked how life was, the answer tended to be that they were eking out two meals a day.

This need is even more clearly on display in conversations with the Almighty. Bhajans refer to the devotee in terms of abject humility, where any impression that God may have got that the individual was getting 'above himself' was promptly and vehemently denied. It was not uncommon to see signs in shops or sometimes behind cars that proclaimed, 'Not By My Merit, But By His Grace'; a public disavowal of any pretensions to personal achievement. To take overt pride in one's achievement was to challenge the wrath of God, and no one was rich enough or powerful enough to risk that.

The desire not to stand out as an individual and to instead huddle together in an undifferentiated collective helped us cope better at a time when straying away from the folds of the community was fraught with uncertainty. The distrust of individualism runs deep and it is only with time and the opening out of opportunity that we are beginning to celebrate the individuality of our achievers. A Sania Mirza or a Dhoni do not need to play down what they have done, but this is as yet only a small beginning. Contestants on talent shows continue to plead with audiences (please, please, please vote for me; they also ask in the name of the collective – the community, the region, the state) for their talents to be recognized. Things are changing but it might still be a while before we end our sentences assertively. Right, no?

SCRATCHING THE ITCH

It is unfortunate that civilization has taken a firm position against the institution of public scratching. Apes do it, lions do it, squirrels do it with abandon. In this context, I am happy to report that the Indian Man, particularly the North Indian variety, has refused to submit to the arcane ways of civilization and continues to scratch away at himself with some diligence. In his case the scratching is localized in a part of the anatomy that occurs frequently in his conversation, often with reference to some close relatives.

To the lay eye, there are three distinct ways of practising this endangered art. The first is the art of the Sprawling Scrawl. Here the hand moves expansively and builds up a nice rhythm of sorts. The concerned area is strummed extravagantly and the nails are used to provide additional texture to the pleasure. The Sprawling Scrawl occurs during conversation, acting as a sort of mental percussion to keep the conversational ball rolling.

The Precise Pinch, however, comes from a completely different school of thought. For the Precise Pincher, the quest is more analytical as he methodically closes in on the itch and nails it in a soul satisfying pinch. This is an act that requires a great deal of concentration and is therefore unlikely to be accompanied by much conversation. This is the solitary brooding thinker among the scratchers, doing what he must with intensity and passion.

A completely different world view drives the third way of scratching – in fact, in many ways this is not really a scratch.

The Adjusting Shuffle is a hop-step-and-jump routine performed to make sure that the right thing is in the right place. Alignment is key to the exponent of this craft and he is not satisfied till he gets it, so to speak, just so.

What is notable is that all these acts of self-contact are not gestures aimed at the outside world – these do not contain any overt sexual aggression. They appear instead to be acts of narcissistic self-gratification; think of these as the adult version of sucking one's thumb. Some psychologists argue that Indian men retain the sense of being the centre of the universe that a childhood of being doted upon fosters. The boy can do no wrong; he is rarely chastised and thus grows up believing in the legitimacy of his own impulses.

It also points to a larger comfort that we feel with our bodies – witness the ease with which we relieve ourselves of our various burdens in public. Or, for that matter, the nonchalance with which we explore various cavities in our body. We spit, dig, burp and fart freely and frequently without feeling any great shame. Perhaps this has to do with the fact that we see our bodies as an extension of the universe whereas the Western view of the body sees it as a source of shame.

Whatever the reasons, it is unlikely that this enthralling public spectacle is anywhere close to extinction. I guess the only remaining question is: Are you up to scratch?

BOUND BY SOUND

Holidays are great places to observe the Great Indian Family at work. Qualises or Innovas are hired (as against Matadors, that contraption made by a sadistic prison designer, so popular once), large numbers of Chintus, Sweeties, Montys and Bappis stuffed in at the back, music systems play non-stop and ten people squeeze into a hotel room. Food is consumed with steady determination, and every meal becomes a massive project, with some people 'taking charge' and ruthlessly organizing everything from soft drinks to softies. Empty chips packets are left as markers of the Great Indian Family's adventures and no tourist spot in India, however remote, can escape the onslaught of Lay's chips (Magic Masala).

But by far the biggest sign of family kinship is the enormous noise that gets generated by the family as it cranks up for its annual migration into cooler climes. Everyone speaks at once, each in different pitches and for different purposes, but they choose to do so simultaneously. Bellows, hoots, squeaky plaints, screams, screeches, beckoning hollers, loud ministrations and barked instructions fill the air as the family embarks on a new day. No shout is loud enough and no shriek too shrill. The family engagement is entirely and stridently public with not a trace of self-consciousness.

Earshot determines distance, with anything within its perimeter being considered as no distance at all. If one's voice can reach there, it is right here. The family is bound by sound; togetherness is determined not by physical but by aural accessibility. We can cope with people being out of sight but not out of earshot. If the ability to hear each other measures distance then the volume of sound generated determines the strength of family ties. Happy families are somehow pictured as loud families; Hindi cinema is replete with families that never stop talking as a sign of kinship. The cacophony of kin is a sign of its engine humming, no make that, rattling along.

This need is not confined to holidays. There is a craving for life to announce itself loudly in many things we do. Our TV sets are louder as is the music we play. International manufacturers have understood this very Indian need for loudness and we can see a reflection of this in the specifications of TVs and audio systems, with the latter being marketed almost exclusively on the basis of PMPO, popularly seen as an index of volume. In everyday life too, we think nothing of yelling for someone from the street; street hawkers in any case have made an art form out of their plaintive cries. No bazaar is credible without noise; it is as if the market must advertise its commercial churn through the sound it makes. Like the stock market, which is characterized by an unearthly cacophony of simultaneous voices, to be a market is to accommodate the untidy desires of many simultaneously and this can scarcely be achieved silently.

Perhaps the Indian fondness for mobile phones, as evidenced by the incredibly large number of people who have taken to it, is in part fuelled by this deep need for constant connection. Separation is denied by the mobile phone and we see it being used in situations that do not really call for conversation (The 'I have landed' phone call that so many people make immediately after the flight lands, for instance).

The need is not a new one. From the time that people carried transistors in their bicycle baskets, the preference for being accompanied by sound has existed in our lives. Hindi cinema rarely uses silence in its narrative, for that makes us deeply uncomfortable. A more telling motif in cinema is perhaps the echo, the Sunita..Sunita..ta..ta that our hero hopefully beams across to his tight-salwared heroine. Here one is able to embrace a larger world as it comes within earshot.

The fear of being alone, of being separated from our close ones, is perhaps one reason for this need. Sound becomes a sign of the living, and liveliness is signified almost entirely by sound. How can one be alive and silent, how can one be in company of people one loves and not generate some evidence of it? As families we can never draw apart as long as we are within shouting distance of each other.

CHAPTER 5

THE PATTERNS WITHIN

Underneath the oddities of Indian behaviour lie coiled deeper patterns. What implicit world view can we deduce from our everyday behaviour? Making sense of India requires us to cross-connect behaviour from across different arenas in our life and try and piece them together. The Indian mosaic then begins to take some shape.

RITUAL REALITY AND
THE INDIAN

D o we live in the real world at all? This might seem a strange
question to ask in a country where reality, far from being
an abstraction, is an everyday sensory overload. However, in the
midst of all this reality, a lot of our everyday behaviour seems to
be strangely ritualistic and often largely symbolic.

A good example of how our actions have symbolic rather
than real effect is to be found in the area of hygiene. At one
level, we are scrupulous about taking a bath everyday, and yet
we see nothing wrong in dumping our garbage right outside the
threshold of the house. It does not take a genius to work out
that flies, mosquitoes and sundry germs may not recognize the
symbolic sanctity of the threshold and will come right back in.
But the symbolic separation of our house and the rest of the
world is seen as being the real one and therefore one is satisfied
by the dumping of the garbage on the 'other' side.

Or take the way we eat a plate of bhelpuri or chaat. The vendor
'cleans' the plate of the earlier customer with a ceremonial swish
of a dirty rag accompanied by a ritual dip into a pail of even
dirtier water. In effect, he has merely ensured that the germs are
now more evenly distributed across the surface of the plate. But
this is good enough for us. It is not that we do not care about
hygiene; if the vendor had not wiped the plate we would object.
It is only that what we are seeking is not delivery of effect but
the signification of intent.

The need for the symbolic asserts itself in unconscious ways.

V.S. Naipaul in *An Area of Darkness* describes a sweeper thus: 'The sweeper...he must be abashed and silent, yet somehow evident, careful never to open his eyes, squatting crabwise about the room among the dirt which is his livelihood and therefore must be identified with...' The sweeper, he went on to say, was a dependent being, 'whose job was to be willingly dependent; cleaning itself was immaterial.'

The overriding compulsion is to be everything a sweeper should be, without the actual detail of sweeping. A more familiar analogy, at least for those familiar with Delhi, is the Delhi traffic policeman. Every Delhi traffic cop looks like a traffic cop, speaks like one and has in every way the unmistakable demeanour of a traffic cop. The only one thing he does not do is to manage the traffic. His relationship with traffic is pure and spiritual, unsullied by any actual action. In the face of traffic jams and gross violations, he always maintains his sense of detachment and never once gets drawn into action.

The exception is during symbolic periods of activity like the Lane Driving Week or the Anti-Speeding Week, when traffic cops swing into action. The very presence of these weeks legitimizes the lack of action during the other periods.

This phenomenon of seeing one's job defined as an abstract noun rather than a verb is widespread. The Indian clerk is no less wedded to symbolic action, with every fibre of his being intent on signifying his 'clerkness' to the exclusion of any action.

A vivid example of this need is the kind of advertising that the government through the Department of Audio-Visual Publicity (DAVP) is best known for. Slogans on walls ('Plant a tree today'), full page ads in newspapers (100 days' achievements of minister X) are all created with not the slightest possibility of any impact. Often they test the limits of absurdity with slogans in English about some social programme being painted on village walls. My favourite one was on a kiosk on the Delhi-Gurgaon highway; it read 'Think Grid-Interactive Solar Power'. I have no doubt that the world would be a vastly better place if only all of us were to think of nothing else.

Even the way the government deals with budgets is in line with this underlying world view. What matters is that the budget was exhausted and not that it was used effectively. Spending money becomes the surrogate for action; intent substitutes action.

The penchant for symbolic action finds its pinnacle when it comes to finding a method to punish inaction. The institution of the suspension is an inspired one. Any misdemeanour, be it a rail mishap or a custody death, immediately leads to a suspension of the concerned officers. The suspension is a brilliant device, in that it marries immediacy with inconsequence. The action is swift but empty. The suspension as a punishment is a hedge against public memory, an act of indefinitely postponing action till it becomes unnecessary. Most suspensions are lifted once the clamour for punishment dies, and often with retrospective effect, without materially altering the life of the one suspended.

Where does this mindset come from? Perhaps from the many exhortations to our collective psyche that the 'real' world is the one within our minds rather than the one outside. Overall, it seems to reflect a lack of belief in the ability of any person to materially alter the world through individual action. By giving relatively lower importance to the physical world, we place thinking on a higher pedestal over action, seeing the latter as a 'lower' order activity compared to the former. This allows us to be more accepting of imperfect execution and less demanding of getting the details right. It permits us comfort with the token form of action. It also means that we can tolerate with much greater equanimity everything that is wrong around us. Our streets may be filthy but at least our minds are pure!

INDIAN TRAFFIC AS METAPHOR

If the Church is serious about reviving interest in religion, it should sponsor more trips by Westerners to India. For nowhere else is God remembered and prayed to as fervently as it is when they encounter Indian traffic. That India is a hotbed of chaos is part of its charm; most outsiders can smile through the assault carried out on their senses by the overwhelming sights, sounds and smell that surround them. They can grit their teeth and tolerate sundry touts, beggars, holy men and curious onlookers who mill around them with a permanent air of neediness. Where many crumble is in taking a ride through Indian roads. For this is a trip that makes everyone spiritual, at least for a while.

Why Westerners, even for Indians, traffic is not a mere occurrence but a test of some cosmic kind designed by powers higher than us. Several parallel universes descend on a narrow strip of road and conspire somehow not to collide, at least most of the time. Indian roads accommodate a staggering diversity of conveyances – overcrowded buses that stop as and where they like, overloaded trucks that rarely condescend to brake, let alone stop, cars that believe that they are supple acrobats and can twist themselves out of any jam, autorickshaws that are, in fact, supple acrobats that rotate greasily on their own axes, scooters and bikes that have foresworn any form of linearity, bullock carts that sedately lurch down the middle of the road, tractors that for some reason always travel down your side of the road, bicycles that make up in daring and agility what they lack in speed, pedestrians who jump out of bushes or behind buses to keep us honest and, of course, cows who do absolutely nothing in order to teach you some profound but as yet undetermined lesson.

Everyone drives focused only on their own objectives, deigning to take the road if it falls in their way. Relentless honking greases one's path, with the horn being seen as the accelerator worn on the outside. The horn magnifies the size of the vehicle and makes pesky tempos seem like steam locomotives urging you to step aside. Size does not really matter, and given the extreme absence of any organizing principles on the road, anyone can play. Scooters hog up the right side of the road, while cycles bisect any two points, however small the distance between them.

Indian traffic trains one to see time differently. Time is no longer a river that flows continuously but the intermittent spattering of rain. Every moment is individual and unconnected to the next. Anything can happen in the next instance, including a giant crane backing into you at fifty kilometres an hour. There is no fear of consequences because that needs continuous time. It is significant that in spite of the nature of Indian traffic, not a single brand of vehicle is sold on the basis of safety. The idea of safety is relevant only for those who acknowledge the relationship between cause and effect, between one's action and its consequence. Driving successfully in India is an act of recursive adaptive calibration. The mind must process all the variables at all times. In other countries, rules create an air of predictability that limits the extent to which the driver needs to exercise his or her mind. Deviation from rules are rare and hence when they occur, the consequences are often disastrous.

Perhaps the best way to see Indian traffic is to see it as a metaphor, which has the additional advantage of rendering something real and terrifying into something abstract and profound. Indian traffic is a miniaturized version of the world we are increasingly inhabiting; one where unpredictability is ceaseless, the source of attack can come from any quarter, where flux is not transient, and where the rulebook changes with every game that is played. To make one's way in this kind of world without being overwhelmed or losing a sense of control is a remarkable achievement. Traffic in India trains us never to rely on rules, more particularly on other people following them. It is a state worse than anarchy for anarchy means an absence of rules, and there is a measure of predictability in that. In India, the driver needs to be aware of all possibilities and violation of rules is an expectation, rather than a surprise.

However confounding Indian traffic is, the truth is that there is always a way. By fracturing rules, by manoeuvring ceaselessly, by inching forward sneakily, by pushing back crowds through the sheer willpower of honking, a way is conjured up. Maybe the success of Indians abroad, the unique ability to find a way in any environment, has something to do with dealing with traffic in India. For the one thing the Indian traffic is guaranteed not to do is make us take anything for granted.

THE RATIONALITY OF INDISCIPLINE

It happens every time. You are waiting for what seems like days at a level crossing waiting for some vitally important goods train to pass when some idiot goes right to the front on the wrong side of the road. Soon the other side is jam-packed with vehicles of all descriptions and what was going to be an interminable wait becomes an intolerable one. You rave and rant, pass scathing judgements on the morons who screw up things for everyone else and quickly move to denounce Indians as a race who cannot hope to do well without some discipline, civic duty and common sense. Underneath all the bombast, what really upsets you is that you thought about doing it yourself, restrained yourself knowing all the while with sick certainty that someone else would go ahead and break the rule and you would be sitting and ranting. The most galling aspect of this situation is that the person who breaks the rule is the smartest – there is no way the traffic can move until he gets to move. The system as a whole suffers but the individual gains – people who show collective rationality end up feeling like prize chumps individually.

This pattern of behaviour can be seen in various forms. A small jam becomes a large jelly in no time because some enterprising motorist blocks up the other side; red lights are seen as commas that open negotiations rather than full stops that conclude proceedings, garbage piles up in the colony because it is no one individual's problem. The individual's need always comes first – the interests of the collective are always subordinated.

In many ways, the city for us is an empty collective without the intricate network of mutuality that characterizes systems that are interdependent. The city is the arena of multiple singularities, packed densely with each intensely individual life living out its deeply personal destiny. The city happens to be a shared space but comes unaccompanied with a sense of the trade-offs that all communities inevitably involve. Interestingly, when it comes to the family, we understand this need marvellously; Indian family life is built around the idea of small mutual sacrifices that keep the collective together.

It is almost as if over the years we have lost the ability to organize ourselves into new communities. We are good at following rules, especially in the social arena, even better at bending them, but seem to be inept at making and following any new rules of engagement. The modern city calls for a new behaviour code to be evolved by us and this has clearly proved problematic.

Which is why we are so comfortable being model citizens internationally – the responsibility for framing those rules is not ours. Also, it is possible to know for sure that others will follow rules. The problem in India is that of never being sure about reciprocal intentionality. If there is a small chance that someone else will break the rule and screw things up for me, then I might as well break the rule first and reap the rewards. Low levels of trust breed high levels of selfishness, which guarantee even lower levels of trust. Which is why we live in cities as users, scavenging what we can from it.

There are two ways by which things can change. Either we will be forced into mutuality because things will break down otherwise, as is the case with Mumbai, the only city in India with a sense of shared destiny. Mumbai understands that the city is a zero sum game – every take needs a corresponding give. The other way is for us to have plenty – to erase the ingrained memory of scarcity that makes us grab what we have today, for who knows what tomorrow might bring. That is likely to take a while, so in the meantime, dream up some new swear words you can use the next time the idiot in the gold Santro jams up the level crossing. Happy cursing!

UNDERSTANDING HYPOCRISY

When Indian cricket selectors want to drop senior players, they choose to 'rest' them. It is an interesting idea, this whole business of 'being' rested. The players are not opting out of their own volition nor have they been dropped, in spite of their desire to play. They are instead being asked to take a break. Resting, which was hitherto an action engaged in by human beings of their own free will, is now an involuntary imposition. However, the blow is softened by a linguistic contrivance, by the use of the gentle label of resting. They have been cast in featherbed exile, having been patted on the knuckles by a chiding caress. In doing so, their seniority has been respected even as they receive their share of punishment. By the cunning use of linguistic hypocrisy, they have been reprimanded, but not shamed.

India is full of these dotted-line contrivances that manage to reconcile the irreconcilable, often in a maddeningly frustrating way. They offer an alternative mode of existence that defies the categories that language otherwise imposes on us. The 'stay' order is another such Indian classic. It is a court order in response to a plea that enforces a temporary status quo. It is a decisive piece of action that chooses not to decide, for now. This state of stasis is indefinite; but conjures up an air of certainty while breeding the exact opposite. Illegal constructions thrive for decades under the benign protection of a stay order. Occasionally it gets 'vacated', another fascinating use of language. It is as if immobility was an occupation; indecisiveness had become a form of residence which needed vacating.

And, of course, as earlier explained, we have the suspension, another idea that floats in a universe where time and space are fluid and indeed reversible. The suspension allows for action detached from its consequences. You can punish someone 'on the spot' without inflicting any real damage. Time is shushed and can later be reversed, by reinstating the suspended retrospectively.

All these devices create a new classification of existence, one that defies the usual binaries of life and death, good and bad, cause and effect, being and unbeing. The problem is temporarily extracted from its context and dealt with symbolically. The appearance of order is maintained and time is given for things to work themselves out. This does not always happen, and hence so many things in India hover above reality and beneath illusion.

The comfort with the indeterminate intermediate state of being is visible elsewhere. Being 'inter'-pass is another such instance. The 'Intermediate' college is between school and college, between having a degree and not having one. In India, being inter-pass or matric-pass or even 'chauthi-fail' is a qualification. Similarly, there are a large number of people doing MPhils and MComs, if not 'studying for the IAS' or 'doing articleship', all euphemisms for living in a condition suspended between idleness and employment.

The inspired use of liminality, the state that exists between defined states of being, allows India to be comfortable with resting positions that the world considers inappropriate. The creative use of liminal concepts allowed a Hiranyakashyap to be killed as he was. In the Mahabharata, the deaths of both Dronacharya and Bhishma are contrived in this manner; Drona is told a neither-lie-nor-truth and Bhishma is slain using someone neither-man-nor-woman.

The ability to find room for manoeuvre, to prize open opposites and reveal space for play and time for negotiation allows both for stasis and manageable change. It rejects the necessity of change in response to an immediate stimulus. It responds to events in a subtler, deeper way. Change is seen as far too important a force to be held hostage to the morality of the day. The prevailing moral and legal ethos is paid lip service to, but action is freed from its immediate context by the cunning use of 'hypocrisy'. The long term is rescued from the pressures of immediacy by speaking through both sides of the mouth. And in due time, most players who were 'rested' would be back in the team and doing very well.

THE POWER OF THE IMPERFECT SOLUTION

If there is one idea that as a nation and as a culture India can lay claim to, it is that of the Imperfect Solution. Things in India always sort of work and never quite do. Whether it is the way we practise our special version of Democracy, or the way we resolve the discipline issue in cricket, or how we manage the contradictions inherent in coalition governments, we always find a dissatisfying way to move forward. Usually, this is what we like to tear our hair about – the lack of desire for quality and the acceptance of the almost-good-enough. The 'chalta hai' attitude is widely seen to be responsible for many of India's ills, and understandably so. But there is perhaps a more profound understanding tucked away inside this seemingly unproductive characteristic.

India understands time. It understands the transience of all things, including solutions. It understands that there are no final solutions to problems; at best there is a temporary equilibrium that must eventually get destabilized and give way to a new equilibrium. Imperfectness is a permanent condition that we must learn to work with for it is conferred on us by the flow of time. The desire for lasting solutions is nothing but a desire to freeze time; and in that sense only death is a lasting solution. By definition then, solutions cannot stay perfect; keeping a solution perfect will take an ever increasing amount of effort that eventually becomes unsustainable.

Western analysis operates by reducing a problem to its

components and freezing it in time. Things are classified, labelled, put in boxes. Similarities and differences are noted; cause and effect is attributed by isolating phenomena from their context. In doing so, the individual becomes the fundamental unit of the world. The world gets defined from the perspective of individuals and their needs. The individual and his actions solve problems. The world we come into is an unfinished job list that we must strive to complete before we are done. Our life must mean something; we must make a difference.

Instinctively, the Indian mind sees the world very differently. Our perspective is ecological; we have a natural grasp of the totality of the system and operate within that framework. The world is not seen through the lens of individuals; the ability of individuals to significantly and permanently change things is seriously doubted. In this framework, imperfectness of solutions makes perfect sense. Allow time to rub against things, align them, and make them fit together somewhat loosely but with a sense of natural inevitability.

Some of our leaders reflect this astute understanding. Vajpayee saw his role as that of nudging time in the desired direction through strategic, if enigmatic, interventions. His solutions depended on the power of time to erode positions; they were dissatisfyingly indecisive and appeared to be riddled with compromises but often provided the only way to move forward in an extremely complex political environment both inside and outside his party. Manmohan Singh's view on the Kashmir problem reveals the same nuanced understanding. The resolution is sought by shaving the problem of its troublesome edges; this involves a complex set of actions that involve very many small adjustments, minor shifts in posture and the smoothening of troublesome characterizations to create an environment where an Imperfect Solution can hopefully emerge.

If there is one country that has trouble with the idea of time, it is the USA. A country without a history that it can acknowledge, everything for the US is rooted in today. The consequences of its actions today and how time will potentially multiply those consequences is something the US, particularly the Bush administration, seemed unable to comprehend.

Is this an argument for passivity? Perhaps, for implicit in the question is an implied pejorative. Implicit in our fear of being labelled passive is our hormonal need for red-blooded action. We need to do things to solve problems; whether they actually get solved or not is secondary. In any case, the question is not one of inaction but one of the power of nuanced action. Action need not be palpable, dramatic or newsworthy; what it needs is to take the totality into account and do what it can do. In fact, sometimes it is important to engage in frenetic apparent action, not for what it will achieve, but for what it looks like. The aura of disorder that surrounds VIPs in India is a small example of how a flurry of entropy creates a sense of importance. The action is enacted, not for a functional purpose but for a symbolic one. Action, immediate impact and eventual systemic consequence are complex, multidimensional questions that are confoundingly difficult to grasp.

Perhaps a good place to start would be to stop labelling situations and conditions indiscriminately as problems. Moving beyond the simplistic problem/solution mode into the process/time mode will allow for a much more realistic understanding of how things change and how little they do. That we understand this is a huge advantage; let us not take to the flashy shallowness of other modes of thinking in our quest to be seen as successful in the short run.

THE DISINTEREST IN
PUNISHMENT

If revenge is a dish that tastes best when cold, India should have been smacking its lips at the death of Prabhakaran and the virtual elimination of the LTTE. For here we had finally seen the end of someone who ordered the assassination of an Indian prime minister, a young and likable man trying to live up to the burdensome legacy of his family. By any account, given Rajiv Gandhi's lineage and popularity and the fact that ours is the most powerful country in the region, a show of strength by way of some retaliation was hardly unreasonable to expect. But there was a remarkable lack of interest in pursuing any such course of action. Of course, Tamil sentiments have something to do with it, but that didn't prevent India from sending a peace-keeping force to Sri Lanka in the first place. At a certain level, there is an intriguing indifference to the idea of punishment that underpins the Indian reaction.

We see the same passivity when it comes to executing Afzal Guru. There is a section that is baying for his blood, but for the most part, the dominant reaction is to muddle through without doing anything very definite. One reason why we can discuss with apparent nonchalance the idea of mercy for the perpetrators of a crime designed to wipe out the cornerstone of our democracy – the Parliament and its members – is that we are not really driven to seek retribution beyond a point. We cannot imagine the US granting clemency to anyone involved with 9/11; they have gone to the extent of punishing an entire country, one that had nothing to do with the attacks on the World Trade Center, in their bloodthirsty quest for revenge. And here we talk of letting off the one person we have managed to nab alive in a conspiracy of similar proportions.

We can see evidence of this trait everywhere. Rahul Mahajan emerged from his indiscretions as a page 3 celebrity and a judge in a reality show. Fardeen Khan shows no scars of his tryst with substance abuse. Charles Sobhraj became a minor celebrity before his re-arrest in Nepal. Phoolan Devi became a Member of Parliament before meeting her version of retribution. Sanjay Dutt bears no stigma for his alleged involvement in the Mumbai riots; he is at the peak of his popularity instead and fashioning himself as a budding politician. Even Shakti Kapoor has regained his original cult status with the masses (just kidding, but you get the point).

Take the cricket betting scandal. The interrogation of Herschelle Gibbs was followed by a remarkable absence of moral outrage. And why not, considering that the dramatis personae from the Indian side seem to doing so well. Azharuddin has received full rehabilitation, having morphed into a Congress Member of Parliament, and Jadeja is a respected commentator. The absence of deep emotional trauma in this case is truly astonishing. We follow our cricket team with a passion that is absolute; every run is celebrated and every wicket that we lose mourned for. The revelation that for years all our emotional investment was manipulated cynically by a few allegedly corrupt players has evoked no major backlash. We still revere our cricketers and they still make millions on endorsement deals. We find it easy to forgive their cravenness; it is their poor performance that we cannot stand.

Of course, the disinterest in punishment is restricted to a few arenas only. Caste-based violence is often retributive in nature. Perceived indiscretions here are ruthlessly punished and the cycle of violence can, in some cases, last over generations. The violence here is institutional and aimed at keeping the existing structure of hierarchy intact. The individual, be it the one handing out the punishment or the victim, is not by himself the key; he is merely the instrument of a larger intent. The punishment is ritualistic in nature in this case and comes from an urge that is collectively implanted. The individual does not really have to think too much on his own; the action dictates itself.

Where does this indifference to punishment come from? It is easier to explain this, in part at least, in the case of celebrities, where the size of celebrityhood is measured by the amount of public attention one can garner, regardless of whether the reason is positive or not. This is not a uniquely Indian trait and the world over celebrities emerge with their auras undimmed after bouts of alcoholism, drug abuse, public rants about race, anti-semitism and extreme misogyny, wife-beating and even murder raps.

But there is something else at work here. The disinterest in punishment becomes marked when we measure it against the involvement a country like the US has in extracting just retribution for crimes. There the quantum of punishment is followed with extreme interest, and whether the death penalty should remain or not is a hotly contested issue that determines the outcome of many an election. Presidential candidate Michael Dukakis is famously believed to have lost the election when he answered in a reasonable and a rational way a question about how he would feel about the death penalty if his wife were raped and murdered. That his answer was too clinical for the American public is understandable, but that it should play a role in disqualifying him as a future president gives us a sense of the importance attached to this factor.

It is possible that the Indian response comes in part from the absence of a pronounced heaven/hell narrative in Hinduism. We do not really have a day of Judgment to reckon with; we do not think of justice in such binary terms. In the context-dependent world we live in, everything has a reason that is embedded in its context and thus judgement from the outside is always difficult. We do not arrogate to ourselves the right to determine absolute right and wrong and hence live in a world of moral ambivalence. Even Ravana had his reasons; so who is to say what is finally good or bad?

It is this ambivalence that creates the Hindu rightwing reaction. Attempts are made to whip up feelings of retributive justice, to try and ensure that we speak in a language of 'strength'. The attempt succeeds occasionally, but by and large the going is tough for the indifference runs deep. We are good at forgiving and even better at forgetting.

SECTION TWO

NEW ADVENTURES IN MODERNITY

CHAPTER 6

LOOSENING THE PAST

*G*iven that society in India had built up a formidable and self-reinforcing system based on restraint and self-regulation, the idea of ushering in change needed to be made acceptable gradually. This involved loosening the clammy grip of the past without causing too much offence. A variety of strategies have been employed, most of which work subtly.

THE MORAL OF DRINKING

Forty-one years ago, when I was six, I first saw a man drinking. Or, at least, I think I saw a man drinking. It was in Ahmedabad (yes, liquor was apparently as freely available then as it is now), and I, along with a group of cousins, hid behind a hedge and actually saw a man drinking what was purported to be brandy. It was the high point of my summer holidays, this encounter with this dastardly consumer of evil spirits. There was no other way to describe this, such was the fear and disgust that the idea of alcohol aroused in my family and in large parts of middle class India.

In time, of course, I realized that some of this disgust did not quite translate into action, as evidenced by the mysterious absences of assorted uncles presaged by cryptic codes and much rolling of eyes and followed by their subsequent sheepish odorous reappearances. But these were lapses barely tolerated, and were regarded with disgust as signs of masculine sewage leaking into and polluting the otherwise chaste discourse of middle class morality.

Bollywood too showed liquor belonging to the realms of failed lovers and successful criminals. In the first case, liquor was the only means of escape available for those whose desires came in conflict with the constraints imposed by the social order. The self-pitying hero dissolving in Mukesh-throated dirges was emblematic of a time when, in a fight between the individual and his circumstances, there was little doubt as to who would prevail.

Liquor detached one from the safe embrace of the collective into the blurred haze of self-forgetfulness.

The other prominent liquor association was with criminals in their colourful dens. Drinking Vat 69 from curvaceous goblets of many kinds, these sultans of sin showed us that a life drowned in pleasure could only lie outside the bounds of legitimacy.

The role of liquor in both cases was to underline the consequences of departing from social conformity. Once you started doing what your heart told you to, you would have no social cover anymore – alcohol was the destructive mistress leading you away from the comfort of society towards ruin.

The underlying discourse at work was the fear of becoming who one really might be underneath the civilizing veneer of society. For that was why we feared alcohol so much; we were afraid of what we would turn out to be under the influence of this hypnotic truth serum. If today the opposition to alcohol comes from a health perspective, yesterday it came from a feared loss of control and the subsequent anarchy that was anticipated.

It is instructive that even then, the military was exempt from these proscriptions. We needed the men who protected us to be in touch with the more 'animal' side of their masculinity; we were happy to ply them with heavily subsidized rum so that the rest of us could lead lives of civilized self-restraint.

The other justification of drinking was when one travelled abroad, ostensibly because of the 'cold' climate. The idea of 'heat' producing alcohol is consistent with its ability to arouse baser passions, which we were only too happy to lock away.

In many ways, these attitudes towards alcohol were seen by the middle class to be the burden it needed to carry. In this easy generalization, the poor were 'below' these boundaries and the rich 'above' them. The frugal world of the middle class was held together by an implicit conspiracy of self-restraint. And alcohol, with its hot bestial masculinity, was too potent a force to be allowed in this fragile equilibrium.

This is what makes the change in our perceptions about alcohol particularly dramatic. The casualness with which one asks a visitor if they would like anything to drink (without the winks, nudges and the thumb signs) is a pointer to how far we have moved in this area. The real change lies within; we are no longer that afraid of our desires. The belief today is that giving in to these is not an automatic invitation to anarchy, nor are we likely to find dragons inside our mental closets.

If anything, we have begun to believe the opposite – that growth will come through the pursuit of pleasure. Far from being a sign of isolation from the social mainstream, alcohol is increasingly becoming a sign of social integrated-ness, of a desire to be an active participant in that part of society that is embracing its tomorrows. Today, alcohol is seen as a device that enables the experience of freedom as it greases the doorways to pleasure. Alcohol makes things easier, allowing us to unwind, let go and to use the word that there is no running away from, chill.

Even now, however, we continue to fear the talismanic potency of alcohol. We stopped serving alcohol on flights after a few experiences that confirmed to us that alcohol brought out that side of the Indian man which could not be safely handled in the restricted habitat of an airline cabin.

But elsewhere we drink less to escape and more to fly; we want alcohol to heighten our experience of the world around us. Now when we say cheers, it seems that we really mean it.

SUNITA ON THE BEACH

The hills are alive with the sound of music. You better believe it. In the hotel where I stayed on my recent trip to Manali, the hills were indeed remarkably alive with the sound of bhangra music. Every evening the lawns of major hotels get their own special DJ Jazzy, who gets Pammiji and Ashokji moving to the thin voice of some burly man exhorting us to Nach Le.

For any Indian worth his pickle, summers ideally meant a trip to a hill station, another English phrase that has long since become Indian. We were a race obsessed with the hills – you only have to look at our cinema to understand the depth of our infatuation with them. For a long time it was a contractual obligation for all Hindi film songs to be shot in the hills (low-budget films made do with the neighbourhood park) and almost mandatory for the hero to echo out 'Sunita, Sunita' till he received 'Shekhar, Shekhar' in reply. With time, the hills of Shimla were replaced with the mountains of Switzerland but the fascination with cool climes and wide open spaces remained intact.

It is only of late that the beach is beginning to come into its own and the pools of Goa are filling up with dupattas of many hues. Movies too are leaning a little more towards the sea, although for a while there was a class distinction with the *Dil Chahta Hais* (and films with Bipasha Basu) favouring the sea while the mass market Yash Chopra continued to look to the hills. Now even that has changed, thanks to the new breed of Yashraj directors.

The hill station was everything that real life was not. It was cool, extremely scenic and gave us a sense of space that we were unused to. In a tropical country like ours, coolness was the antithesis of everything our lives were about. The escape to a world away from sweaty struggle, away from the overbearing presence of other people's eyes and the constant sense of being hemmed in was highly desirable. But by far the most important aspect of the hill station was that it came without the rules that most places in India come accompanied with. Till a decade or so ago, holidays meant going back to one's home town or, at best, to a relative's house. Going to the hills was a licence to behave irresponsibly. We didn't go the hills to be one with Nature or to contemplatively regard its magnificence; we went to the hills to go to Monkey Point, eat chana bhaturas and drink cold coffee while being photographed wearing ridiculous hill costumes. We took an open, beautiful, serene place and made it an arena for chaos-infested outings that pass for family fun in our scheme of things. We went to the hills because they were everything we didn't find in our everyday lives and then derived pleasure by converting it into an overdose of precisely that. So we ate Gujarati thalis, honked impatiently at pedestrians, bargain-shoppped through the day and danced to the sound of the thin-voiced Punjabi man.

The hills were an arena of release; we were allowed to play out our repressed fantasies in a place that sanctioned such behaviour. We lived out a more impulsive life homeopathically; a boat ride here, a softy there. Indulgent consumption was the key to the appeal of the hill station. Till recently, the popular beaches too were used similarly. The archetypal beach experience was not Goa, but Chowpatty. Families eating themselves sick while jostling with other families determined to do the same.

The beach in its pure form was a daunting thought. While across the world the beach represents the liminal greyness of a place that is neither land nor water and hence without a rigid set of rules, we feared the brazenness that it demanded of us in order to enjoy its pleasures. We needed to become someone else

before we could partake of it. It was a licence to drive at a speed
we were petrified of. Also, it was not a family place nor did it
have a Mall Road.

It is only very recently that we have started becoming more
comfortable with the outside of our own bodies. The beach has
begun to feature more prominently in our consciousness and
signals a growing comfort with the pleasures of the lower body.
Our role models in cinema too have started rubbing against each
other in lycra on the sand rather than in striped polo necks down
slopes and this has given us a new site to locate our fantasies in.

But if we were to be really honest, it is still a stretch. Pristine
beaches are too minimalistic for our liking and the activities
they offer involve either too much passive lolling or too much
physical effort. The beach celebrates the culture of the sun.
The West looks to the sun for warmth that unlocks the body
and allows it to celebrate life. The beach is the arena where the
body soaks up the energy of the sun and expends it without a
sense of restrictions. For us, however, the sun is the overbearing
father whose occasional absences are looked forward to with
avid eagerness. If the Western song looks to the sun amidst the
rain, and where summer signifies an all-too-brief dalliance with
outdoorsy fun, the Hindi film song longs for the 'chhaon' to
escape the 'dhoop'. For the sun is the harsh truth around which
we are forced to construct our lives. The hills welcome us with
the toothless indulgence of doting grandparents and we revert to
being attention-seeking ten-year-olds in their presence.

Of course, one doesn't have to choose between the two. In
true Indian style, there is a great compromise at hand. The other
day, I happened to catch a TV show shot at a water park, where
a Hindi film singer on a mock cliff belted out the latest hits
in Hindi and Gujarati and scores of Kalpeshbhais in undress
frolicked amorously with fully clad Hansabens. Talk about being
in Nainital and Goa simultaneously and with live entertainment
to boot!

UNITED WE DANCE

I could be back in Baroda. The number of reports on dandiya festivities in Delhi make me feel homesick. Till some years ago, during Navratri, a few Gujaratis huddled together in some favourite haunts and engaged in polite stickplay every year. Now, of course, dandiya has been acquired by the larger community and is considerably more colourful, loud and inclusive. Monty does garba while Bappi likes to dandiya, and Falguni Pathak is known to one and all. And this is not the tap-tap-tap-these-Gujjus-are-crazy participation of the bemused outsider coming in for a cultural stroll but the robust let-me-at-those-dandiyas immersion of the insider straining to wear those mojdis and start dancing.

Of course, dandiya in Gujarat makes the word excessive feel like a wimpy underachiever. Everybody is dressed in the most impossibly colourful and elaborate outfits, is up all night and eats everything that doesn't talk back to them in Gujarati. Every sense is catered to, preferably simultaneously. Interestingly, the outfits are all stridently, almost hallucinogenically, traditional. If tradition dropped some acid and decided to make garba outfits, Gujarat would buy up the whole lot. Men, in particular, wear things that make them look like gigolos for the colour blind. Dressing up is now an important part of festivals – we do so consciously, as if we were playing a game of 'tradition-tradition' and want to look the part.

In a larger sense, we mark our festivals through our senses and express ourselves through acts of consumption. Colour unites most of our major festivals and today we express ourselves vividly in this medium. Every festival now calls for greeting cards, sms messages from obscure people celebrating obscure festivals, gifts, new clothes and lots of things to eat.

Of course, in some ways this has always been the case. Festivals were the safety valve in our otherwise austere middle class worlds. The Diwali bonus was the one time there was cash in our hands and we used this with the wise largesse of those secure in their constraints. For most who grew up in middle class India, our lives were marked by a succession of 'occasions' and we lived in anticipation of them. The legitimacy of festivals came from the rituals embedded in them, which would be gravely performed before the pleasurable bits would begin.

What we have done today is to dispense with the serious bits and gather all the pleasure notes resident in a festival and proceed to amplify them for our pleasure. To this end, we recruit festivals from everywhere and convert sombre festivals into joyous ones.

All festivals that are expressive in character have got appropriated by a growing community of urban cosmopolitans. Durga Puja, for instance, has begun to attract large participation from an ever wider cross-section of India. Delhi's Durga Puja festivities now routinely include rock acts that are as Bengali as dhansak. The growing metro fascination for Christmas is another case in point. Again we seem to be effortlessly celebrating something that most of us have no instinctive knowledge of. We have read about it, heard about the Christmas spirit and know the trappings that go with it. Our interest is not in Christmas but in the licence it gives us to have fun. The same holds true for all the festivals that we are embracing with such fervid openness. We are looking for excuses to enjoy ourselves and are ready to co-opt any likely candidate in this quest for a new reason to party.

It is interesting that our sense of being 'Indian' is at its peak when we are in celebration mode. We need the emotional high of festivity to allow us to step outside our narrower regional identities and immerse ourselves in a more inclusive national one. It is interesting that festivals that hitherto promoted our own regional cultures are now an instrument of shared good times. Of course, this also means that all celebrations are beginning to take on a similar hue. Be it winning at cricket or a wedding or a regional festival like dandiya, if we can take to the streets, surround ourselves with colour, eat incessantly and most importantly, find some reason to dance, we are all one. United, we dance.

MINCED PUNJABI CHIC

What on earth do the words Baliye, Mahiye, Shava and Soniye mean? I know everybody has a responsibility to go Shava Shava every now and then, but why? Karan Johar is single-handedly responsible for this; apart from making his heroes dress up like mithais and discovering that the word disco has many rhyming equivalents in Hindi, he has contributed to the arrival of a new minced version of Punjabi as our lingua franca.

And this is not the Punjabi as we knew him. We saw the Punjabi as a robust man, full of body hair and back-slapping gusto, cheerfully shouting out endearments about the biological apparatus of sundry relatives when not engaged in polishing off a leg with a peg. The Punjabi stereotype was of someone who lived life fully and made sure that we were all within earshot. The language rolled off our tongues like boulders in mating season, irrigating our lives with its rustic simplicity. The rest of India knew very little Punjabi except for the odd mention of puttar and balle-balle. Hindi film songs, while drawing heavily from Urdu, considered Punjabi not poetic enough and barring the odd exception, gave it a wide berth.

Punjabi today is revealing a new side; somewhat like a well-epilated Karan Johar, it is coating its once-hirsute exterior with a sheen that comes from rigorous exfoliation. The made-over Punjabi is minced, not spoken, lisped, not uttered, and is often accompanied by limp wrists rather than hairy forearms. It no longer has as its inspiration Anil Kapoor's back but Salman Khan's front. It is spoken with a barely open mouth, allowing words to slither out instead of being hurled out.

In a larger sense, things Punjabi are becoming modes of expression across many parts of India. Be it the naan-roti-dal-chicken combination in food, the salwar kameez as the default national attire for women, the bhangra or dances-that-consist-of-armpit-exposure as the national dance, the baraat as the official mode of getting married, the Punjabi influence is everywhere.

Perhaps the Punjabi spirit captures who we want to be right now. Part of the reason why this is happening could be attributed to the Hindi film industry and the strong Punjabi clique that runs it. But that is, at best, a partial explanation, for the Punjabi stranglehold on the industry is not as strong as it used to be, and we are seeing a much wider depiction of other regional cultures than ever before.

The Punjabi belief in the power of the individual to shape his own destiny and a general unwillingness to stay mired in the past is perhaps attractive right now. The uninhibited expressiveness that we seek in our lives today seems to have been hard-wired in the Punjabi ethos and we find ourselves drawn to it.

Minced Punjabi Chic, or Punjabi from which rusticity has been squeezed out, makes it easy for us to buy into this spirit without shame. In many ways it is a metaphor for what we want consumerist India to be. It celebrates our new-found zest for life and in things material. It allows us to see the modern as an amplification of tradition and it expresses itself in the blow-dried brogue of the newly sophisticated. It also brings us a new epilated form of masculinity, one in which aggression is streamlined into something resembling refinement.

The lyrics of Hindi films are a powerful source of reading change in India. We grew up in a time where we didn't understand the words of songs because they belonged to the drenched-in-pain-and-self-pity world of Urdu poetry. After decades of rhyming izhaar with ikraar and wafa with jafa, whatever that means, we have discovered a new source of ignorance in Punjabi. The cultures that the two languages reside in are, of course, completely different. So we might as well go Shava Shava one more time. Who cares what it means; one can at least dance to it.

THE DEATH OF THE BARITONE

This is All India Radio. The News, brought to you by Borun Haldar/ Surojit Sen/...,' my earliest memories resound with the echoes of powerful voices on the radio. Rich definitive baritones resonant with authority, telling us about what was happening in the world. Voices that broke through the stillness of our as yet uncluttered-by-media lives. Voices of people like Melville D'Mello, Berry Sarbadhikary, Tejeshwar Singh, Jasdev Singh, Pratap Sharma and many others who defined for us the sound that media emitted. Whether it was the news, commentary or advertising voice-overs, the only voices that ruled the airwaves were the voices of authority. Voices that electrified the ether with the static charge of certainty as they spoke to us in tones of clipped correctness. Voices that hung in the air long after the words were over. Voices that were above all Voices; no attempt was made for the person behind the voice to ever break through. An entire nation waited for Salma Sultan to smile once at the end of the News, such was the scarcity of any sign of a human presence behind these voices. Communication, when carried out through voices of such obvious power, was a formal affair, conducted with ceremony and mindful of ritual. The language used was replete with official flourish and decorated with cliché.

Recall any Republic Day parade commentary, for instance, and you will know what I mean. Yards of verbiage surrounding every ordinary action spoken of in tones of excessive reverence.

To the baritone, nothing can be trivial. The act of speaking about anything makes it a Matter of Vital Importance. Think of Pratap Sharma's advertising voice-overs that made Haiiiiir Caiiire seem like a subject of geo-political significance and it becomes clear that the key function of the baritone is to make the act of communication itself significant.

The baritone is the preferred voice of the state and of all institutions in general. It makes all content appear credible and vested with an implicit authority. In a time when all media spoke for the state or for established institutions, all communication too was delivered down to the individual and the voices that dominated at that time were the voices dripping with power.

The formality of communication was pervasive in its influence – in the Doordarshan era, the TV announcers dressed formally and spoke in the bureaucrat-approved argot that passes for shudhh Hindi. Interviews were formal; no starlet could escape being asked what her message to the youth of the nation was. Entertainment needed to be cloaked in Some Larger Purpose – election time legitimized the airing of more than one film per day (sometimes a staggering three films were shown, it is true) and millions of radio listeners enjoyed the weekly special Jaimala presented by a film personality, ostensibly aimed at our brave Fauji Bhaiyon.

The one voice that subverted the comfortable reign of the Deep Baritones was that of Ameen Sayani. From his guerilla outpost of Radio Ceylon, Ameen Sayani was the Baritone Who Wasn't; someone whose humanness shone through inspite of the resonant timbre of his voice. His Behnon aur Bhaiyon signature may seem a little contrived by today's standards, but at that time it was a radical and refreshing change. True, Sayani spoke to his audience as if they were children, but he at least acknowledged that they were human children. This was the first attempt to communicate in a person-to-person kind of way and no wonder he became the icon he did.

The breaking down of the formal stiffness that surrounded communication has much to do with the commercialization of media. As advertising revenue began to matter, the individual viewer and his preferences began to take precedence. In a larger sense, the commercialization of the economy has made the consumer the central unit of the country. As media becomes a consumer product, it needs to engage its consumer in a dialogue. The voices of today do just that; gone is the stiffness of the rostrum-voice and replacing it is the cosy chattiness of the personal dialogue. The newsreaders of today are not required to have voices that crack glasses when they quaver; instead what is sought is an ability to connect. The TV announcer today is a hyper-performer, who needs to keep saying things very quickly in very many different ways to keep us from changing channels.

Nowhere is the change as dramatic as it is in advertising, where the voice-over today is likelier to be in tapori-twang or Tendulkar-treble than in a sequinned baritone. Advertising voice-overs now seek out voices that ring with human whimsy. The source of inspiration is now the chaiwallah, nor the boxwallah.

From the baritone that represented stability and authority, we have moved to a more de-centred world where the anarchy of the individual spirit gets a free hand. A fixed centrally determined version of the world is giving way to an open version formed by a multitude of very different voices speaking their own minds. Today's voices boil over with the irrepressibility of desire and not the self-importance of correctness. The result is by no means pretty; a part of me cannot help but get nostalgic about the simplicity of the Baritone Days, but the truth today perhaps is shriller and more discordant, and that's how we are hearing it.

FATHER AMITABH

We can't get enough of Amitabh Bachchan. We see him in every other ad, we see him at what seems like every award function, we see him espousing all kinds of public causes and we see him in more films today than at any other time in his career. Instead of diminishing his stature, we find it growing. He does everything iconic superstars should not – he is in our homes several times a week on the small screen; he endorses dozens of products, and not always with dignity and grace. His film career has seen him experimenting with a freedom that some would argue borders on the reckless. It is almost as if far from being diminished by any of these, he seems to magnify everything he touches. What explains the power he exercises over our collective consciousness? What does he give us that we so badly need?

And it is only in the last few years that Mr Bachchan is back in public grace. There seemed to be a time when we watched with sadness the apparent decline of a once great hero into a caricature, of an idol flailing his way into buffoonery. In film after film, he played the ghost of greatness, relying on memory more than conviction. What has helped him become an icon all over again?

To understand the power of Amitabh Bachchan, we have to understand the hypnotic power of Salim-Javed's Vijay, a character that dominates our consciousness like no other screen character. The angry young man, who was in reality much more hurt than he was angry, told the story of a failed quest to believe in a credible father figure and in turn be accepted by him. In film after classic film, Vijay is let down by the father – in *Deewar* he is disgraced, in *Lawaaris* disowned, in *Shakti* abandoned and in *Trishul* discarded. The escape to the mother's womb too was always doomed – eventually there was no permanent sanctuary even there. Vijay spoke for a generation that felt let down by its father-figures but one that was doomed to comply with their authority.

Today's Amitabh has come a full circle – he is, in many ways, the father Vijay yearned for. His authority comes from active performance and not ossified custom. He can out-sing, out-dance and out-fight anyone else and yet be inclusive, accommodative and gracious. It is important for him to be affluent – his legitimacy comes from his success more than from the ideals he holds dear. For today's urban India, he reconciles our ritual respect for the past with the need to build a future. Amitabh Bachchan is what we want in a father figure – an imposing pet, house-trained in dignity.

It is interesting that the difficult years for Mr Bachchan were those when he was neither the angry son nor the accepting father. *Kaun Banega Crorepati* marked the transition – physically the attempt to stretch a long-lost youth gave way to revelling in the still self-possession that age can bring. His beard made all the difference for in wearing it, he discarded the overt attempts to powder over the sagging skin, choosing instead to embrace an air of benign gravitas. Instead of fighting age, he embraced it, wearing it as a badge. Amitabh Bachchan's beard was a mark of distinction and almost instantly, the meaning he transmitted was transformed. He was the Father Inquisitor standing at the doorway of untold wealth – testing ordinary mortals with an understanding twinkle in the eye.

Becoming a father figure in today's time is very liberating. When he experiments with his roles, he opens the doors wider for the rest of us. The travails that Vijay has gone through give Amitabh Bachchan a legitimate right to test the boundaries.

What Mr Bachchan gives the Indian man is a sense of belief in his own significance. As Vijay, he strode tall all by himself and made India's marginal men believe briefly in themselves. Today he helps us believe in an India that does not need to struggle with itself.

As India seeks to move forward, we constantly need reassurance that the past is with us and that it approves. We need Amitabh Bachchan because he is both credible and inclusive. He tells us that things are fine and leads us into a more inventive future. As the Pied Piper of modernity, he plays a compelling tune. We follow him because we for once have a father we want to believe in. Which is why we will always pray fervently for his well being.

IRRIGATING OUR ROOTS

This is the time for nostalgia. We have recently seen several films with old songs as titles – for example, *Om Shanti Om* and *Khoya Khoya Chand*, both set in a recognizable past. *Sholay* was remade (well, sort of) as was *Devdas*; and Gabbar skits still rule comedy shows and ads. At a time when there is so much talk about the future, something otherwise unheard of in India (my generation, at least, has grown up on stories of our allegedly glorious past), why are we looking so much to the past? Shouldn't this be a time to reimagine the future in new terms rather than sigh nostalgically about dog-collar shirts and polka-dotted trousers? Is this really the time to become nostalgic about Leena Chandravarkar? For that matter, should one ever become nostalgic about Leena Chandravarkar?

Or is it that this nostalgia in not really about the past? Take *Om Shanti Om*. It is hardly a faithful account of one era but more a pastiche of generalized memories about growing up at a certain time. The seventies it imagines are more vividly ridiculous and more engagingly endearing than the real deal. The colours are more pointedly flamboyant, the hairstyles more fulsomely absurd. It is as if we take the reality of the seventies and paint on it another coating of the hyper-seventies, the memory that we have of that time. Which is why we remember the past not as it was but as we saw it on screen. The seventies we remember is all electrons and sound rather than flesh and blood.

An actual seventies movie is not aware of its temporal

displacement and takes itself seriously. In doing so, it becomes fodder for retrospective irony. What we like the most about the seventies is that it is behind us safely enough for us to enjoy it. It exaggerates our bumbling inadequacies and now that we are perched atop some affluence, now that our vantage point is lofty, we can chuckle with affection at who we were then.

We rifle through our past to find benchmarks that allow us to measure the distance we have travelled since. If earlier the past was evoked through prices (remember when petrol was Rs 3 a litre) and geographies (Deer Park was considered on the outskirts of Delhi when I was young), both forms of physical reality, today we do so with images. In a world mediated by images on various screens, our mode of memory too is changing.

But the question still is whether nostalgia is at all a form of memory? We have no desire to remember the past in most other arenas. We are not interested in the cricketing legends of the past, for instance. I grew up listening to stories of Vijay Merchant and Mushtaq Ali and the alleged fearsomeness of Amar Singh and Nissar, and for all the popularity of cricket today, that is not our current mode of engagement with it. We follow cricket not to celebrate the game but to celebrate ourselves. Chak De etc. Similarly, we are not particularly fond of seeing reruns of old Hindi films; the original Devdas has no takers. Naya Daur sank without a trace when re-released. Mughal-e-Azam was coloured, but even that was found too old. Memory when intact seems to be inadequate; it is only when it is reconceived that it interests us.

And that is perhaps the key to the nostalgia we are seeing today. Om Shanti Om celebrates our present by going back and irrigating our past. We want a Sanjay Leela Bhansali to reimagine our past through the eyes of today. We want our current frame of mind to engage with our own past and rediscover the magic that we did not quite grasp when we went through it the first time. The nostalgia for an imagined past is the assertive celebration of the present. The images of the past, when examined closely, reveal themselves to be pixellated with sensibilities of today. We look back as a way of looking ahead. In that perhaps *Om Shanti Om* is set in the future.

OUTSIDE THE CLOSET

Sex doesn't know this but when it decides to come out of the closet in India, it is likely to face a barrage of flashbulbs and a slew of television interviews. For the media has been waiting fretfully outside, bemoaning the long wait and amusing itself by making many false-start announcements about its alleged escape, only to go back defeated and wait some more outside sex's closet. Is it possible that in the meantime sex has actually slipped through some inconspicuous back alley and roams free within us?

For that is a hypothesis worth considering. The reason why India is going through such a period of feeling good about itself, why 89 per cent of us want to be reborn as Indians, why most of our blockbusters are about disgustingly rich people leading disgustingly happy lives, is simple – we are getting better sex than ever before. Ok, so maybe there are other reasons but those have been discussed threadbare by now so let us for once talk about sex.

One defining aspect of the change we are going through as a society is the rediscovery of our senses. Having grown up in an era where we were taught to distrust our senses and every impulse was seen as a warning sign, our attitude towards all kinds of pleasures has been a complex one. We were lured towards things pleasurable only to find that our minds quickly stepped in to ensure that our senses were thwarted. Sex as the ultimate pleasure, naturally, was the subject of most repressions. Sexuality needed to be tightly controlled and ceaselessly monitored lest it rupture the delicate fabric of our family system. In a world full of constraints, impulsive urges were the ultimate enemy.

Sex in India therefore has had a tortured upbringing. Denied any sunlight, it mutated into a distorted demonic version of itself. In films it was presented in its vilest form – through the device of rape. Under the guise of righteous horror, we consumed the salacious pleasures of sex in this manner. Within marriages too, it was an area of darkness, a corner cold and dank festering with fungal misconceptions. In the chilling words of Sudhir Kakar, sex in a lot of Indian marriages was 'a sharp stab of lust' that women stoically tolerated so that they could go on with their lives. Men too were full of despairing doubt as evidenced by the whole host of wall paintings that dot our landscapes peopled by virile men with tumescent moustaches offering tensile strength for those allegedly weakened by 'hand-practice'.

As earlier explained, what our recent affluence has done is to set our senses free. We are more willing to consume the world through our senses and this shows up in all arenas of life. We wear more provocative colours, experiment with cuisine, dance in manic self-forgetfulness and yes, enjoy sex with less guilt. Witness the change in the colour of lingerie and the preponderance of red and black. From the earlier days of white underwear that were soggy with disbelief, we have quickly moved to a colourful world bristling with sensual promise. Honeymoons are on public display with couples from conservative backgrounds showing alacrity in embracing the pleasures of flesh. Ask any ski guide in Manali or go to any beach in Goa and you will know exactly what I mean when I use the word embrace.

Then why is media still sitting outside sex's closet? Possibly because it defines sexual freedom in terms of promiscuity. In India sexual freedom today is about the freedom to enjoy sex and not about the freedom to have it with different people. The real change in our attitude towards sex is seen within marriage.

Of course, there is change outside it too, but that is more gradual. The reason why this kind of sexual freedom results in an overall euphoric sentiment is because it allows us to enjoy sexual freedom without paying its costs. Sex in India is not yet a watchful game of one-upmanship where numbing conquests overwhelm the need for frank pleasure. Sex in India, for the moment, is like a child sliding down a banister – someone full of exhilaration at having discovered pleasure that is always at hand. The complications of sexual politics will perhaps follow but for the moment it is the time to, well, disco.

CHAPTER 7

THE HEADINESS OF MOBILITY

The sudden opening out of economic and social mobility has created a new sense of possibilities in India. From a time when motion of any kind was not really an option for most Indians, and where one found ways of finding meaning in one's existing circumstances, the idea that one could refashion the variables that defined one's life has been a heady one. This freedom has found interesting new modes of expression as it navigates the space between the old and the new.

LIFE AS ARENA

It is as if something fundamental has changed. The clichés are many – a tiger has been uncaged, the elephant is dancing, a sleeping giant has risen – and they all describe the new energy that we are seeing in India. And whatever be your ideological persuasion, it is difficult to deny that there has been a big change in the essential character of the Indian view of itself. There is a new hunger, a surging sense of self-belief that borders on fantasy, and a desire to extract out of life all it has to offer. We see this at work in our growing fascination with the world of consumption, the rising concern about personal appearance, the interest in making money and doing so quickly, and in ensuring that India is seen well by the rest of the world.

It is easy to attribute this to changes unleashed by economic reform, which allowed us to give free vent to our innate sense of enterprise. After all, this is the first generation that believes that its tomorrow is going to be better than its yesterday. Till my generation at least, it was clear was India was once a great country, the 'sone ki chidiya', and textbooks were full of wistful references to our ancient greatness, when India was admired as a benchmark by the world. This meant that the future could never really measure up to the past and we lived in the hope that far from embracing the future, we would one day be able to go back to our past. Memory became a magnet that pulled us back, and as for the present, the best we could do was cope. Today, that fixed idea in our collective psyche has changed. Tomorrow is seen to be bristling with promise, and from a mindset of someone to whom things were done, we are now seeing ourselves as subjects who have the ability to make a mark and influence the course of our own lives.

The most fundamental change has occurred in our mental model of life itself. So far, for most Indians, life was a condition into which one was born. It was an act of fait accompli that needed to be complied with. We were embedded inside our lives; we were the play and not the actors, the book and not the readers. We lived without too much concern about the content of our own personal lives. Existence was all about aligning oneself with the ebb and flow of life and not trying to impose one's will on it. We lived from season to season, family event to family event. Age was embraced, and life roles were adjusted in line with the progression of natural cycles. The idea of aspiration was weakly felt and rarely articulated. For most, a successful life meant that they had ensured good education for their children, and that their 'daughter was married, the son had a good job and both were well settled'. A man's life was successful if he had passed the baton successfully to the next generation. We lived life not for our sake but for its sake. Continuity was the key, not personal achievement.

This also meant that a strain of passivity was visible in the way we engaged with life. As the Mother India song goes, 'Duniya mein hum aaye hain toh jeena hi padega, jeevan hai agar zeher toh peena hi padega' (Since we have been born, we have no option but to live. If life is poison, we have no option but to drink). The fatalism of having to endure a difficult life, once one was born, was a widespread one, and Hindi films, for one, were certainly full of self-pitying laments about the cruelty of the world (bedard zamana, zalim duniya) and the sense of being trapped inside life.

One way of reading the India of yesterday is to see it as a wonderful example of a functioning zero-growth model.

Meaning in life was not predicated on making material progress within one's lifetime but came from the minutae of life. Life was broken up into an endless series of events and activities and one lived inside this cocooned habitat, without asking what it all added up to. Introspection in India has been about the nature of life itself rather than the nature of one's own life. Sudhir Kakar points out how the Socratic prescription of know yourself means such different things to the Westerner as compared to the Indian. The Westerner focuses on the self while the Indian attempt is to transcend the self. Kakar also uses the evocative example of the Indian disregard for autobiography. While Western writers dwell at length on the childhood influences that shaped them, Indian autobiographies tend to dismiss an entire childhood with a laconic 'Mother was loving, father was kind'. One's life by itself was not worth reflecting upon.

The big change today is that life is no longer seen as a condition but as an arena. The individual has detached herself from her life and has the ability to regard it from the outside. Life is a canvas on which one needs to paint the story of one's life. We have the ability and indeed the responsibility to fill our own lives with meaning. This we find in personal achievement, in the relationships we build, the things we consume and the legacy we leave. Being able to see our own lives as a movie in which we star also gives us the ability to see ourselves as others see us. This means that instead of being stuck to our inner worlds, where our actions were reflexive, we start inhabiting our outer world, where we do things in a discretionary manner. Earlier we ate what we always did (sweet dal because we are Gujarati), wore what people like us always wore (vesti, saree with straight pallu), and followed the customs that were always followed. Today, each of these arenas of our lives needs us to take decisions. Living our lives and populating it with meaning has become our responsibility.

The interaction with the outside world has grown manifold.

The desire to live life to the full is the most commonly articulated desire of today's middle class Indian. This new awakening to the idea of life as a gap in time that we need to fill up is at the heart of the many changes we are seeing in the mindset of the New Indian.

THE DISAPPEARING PIGTAIL

Sometimes, the biggest changes are presaged by the smallest signs. In the last few months, in the several trips by road I have had to undertake across parts of the country, I have made a remarkably inconsequential discovery. The pigtail is disappearing.

Remember the pigtail? The well-oiled cording of thick long hair into single or double plaits held together tightly by a red ribbon with oily residue? The 'choti' that usually trailed a woman wherever she went and occasionally made its coy appearance in the front? The envious oohing and aahing that accompanied women with long hair, the stories about your mother's plait 'reaching right down the back' when she was a little younger? Film actresses tossing their pigtails in romantic thrall as they sashayed ahead of a panting hero with fop hair?

In parts of metropolitan India, its presence is already marginal, but even in the smallest towns across India, more and more little girls are wearing their hair shorter. To be sure, the pigtail is still very visible here, but is no longer the dominant force it used to be once upon a time.

The pigtail was a strong cultural sign that was an integral part of the larger world of women's hair. Hindi film songs that pay tribute to a woman's zulfein that are like 'saawan ki ghata' are too many to recount, but it is clear that hair played a big part in signifying femininity. Long hair was intrinsic to the idea of 'good' female beauty, but it was rarely left open.

Long hair was as glorified as it was contained. In part this could be because long thick hair was a sign of fertility, and evoked the schizophrenic response our society has towards female fertility. It is both revered and feared; we want the fruits of fertility but are afraid of the potency of the sexuality that accompanies it. So long hair needed to be governed tightly, it needed to be steeped in heavy aromatic oils and tied into coils simmering with passivity. The aroma was in some ways a substitute for mobility. The hair was tied down but the aroma acted by creating an aura of attention around the hair. The hair did not move, you were drawn to it. Hair represented a powerful force field of fragrant femininity, as bewitching as it was static. It made up in depth what it lacked in motion. Long tresses were an elaborate trap, an intricate net of feminine murky depths waiting to ensnare a man. Think of Meena Kumari combing her hair in front of a mirror in *Sahib, Biwi aur Ghulam* and you have the archetypal picture of an enigmatic, seductive woman tied up in the rapt loneliness of her one-person universe. When her hair was left open, it was usually a sign of a woman losing control. It either signified awakened sexuality (think of a plump, as-yet-unwaxed Mumtaz trying to seduce a waxed Biswajeet with a 'Yeh hai reshmi zulfon ka andhera') or of uncontrollable anger (Kaikeyi's almost menstrual tantrum in her kop-bhavan).

Short hair, therefore, represents much more than merely style. It is a form of unburdening of the feminine baggage that women have carried for long. It short-circuits the set of meanings that were woven into a woman's plaits and frees her from the roles that are embedded in her hair. No wonder short hair evokes some cultural anxiety. Even now, the first time a woman sheds her tresses is usually accompanied by some guilt, as if somehow she has betrayed her gender by this act. The safer option, therefore, is the midway ponytail, which needs feminine managing but a single rubber-band suffices. 'Bob-cut' or 'boy-cut' hair is seen as a sign of assertive femininity that is resented by some. I think it was Sharad Yadav who used the label 'parkati' (one without wings) to describe the modern woman – a truly ironic inversion of meaning, considering what he meant was the opposite.

The vocabulary of hair and the products used to groom it have both changed in the last few years. Hair oils have become lighter and less oppressively perfumed; shampoos have penetrated into all parts of India. Ads now talk about hair that is 'bouncy', 'lively' and 'manageable'. The accent is now on the mutability of hair and the degree of personal control one can exercise over it. Unlike the past, where the attempt was to immobilize the woman with the perfumed heaviness of her hair, today the focus is clearly on elevating her with its girlish exuberance. In some senses, a woman's hair today belongs to her and not the other way round. It is possible, of course, that long hair may always be in vogue – but today, it will come unaccompanied by the culture that once surrounded it.

So as more and more ten-year-old girls across the country choose to, and are allowed to, keep their hair short, some change is surely brewing. The pigtail is part of a world view we are leaving behind us. It is nobody's case that women can become freer by getting a haircut, but when more and more mothers across the country allow their little girls to rid themselves of the need to signify their femaleness by wearing their hair long, surely that tells us something.

SCOOTING TO FREEDOM

Can a scooterette cause a revolution among young women of small town India? Can it be responsible for sweeping changes in the mindsets and lifestyles of a sizeable segment of our population? History is full of examples of powerful changes unleashed by the cascading effect of seemingly small ones. It has been argued that Gutenberg's invention of the printing press made printing of books possible on a mass scale, thus allowing a much wider audience for the Bible and thereby reducing the power of the Church by eliminating the need for the middleman.

The car is credited with many changes, including the creation of the suburb. The automobile allowed us to separate our work and home lives by putting physical distance between the two. It has been argued that by isolating the woman from the rest of the city, the notion of the housewife-wrapped-up-in-her-home was constructed. The home became the arena of performance for the woman who scrubbed, cooked and washed her days away in the quest for the idealized home.

In this context, it is easy to see how personal mobility is radically changing the face of the small town Indian girl. A visit to any town of middling size in India will reveal the astonishing preponderance of girls on their mopeds and scooterettes whizzing around buzzing with dragonfly energy. They ride with nonchalant confidence; there is a sense of control as they navigate their crowded everyday lives.

Earlier, the navigation of the Outer World was primarily a

male responsibility. Women were dropped to and from their destinations and needed to depend on men to do so. Mobility was a male prerogative which they conferred on their women. When women used public transport, it was usually with an air of hesitancy; one needed to be mindful of male attention at all times. Public transport created zones of comfort and familiarity; there were designated routes and 'stops' that one was familiar with and comfortable in. The world outside was inaccessible and a little daunting and needed to be entered one hesitant step at a time.

Personal mobility changes all that. Every place becomes accessible, every road navigable. The topography of the woman's comfort zone is made continuous; there are no gaps where one cannot go. One is free to stop anytime and anywhere one feels like. One can explore all that the city has to offer almost without any extra effort. The fear of the unfamiliar place diminishes; the idea of the outside world being inherently hostile is revealed to be an exaggeration.

Personal control over one's movements also provides some freedom from the claustrophobia induced by the unblinking male eye under which women find themselves trapped when they are stationary. On a two-wheeler they are a blur of individuality; the male gaze cannot pin them down.

More fundamentally, the two-wheeler offers the young girl the most direct proof of her power. The gearless vehicles seamlessly connect her wrist with her mind and make the vehicle respond to every touch. Thought translates effortlessly into action; the ease of realizing one's ideas is demonstrated. The sense of being in control, of being in charge of one's immediate destiny, of being able to navigate in real time all that the world has to throw, is experienced directly.

The scooterette is designed for the girl. It is usually gearless, is styled with expressive fluidity, and has enough power to move quickly without drawing too much attention to oneself. The vehicle does not set out to conquer the places it vends its way through; inherent in its construction is a 'softened' conception of the Outside World.

It offers freedom that is not aimed against anybody. In some curious way, today the girl in small town India is arguably freer than her Metro counterpart. The big city contains its women by its combination of distance and danger. It is too large to be traversed by a small two-wheeler and too anonymous to feel safe in. It is in the smaller town that it is possible for a girl to feel that she is comfortably in control of her own destiny. She experiences another side of freedom – not to do what is forbidden but to do what one feels like in the here and now. This is the freedom that is increasingly unavailable in the larger city. The future could well belong to the small-town girl, who is growing up today getting used to going where she pleases when she wants to. Thanks to a small hornet-like vehicle.

SETTING FREE THE OLD

Were films like *Baghban*, *Jogger's Park*, *Nishabd* and *Cheeni Kum* trying to tell us something? Are we seeing some new meanings being attached to the idea of ageing in India? Cinema is not alone; the world of advertising too is full of new images of the old. We see the retired generation on rollercoasters, playing cricket and gifting diamonds to their bewildered wives. Is this a real change that we are witnessing?

Historically, of course, the old have played a very different role in cinema. One of their prime functions was to symbolize authority, and generally act as grim protectors of the family's naak. This resulted in their frequently standing at the top of double helical stairs and bellowing Barkhurdar at their hapless progeny, while wearing a satin dressing gown. The other role they fulfilled was to evoke guilt and sympathy, with the mothers being particularly tubercular and coughing constantly when not becoming human bait at the villain's den. The old defined the values that we were meant to follow and elicited obedience through fear or emotional blackmail. The father governed the actions of the children either in person when alive, or by proxy through a photograph in the drawing room when dead. The mother used her lap, tears and paranthas for her purpose, although not necessarily in that order.

Given this context, it is instructive to look at recent representations of the old. Let us take a closer look at *Baghban*, because it is perhaps the closest to the older depiction of the aged, as also because it found favour with more people by presumably connecting with them. At one level, *Baghban* updates the Hindi family social typified by films with titles like *Ghar Ek Mandir*; telling the oft-repeated story of a an ideal family torn apart when the sons grow older and their personal ambitions reveal their venal characters. The key difference between a *Baghban* and say, an *Avtaar*, lies in the relationship between Amitabh Bachchan and Hema Malini. Both radiate agelessness, without being in any way youthful, and are unembarrassedly and utterly in love. The older version of Shabana Azmi in *Avtaar* was a hollow-eyed woman bereft of all meaning in life once her children left her. Hema Malini, on the other hand, derives meaning from her husband rather than her children. She is able to walk away from her sons, not for a lofty purpose, but for her own peace of mind.

At one level, *Baghban* is the story of the old asserting their independence and their right to live life for themselves rather than for their children. Another reading of this is less cheerful. Films like *Baghban* help free the younger generation of the moral responsibility for their parents. The parents are pointed away from their progeny, towards each other or towards their peers. Is *Baghban* a cautionary tale, aimed not at children but at parents, asking them to leave their kids alone? In the guise of the revenge-of-the-old formula, was *Baghban* a sign of a new prescription?

Advertising representations of toothless tomfoolery too help de-fang the old seductively. By reimagining old age as a playground without rules, we convert the authority of the old into harmless idiosyncrasies. The old must be left to have a good time with people of their ilk; for that is what they enjoy most, we are able to tell ourselves. The old now need indulgence that is discretionary rather than obedience that is not.

Of course, a *Nishabd* and a *Cheeni Kum* do more than put the old in their place. But do they really tell the old that all life continues to drip with the old promise? It is likelier that they speak to the young by reassuring them that growing old does not mean giving up on the pleasures of youth. Amitabh Bachchan is Sexy Sam, feeding the fantasy of agelessness for those who have not yet got there. For those who have, the mirror tells another story. At this stage in India, the premium on youth is such that every story we tell is implicitly told from its vantage point. The old become the 'other', the people we are not but might one day turn into. The young need ways of insulating themselves from the idea of age.

In a society like ours, the question of how to treat the older generation is going to becoming a defining one. As we move to a more individualistic mode of engaging with the world, traditional roles and expectations will need to be redefined. What we are seeing is a process of negotiation, a feeling out of the space available for both generations. If only we could all be Amitabh Bachchan at sixty-four.

LOOKING BACK AT THE MARUTI

If there was one moment when India changed, when it decisively moved from one set of aspirations and mindsets to another, it was when we first saw the Maruti 800. For it was virtually the first product available in India that one lusted for. I remember being transfixed when I saw my first Maruti (it wasn't even the car, it was the van); I had never seen anything shinier, anything more radiant with bliss. Twenty-five years on, that seems difficult to believe, so completely have our eyes been jaded by all the cars that clog up our roads now. But to a generation that grew up watching other people drive their Ambassadors or Fiats (Standard Herald for the less lucky ones), the dinky little bit of plastic, all shiny and red, was an invitation to a new kind of paradise.

The Ambassador was the reigning deity till then. Its lines were inspired by a matron's commodious petticoats and its interiors had the well-worn comfortable shabbiness of the Indian drawing room. It drove you with the laconic recalcitrance of the father while offering you the familiar comfort of a mother's lap. You sprawled inside the car when not carrying your entire brood of third cousins and their family friends to the railway station to receive or to see someone off. The car was large, solid and rounded. Nothing about its design acknowledged that it was an object designed to move. The Ambassador squatted on the ground, embracing its own centre of gravity. It was a car that clearly believed that it was better to waddle than to race, and moved with stolid disregard for one's surroundings or one's intent. The Ambassador was status quo on wheels, a car that allowed one to stand still even as one moved and do so with one's entire way of life intact. It pointed nowhere and took us nowhere, which was where we wanted to be.

The Fiat was a modern car in the way that a transistor was modern. It detached itself from the collective, being designed for a nuclear family, and it had a shape that actually pointed somewhere. It was a car that moved, albeit with extreme self-awareness about its limitations. Like the educated Indian, mildly successful, and keen not to underline that success too much, this was a car that took a small step forward without taking us anywhere new. If the Ambassador was a pyjama, the Fiat was a pair of creased terrycot trousers worn with a nondescript shirt.

The Maruti came as a plastic shock out of the blue. It was all electric compactness, bristling with impudent desire. It looked like it was made as a seamless whole by technology instead of being painstakingly riveted together by a combination of lathes and welding machines, as appeared to be the case with the older cars. If the Ambassador and the Fiat at best deigned to confer broad agreement on our travelling intentions, the Maruti leapt to our commands, converting even transient whims that barely crossed our minds into spittle-spraying feats of fierce manoeuvrability. We squeezed into our little dream machines and rocketed off to newer destinations on the road as well in the mind.

The Maruti freed us from our scripts. For most of us, who were born in the middle class only to die there, the car was a border we could not imagine crossing. Only the haves could dream of owning a car, but for the rest, a Bajaj Chetak after eight years of a waiting period was the best one could hope for. The Maruti compressed the promise of consumerism in its appearance, performance and price. It flung the doors of aspiration wide open and made us believe for the first time we could escape the middle class, tyres screeching. In a larger sense, it made us experience the power of desire and the exhilaration of being in the driver's seat.

The Maruti 800 made us believe in plastic. We were able to tear ourselves away from a world which measured performance in terms of the thickness of gauge or hardiness of form. Mutability, flexibility and speed came to be valued as did the overtness of external appearance. We understood packaging even as we redefined the meaning of performance. Substance was no longer opposed to style, and price no longer extracted for performance. The Maruti sold us the idea of consumption with irresistible glibness.

Seen with today's eyes, the Maruti 800 is a somewhat basic piece of machinery that seems oddly outdated. But if we have driven as far as we have from it, let us remember that it was in the Maruti.

NO RUNGS IN THEIR LADDER

Mahendra Singh Dhoni has an eerie sense of calm around him. He has an innate sense of wisdom that seems to come from no discernible source. Nothing in his background explains his ease with success and equanimity with failure. He continues to do what young men of twenty-six tend to, viz., experiment with their looks, drive fast bikes and meet lots of girls. And yet, he exudes a self-assurance that borders on the sage.

He exemplifies an attitude that small town India seems to possess in plenty – the lack of fear of failure. It lives in an environment where success is often about landing a government job or running a small business. The yardsticks of success are not very well established and expectations from the young are modest. Failure as a burdensome fear is neutralized for the default option would at best yield a very minor success.

Contrast this with the large metropolises where success is an intricately structured industry, where the young prepare to be successful from an early age, where every action from infancy is fraught with consequences. Being successful is a responsibility; it is a marathon run by the young supported by parents and sundry friends and relatives shouting out conflicting advice from the sidelines. Here success is a ladder to be climbed one rung at a time, in full view of so many others trying to do the same.

The change in the mindset of small town India has come with the availability of a new vehicle for social and economic mobility – talent. Hitherto in India, the only way to vault out of one's immediate circumstances was through education. Now this is a vehicle that is in extremely short supply in India and is mediated through a Brahminical hierarchy. We still have a disdain for vocational courses, deeming them intellectually inferior, and hence produce millions of graduates in disciplines that have no productive use. Good quality higher education was restricted to very few centres and here the larger cities helped prepare their young much better to compete for the few seats available.

Talent, on the other hand, is an alchemic idea. It springs from within and while it needs to be spotted and nurtured, it has a compelling raw energy that spills over. Media has unified ambition in India by populating all our minds with the same benchmarks of success. It has also allowed all of us to rehearse our success by giving us an intimate glimpse into what it looks like. The young today embrace success well before it embraces them. Small town India, in particular, knows what success looks like without tasting what the fear of failure feels like. For unlike the metros, small town India is not bogged down by expectation – it trades largely in hope. Also, growing up in a small place gives one a sense of mastery over one's terrain that is elusive in larger cities. And while there are few role models in one's immediate vicinity, there is virtually no one who knows better and who must be listened to. The ladder here has no rungs; talent pole vaults its way into recognition, marked by a sense of retrospective inevitability.

Having grown up without being assailed by expectations, in a space where one can feel in control, spurred on by media images of success, the small town Indian celebrates ability without the complications of self-reflective introspection. This is why when Dhoni takes the field, he seems to do so without memory. The past is perpetually erased and the future can only be an improvement on one's past. Memory is the preserve of those who have a past to live within and live up to. The absence of memory creates a freedom that is unmindful of hierarchy, class and past records.

Today in India, the seeds of ambition have been broadcast widely and we are beginning to reap the harvest. The talent map of India is being redrawn and we need to recognize that in this new scheme of things, where people are not climbing the ladder one rung at a time, we need to create a system that recognizes talent wherever it may lie and enable it to blossom. Small town India has just begun to tick – there are many more Dhonis waiting to erupt.

THE MILITANT MASK

A peculiar sight is common in many smaller towns in India. Young girls across Baroda, Jaipur and Pune, to name but a few towns, are going around on two-wheelers fully masked. Typically, they cover their faces fully with dupattas, leaving only a slit for the eyes. The arms are covered with gloves, ensuring that no skin is exposed to the outside world. Now this is not an isolated instance, but pretty much the universal custom. This seems to happen only with young girls when they are driving, and seems to occur primarily in smaller towns rather than metros.

At the first level, it would seem that the reason for this strange mode of attire is an excessive concern for one's appearance. There is no doubt that taking care of how one looks is high on the priority of the young today, and this is perhaps an extreme way of ensuring that one's skin stays protected against the harshness of the Indian sun. This is undoubtedly true, but perhaps not the whole truth, for then one would expect that sunscreen lotions would do exceedingly well in India, and that is not really so. Alternatively, it could have something to do with preserving fairness, but it seems odd that there would be such a dramatic surge in this need in this day and age. Also, it is not clear why this desire should manifest itself only in small towns and that too while driving.

The other possible explanation has to do with a desire to protect oneself from the wandering gaze of men. What is being worn is in effect a veil, and one where the girl covers herself up completely.

Again, this is not an explanation that quite adds up. Everywhere around us, women are dressing a little more freely and if popular cinema is anything to go by, skimpy is the dress code of choice.

The truth is that, whatever the ostensible reason for this strange practice, it throws up a powerful symbol of our times. The girl is in effect reversing the gaze that she has always been subject to; it is now she who sees. The world is consumed by her as per her need. She refuses to offer herself up for scrutiny. The fact that she is mobile makes her withdrawal an act of active assertion rather than passive protection. She chooses to retreat into herself while engaging with the world on her own terms.

Even if the reasons for this withdrawal are cosmetic, it tells us that she believes that her real arena is elsewhere. She does not need to appear in a starring role in the day-to-day arena of her current reality. She is investing in the future so that she plays the game that she is meant to play, one day. She denies herself the immediate sense of presence, of being noticed, perhaps admired, for a day when it will be more meaningful.

Visually, her appearance is a gauntlet that she throws down to the world. There is something more than just a little militant in the mask that she chooses to wear. For this is a veil worn deliberately, and one which inverts the traditional meaning of a veil. It signifies not fear of men but contempt, or in the very least, it communicates to them that their approval is of no great significance.

And the small town is the stage for this drama to get played out largely because the woman here is mobile. Being self-propelled allows her the ability never to be pinned down; she is a free spirit quite literally. Large cities do not allow for such easy navigation; the incidence of women driving their own personal transport is much lower in the metros. It is possible that this practice may be a passing fad and give way to another. But what it points to is not a transient trend. The small-town girl is coming and she doesn't seem to need anybody's approval or endorsement.

THE WONDERFUL WORLD OF
THE INDIAN NIGHTIE

Every morning, in large parts of India, women wake up, have a bath and change into a fresh nightie. This is then worn throughout the day, certainly at home and even for the occasional dart into the neighbourhood market. It is common to find women of all ages and backgrounds breaking bhindi ends together at a vegetable shop resplendent in their nighties. And this sight is not limited to the large cities but in most of urban India. Like the engagement ring, the nightie is an alien habit that we have embraced without reservation but in our own unique way. What has allowed this form of attire to penetrate so easily into our consciousness?

The nightie is designed like a smock, making few allowances for the contours of the wearer's body, but registering its femaleness by means of its design (floral prints, for instance). The nightie does not emphasize any part of the body and is designed to make the watcher's gaze slip off the body without allowing it to come to rest anywhere in particular.

While belonging to the larger family of the negligee, the nightie is an adherent of a different school of thought altogether, being careful to steer clear of anything frilly, lacy, racy or sheer. It is resolute in its modesty and is feminine enough without looking fetching. As the name suggests, the nightie in India, like anywhere else in the world, was originally meant as bedtime wear – its current use as an all-day attire is something that its wearers have evolved. It is interesting that its current popularity has been generated not by any clever marketing campaign but entirely by the user, who has seen in it value not originally intended.

The easiest explanation for this unrestrained adoption of an alien form of clothing is that it makes the wearer feel extremely comfortable. But its popularity suggests that it has struck a deeper chord than that. The nightie is perhaps a deceptively understated banner of revolution. It is a garment of liberation, a freedom smock. The nightie is one garment that does not tie a woman to her body. It has no strings, hooks or knots and falls freely over her, letting her body be. It offers her freedom from shape, from the burden of the gendered curves of her body. Worn usually when the woman is by herself, there is a naturalness that the nightie confers on its wearer, an ease that allows her to navigate through her daily life as a person rather than as a gendered being.

It helps that being of alien origin, the nightie frees women from the coded garments of the past, but in a way that invites no social opprobrium. The saree and the salwar kameez are both garments that are embedded with implicit social roles. Pallus have to be watched and dupattas need to be attentive guardians of the body. The nightie, by virtue of being extremely modest in its design, is as legitimate as these garments, but is more convenient and has the additional advantage of being modern.

More than any other new form of attire, the nightie is perhaps a truly modern garment. The nightie tells us that modernity is at its heart about functionality rather than appearances. By helping detach the woman from the past that she is otherwise embedded in, and by giving her a sense of individual-ness, the nightie helps the woman luxuriate in her 'modern' self. As against a more overtly contemporary garment like the skirt, which is a loud sign of modernity, the nightie minimizes its role as an outward sign and concentrates on delivering a real benefit. It is precisely because it appears harmless that it manages its modest revolution. It brings about change because it displays little desire to do so.

Its power lies in its ability to be both modern and modest; to be both personally liberating and socially legitimate. As an innovation in couture, the nightie may not have a page devoted to it in the history of Indian fashion, but in the ongoing quest of the Indian woman to retrieve some space for herself, the nightie deserves at least a footnote.

MONEY AS ENERGY

Remember the sequence in *Rangeela* when Aamir Khan lands up at a five-star hotel resplendent in a yellow suit that advertises his vulnerability to an environment where his money talks but its accent gives it away? This scene reminds me of an incident narrated to me by a British tourist who, after a great day's outing presided over by a local three-wheeler driver, invited him to his hotel for a drink, only to meet with an embarrassed refusal. The auto-driver knew that in the tacit territorial map of our society, the hotel represented another country and he was a man without the right passport. In both the above cases, the issue was not about money, but about the right to access. The money, though critical, was by itself inadequate to overcome the invisible barriers of class that we have created.

When we think about the past and the way our society was constructed, it is difficult not to marvel at how well we managed to contain what we then saw as the potentially disruptive power of money. First, we constructed a social framework where the highest echelons lived a lifestyle that was conspicuously demonetized. They lived in official quarters, and drove official cars, either officially or otherwise. They went to clubs that served food and beverages at a price that was notionally a notch above free, holidayed in guest houses and circuit houses available only to them and got land allotted to them at throwaway prices to build their own houses.`

Then we made sure that money could buy very little. High

taxes on goods, low access to the best the world had to offer, and an overall air of shortages reduced avenues for expenditure. This process was aided considerably by making the process of using money very difficult. Withdrawing and depositing money was a one-day outing, booking tickets to anything was a well-orchestrated nightmare, getting from one place to another an adventure and so on. The government was deviously stingy not only in giving its citizens any facilities but even more so in collecting its dues. Whether it was about paying taxes, remitting the electricity bill or renewing one's train pass, every effort to pay the government any money was met with heroic resistance on its part.

And, of course, we closed the loop by limiting avenues of making money. Private enterprise was placed under house arrest and glared at with unblinking hostility by several kinds of watchdogs as it fretted listlessly in its confined quarters.

In effect, we were an economy that disowned its fundamental unit, money. We were an access economy, where power was the deity and access its currency. If god had an ambition, it would be to one day become a joint secretary. The size of the queue in front of one's door became more valuable than the size of one's bank balance. An access economy became the fertile hunting ground for the agent, who whispered hot promises of access in our ears. Middlemen brokered everything – be it a driving licence, a manufacturing licence, a school admission, a railway reservation, property registration or a cinema ticket.

Ironically, money became a potent force. It became everything we feared about it – it became an instrument of illegitimate access. People with money bought power and used it to precise personal effect. A licence guaranteed profits; there was no reason to worry too much about the quality of goods manufactured. Capitation fees allowed the unworthy unfettered access to coveted degrees.

But at its heart, the idea of money is inherently a democratic one. When set free, it allows for uniform access universally.

When things operate on the basis of money, they become more transparent and available to all. In a society as fragmented as ours, with as intricate a system for discriminating between people, money can potentially act as a real force of democracy. If in an access economy, there is an in-built mechanism that fosters scarcity as a source of power, here the mechanism drives us towards more being available. Where power was the speed-breaker, money is the accelerator. Money liberates us from the cavernous mysteries of the corridors of power. In doing so, it perhaps sets in motion its own set of distortions.

In the past, our mental model of money was that of a stagnant pool that always needed to be protected – from evaporation, leakage and reckless use. The inflow was limited and the outflow regrettably certain. Except for the trading community, who understood that money generated money, the rest of us saw money as an immobile asset that could only diminish. Even today, our preference for gold is a pointer to the role we see money playing in our lives. Gold is our hedge against an uncertain tomorrow. Our obsession with lockers reveals our strong desire to 'lock up' and 'bury' what little wealth we own. Every month or quarter we go visit the locker to both check if it is all there as also to bask in the warm glow of the twenty tolas we have hoarded up in some basement of a nationalized bank. We go every month in spite of knowing that the gold is going nowhere because in some irrational corner of our mind, we fear the involuntary leakage of what we have so painstakingly accumulated. The reason why we resent our bank charging us for specific services is precisely because it confirms this deep-rooted fear of money evaporating by itself. We cannot bear the thought of money declining for whatever reason in a bank.

In a larger sense, our enemy was tomorrow. Left to itself, tomorrow was likely to be worse than yesterday. Any belief in tomorrow, any expression of optimism, was seen as inviting tomorrow's wrath. Compliment a chubby child on her pink cheeks and the mother promptly puts a black teeka behind her ear, ask the owner of a booming business how it is going and he will tell you about how he just about ekes out two meals a day. It is as if any expression of belief in oneself is an automatic invitation to disaster.

It is interesting that our society is a great example of a sustainable zero growth model. We have been able to find meaning in our lives without depending on economic growth within our lifetimes. In such a context, it is easy to see why money was feared as a disruptive force which could contaminate the fragile purity of our stretched existence.

The conception of money as a stock rather than a flow is evident in the extraordinary number of inheritance battles that clog up our courts. For a society that ostensibly shuns the material, the ability of families to fight bitter feuds over money for decades is revelatory of an underlying belief that wealth can at best be maintained and not created. Which is why we spend so much time, energy and money trying to get our share of the spoils of the past.

The idea that money comes in the way of relationships is grounded in the very conception of money. As a device, money frees us from the burden of reciprocity inherent in a barter economy. When we pay for something in cash, we are no longer bound in a reciprocal relationship – the transaction replaces the relationship. This is the reason why the so-called Relationship Banking services that foreign banks offer is flawed – to our mind a relationship is one where we no longer measure each other by money. The foreign bank sees the relationship as another transaction – deposit Rs 10 lakhs in our bank and buy a relationship, add another 10 and get an even better one. The public sector banks, for all their other inefficiencies, understand the idea of relationships better – old customers, regardless of the size of their relationship, get special treatment.

If money yesterday was a static part of a social framework that sought stability, how has its role changed today? The big change in mindset is really in how we see tomorrow. This is the first generation that sees tomorrow as being better than yesterday, and this fundamental change has transformed the way in which we see money. From being fearful hoarders of money, sick with the certainty of its impending evaporation, we are today willing to be energized by the continuous flow of money in our lives. Today we are beginning to enjoy money in circulation whereas yesterday money was revered in its accumulation. Money is today energy that vitalizes our everyday life. We are still as cautious about the value we derive from the money we spend, we still hate paying bank charges, but we now believe that money will keep coming in.

The stock market has played a key, if symbolic, role in making the idea of continuous growth tangible. The index is a totemic reminder of the validity of our faith in a perpetually progressive tomorrow. First generation wealth creators like Dhirubhai Ambani and N.R. Narayana Murthy have been advertisements for the economic mobility that has become accessible to us today.

Our fear of the contaminating power of money is also on the wane. Karan Johar films are a good place to observe how the ruddy glow of a few crores causes families to huddle together in cosy warmth. In the popular imagination of today, money is the gushing warmth that allows us to lead a brighter, higher wattage life the way we want to lead it. The power equation has changed – we believe in our ability to use money rather than be used by it.

Money has also helped democratize at least one section of society. In the cosy Brahminical world of yesterday, new entrants were unwelcome. You made it by birth and pedigree and no amount of individual achievement was enough. The snooty demonetized club of yesterday has been replaced by the 'money-shouts' hotels of today. Everything can be bought by anybody with money. The energy of New India is in part the energy of the emerging class, which has money and the drive and unrestricted access to many more opportunities today.

Overall, as our conception of tomorrow changes, so does our relationship with money. We fear it less, express ourselves in its language more comfortably, and extract more out of it, not to eke out an ordinary life but to celebrate a magnificent one. This is a time when we have just woken up to the throbbing vitality that money coursing through our lives can bring. At this point in time, we do not want to be reminded about those who don't have money. The poor do not exist – not in our imagination, not in our movies or on our television screens. It is a passing phase, but for now we are incandescent with money.

THE FREEDOM OF ARMY DAUGHTERS

A curiously significant proportion of women who do well in areas as diverse as business, media, sports and the glamour industry come from an army background. There is something about cantonment living that seems to confer a distinct advantage on young girls as they step out into the larger world and try and carve out a place for themselves.

Some reasons are quite obvious. There is a high degree of emphasis on education, activities beyond studies, grooming and social graces that allow young children to grow up in a rounded way, but if that were all, an army background would be nothing more than a decent finishing school. The more Westernized ethic of the military does make for a more liberal upbringing, but perhaps there is more at work here than just that.

The most powerful aspect of a services lifestyle lies not so much in what it offers as in what it doesn't. Army life detaches the family unit both spatially and culturally from the larger social arena. The cantonment is another world – with its own distinct physicality and its own code of behaviour. Postings in each station are of small durations; no roots are allowed to be grown. Often, cantonments are located in remote places where one is far from the comforting and often overpowering bosom of one's larger family. At a time when the home town posting was highly coveted and connived for, the army made sure that the uniformity of the cantonment was the only home you knew.

Army children thus grew up in a cocooned world that bore

allegiance not to larger society but to itself. They enjoyed a freedom that few other Indians experience – the freedom from the past. In some ways cantonment life offered escape in terms of both space and time. Army life was rooted in the now – there were few opportunities to get tied down to a place or indeed to a set of people. Transience made sure that one never belonged anywhere; everything became an experience that shaped one, without being defining. The effect on girls was perhaps disproportionate, given the otherwise narrow and fixed space they get allotted in the world outside. Girls grew up free from the invisible network of tongues and eyes that keep them in check otherwise. They grew up not knowing too well what being a girl in India usually meant. The freedom to live in the present and to be who you are is perhaps the reason why army daughters display the easy confidence of those who do not see the world as a place full of invisible constraints but one of frequent opportunity. It is not that they grew up in an alien culture, for their parents, however Westernized their lifestyle, came from the same traditional social fabric, but only that the relationship that they enjoyed with society was made up of dotted lines. The outside world was a hazy blur which was real but not that consequential.

Army wives did not have it so easy. These were women brought up conventionally who found themselves thrown in a world with very different rules. They needed to straddle two very different cultural universes without having any preparation to do so. At a time when most women got married into families, these were the few who got married out of one. Behind the sometimes awkward short-hair-dyed-jet-black-speaking-in-English-every-fifth-word army wife lies someone who has perhaps made a dramatic transition in her way of life and learnt to be an individual one step at a time, almost entirely by herself. No wonder the word formidable comes frequently to mind when thinking about army wives.

The phenomenon of army daughters shows that freeing the

energies of women in India perhaps requires above all an absence of the overweening community that surrounds us. We can see a similar effect on all the children who had the benefit of growing up in self-contained colonies outside their 'native places'. Similarly, hostels provide avenues for the young to discover their own independent selves and figure out what they want in life. On the other side of the success of army daughters lies the tragedy of millions of others who do not have the advantage of an alternative cocoon. For our social system does not let go of its daughters so easily – it requires a military cantonment to get the licence to do so.

CHAPTER 8

THE BADGES OF
MODERNITY

The modern must reveal itself. Often worn extra-vagantly, the badges themselves tell us about our new engagement with the West. They tell us about our overt desires as also about the things we don't admit to ourselves or don't quite know. The symbols speak louder than our intent-laden actions and they tell us fascinating stories about ourselves.

TERMS OF ENDEARMENT

My parents never once told me that they loved me. No, I have not suddenly decided to unburden myself and finally tell you the sad story of why I have become an axe-murderer. It is a simple statement of fact; growing up, it was inconceivable for my parents to actually spell out something like that. And this is true for most of us; it was not in our nature to baldly say something so basic to each other. There would be no shyness in expressing affection – all kinds of drippy pet names that would hound you to the grave and dollops of laad-pyaar expressed through gestures of varied kinds, but mainly through food, were common, with mothers playing a starring role. But no one would actually say 'I love you' to one's kids.

And this was true even among couples; it was somehow not deemed either necessary or appropriate to articulate one's love in these terms. Even in a relationship that went under the self-conscious tag of a 'love' marriage, there was no room for this. One can understand the Indian reluctance about displaying romantic affection in public; but even in private we held back when it came to saying what the West sees as the three magic words that everyone longs to hear.

And it seemed absolutely corny to do so. It seemed like a laboured self-conscious affectation that we were very uncomfortable with. Even in the early films, where heroes and heroines began to use the word 'love', it was done with syrupy self-consciousness. 'Love' was not a translation of the word 'pyaar' but resided in another universe altogether. Love was an exotic new emotion, chocolate to the Indian mithai, fork to the Indian use of hands. Love needed skirts to be worn and tutti-frutti ice cream to be eaten. Whenever 'I love you' was said, it was said with the quotation marks intact; we were repeating other people's words and not giving voice to our own feelings. Think of the impossibly turgid 'Ilu Ilu' ('Ilu ka matlab I love you') number or, for that matter, 'Angrezi me kehte hain I love you', both of which were actually teaching us how to spell it out.

And yet today, in large parts of urban India, we are happy to spell out our love for our kids several times a day. Young couples are beginning to express themselves more freely in these terms. Is it only an act of imitation – have we finally seen enough Western films and serials for us to feel more comfortable, or is there a real change that is taking place here?

The real question is perhaps in understanding why we were so uncomfortable in expressing ourselves in the first place. It probably came from not seeing ourselves as being separate from our loved ones at all. Our sense of individual-ness was never sharply etched; the boundaries of our selves were fuzzy. Our individuality was like a ladle of sticky porridge that briefly emerged out of a filial pot, but it always brimmed over and kept dripping back. In the absence of this sense of separateness, the distance between I and You was perhaps never large enough to warrant bridging verbally. A feeling of 'I am You' pretty much precludes a need to say 'I love You'.

The fear of enforced separateness haunts us as our worst nightmare. Both the Ramayana and Mahabharata tell us about the pain of separation and the joy of reuniting. Bollywood spent an entire decade on the lost-and-found theme. The idea of being torn apart from people who made us complete was a deeply fearful one. We needed to stay immersed in our communal collective to retain a sense of comfort and belongingness.

Which is why our recent comfort with being able to say 'I love you', at least in some parts of society, is instructive. It points to a growing sense of being separate individuals who are bound together in ties of kinship rather than being a single organic entity out of which we emerge as blurred individuals. It doesn't necessarily mean that family ties are becoming weaker but merely that the nature of the binding is changing. The individual and her needs are being accommodated, new rules of engagement about the public and the private are being framed and adjustments are being made to our mental model of a close-knit family. The house is no longer a free space that belongs to everyone – we have more clearly demarcated public and private zones. There is a tacit understanding about what doors to open when, an understanding that was wholly unnecessary some years ago.

And there is more at work here than the nuclearization of families. Families have been becoming nuclear for decades now. In earlier times, the nuclear family was like a branch outpost – the emotional headquarters were unambiguously located in one's 'native place'. All orders emanated from there and an annual tribute in the form of a mandatory visit was paid regularly. It is only recently that the emotional headquarters too have shifted to the nuclear family.

Even now, our sense of the family as a single entity continues to be strong; but our definition of what constitutes that family has narrowed. It is a noteworthy sign that while we accept, in part at least, a Valentine's Day, we are very lukewarm towards the idea of a Father's Day or a Mother's Day. We have not put enough distance between ourselves and our parents to need such a clunky bridge. But as our sense of separateness gets formed more firmly, we will need more bridges to communicate to our loved ones. More greeting cards, more gifts on birthdays, and perhaps, more celebrations of Father's Day and Mother's Day...

GREASY MODERNISMS

After cleaning Sweety, who had done potty in her nappy, Mandy changed into her nightie and turned her attention to Monty and Rocky, who were struggling with their math. It is clear from the above sentence that the Mandakini described is a woman with modern inclinations, surrounded as she is by people and objects that sound crisply modern. For it is clear that modernity comes along with its own aural signature, and systematically transforms the familiar into the contemporary.

What makes something sound modern? Why does Venky seem more 'today' than Venkateswaran and Sandy feel more comfortable than Sandeep? The idea of shortening names is clearly not a new one. We have all grown up with 'pet names', a fact that some of us go to any lengths to hide. It is not a pretty sight when a Pushpendra Pratap Singh is unmasked to reveal that he was all along merely a Pappu. India is full of grizzled people with gravitas who are in fact fondly called Chintoo, Mintoo, Babloo, Babli, Chhotu, Munni, Bappi, Tutu, Chikoo and yes, it must be said, Lolo and Bebo. Pet names emerged from the simple fact that it was difficult to call, with any conviction, the wriggling, drooling, gurgling, burping thing by its given name Suprabuddha. It was felt, perhaps with good reason, that a Suprabuddha, however young, would refrain from evacuating himself so freely and frequently from all possible exit points in his anatomy. Poopoo, for instance, seemed a more natural fit.

A large number of our pet names are rooted in our childhoods and are nothing but sound images evoked by us in our infant form. They are terms of endearment that seek to enshrine us in a form most cherished by our culture – that of a child. These names are part of the curious lexicon of unintelligible gibberish that adults feel compelled to employ when in the presence of infants. The traditional pet names also retain the character of the language spoken at home – different regions have different pet names.

What 'pet names' do is to make us more informal and accessible. In fact, we refer to the two sets of names as the 'house name' and the 'school name'. To the outside world we stride as Mr Dhurandhar Bhatavadekar, but at home we loiter around as Dhuru or Dhurya or perhaps just Dhu, as the film in question, *Rang Birangi*, suggested. Today's modernisms too serve a similar purpose. A Rags seems easier to back slap than a T. Raghavendra Rao. But there is a qualitative difference in the purpose they serve over and above that of being more accessible.

The modern sound comes from departing consciously from the language of origin. There is a strong desire to produce a sound that sits comfortably with English. The meandering mellifluousness of an Anandanageswaran is transformed into the hard-walled abruptness of Nags. It is as if the alluvial richness of a river gets abbreviated into the concrete functionality of a canal. We pronounce a Kaapadia as a Kapaadia – the subtle shift in emphasis serves to both erase the meaning (Kaapadia meaning those dealing in cloth in Gujarati) as well as harden the sound to make it sound more contemporary.

As part of a modernizing process, it is interesting that today's nicknames seek to freeze our identities as they exist in college as against the child-state pet names of yesterday. We are named by our parents and renamed by our peers in an attempt to update our identity. A Venky does not trap us in the past in the same way as a Chhotu does. Also, unlike earlier, today's nick names are our 'outside' names and not our 'house names'. In keeping with the needs of today, these nick names allow a handle for the outside world to grasp us by.

The nature of transformation sought today is clear from the kind of names we confer on our peers – colleges today are full of Sandeep-Sandys, Harpreet-Harrys and Samir-Sammys. Samir, for instance, is not a name that needs abbreviation – the desire is clearly for Samir to sound more Western. It is never clearer than when we seek to convert an already compressed maths into the Americanized math.

It is interesting that in British times too, we used our names as a signifying device. Pal became Paul, Lal became Lall, Mumbai became Bombay. In doing so, we made the process of assimilation easier for them. Does the act of making the names of people and things sound more Western then merely a harmless part of a modernization process or is it a more subtle process by which we colonize ourselves? Do our politicians understand something deeper when they fight for changing the names of places or are they caught in a time warp? Are we becoming someone else when we start calling mathematics math? Or should we simply accept that modernisms, greasy or not, are here to stay?

ENGLISH IMAGINATIONS

The Indian proficiency in English is routinely seen as a big strength for the country. Although English is spoken by a very small fraction of the population, the role it plays is much more significant. In a country teeming with languages, English is a bridge everyone can cross when attempting to communicate with each other. It is a link language not just in India but across the world, which is a considerable advantage when we try and make our way forward in this rapidly globalizing world. China has taken serious note of this linguistic inability on its part and being China, has launched a concerted programme to ensure that its next generation is fluent in the language.

And yet, there are enough people who would argue that to promote English any further in India is fraught with cultural consequences. As a language inherited from our erstwhile colonial masters, English carries with it an implicit aura of power and serves to create an axis of discrimination. This is visible in so many different ways in India, with our obsession with English-medium schools and 'convented' brides and our deference towards anyone who speaks the language. English-speaking thieves make headlines, as if the knowledge of a language was inoculation against having criminal tendencies. We cringe when an important Indian who doesn't speak the language well interacts with anybody Western; we feel smaller vicariously. The sense of foreboding with which the middle class views the prospect of Mayawati becoming prime minister has less to do with caste (Kanshi Ram would not have evoked the same anxieties) and more to do with an overall demeanour of which her inability to communicate well in English is a big part. Had Mayawati been fluent in English like Jayalalitha is, chances are that our objections would get considerably muted.

English in India has been a device to communicate as well as to separate. As Sunil Khilnani argued in *The Idea of India*, English replaced Sanskrit as the new language of the state, carrying the same mysterious power accessible to only those who knew the language. Its talismanic properties are wonderfully illustrated in a scene from the film *Guide*, when Dev Anand's character gets mistaken for a saint by a group of villagers, something that enrages the local priests who, in order to establish that Dev Anand is a fraud, test him by showering a volley of Sanskrit shlokas at him. Dev Anand's reply is to fire a volley back – in English. The priests are silenced, the villagers cheer, the baton passes. As a language of state, English is both privileged and privileging, conferring wisdom and sophistication on whoever learns it. The editors of English newspapers have historically wielded much more influence than their regional counterparts, in spite of much lower reach. Writers in English are glorified while we barely know of emerging talent in local languages, something that is lamented a lot but rarely acted upon.

So is English an alien language that works on the principle of power distance or is it a vital unifier in a country divided by language? Does it enslave our imagination or does it allow us to speak in the language of today? Does it detach us from our moorings or enable us to become part of a larger world order?

Instead of attempting to answer these questions, it may be time to revisit their validity. Language is an open system and incorporates the context into the way it develops. English itself, some would argue, now has porous boundaries, as do local languages. As we think simultaneously in different languages, we are more comfortable mashing them together in order to create new vocabularies and reach new communication destinations. Hinglish is a phenomenon that diminishes the aura of power around English by bending it in a way that fits our lives better. It opens up the peripheries of the language and allows more people to enter its fold, without feeling intimidated by its alienness. Simultaneously, there is greater comfort with the Indian accent and even theatre productions in English now are veering away from the ridiculous phoniness of the pretend-haw-haw accent and speaking in more natural tones. So perhaps, English is becoming an Indian language now, as many have argued.

Of course, Hinglish itself is neither homogenous nor politically innocent. What we call Hinglish is actually an array of argots, each with its own uses and contexts. For instance, we have the phenomenon of Hindi garnished with English words, where the use of English either gives voice to a concept that was born in English (department, transfer) or underlines the importance of what is sought to be communicated by elevating its ritual status (yeh mamla bahut urgent hai, ise aaap please seriously lijiye; kya main tumhen hot lagti hoon?). This Hinglish is different from that of casual conversation (Tension nahi lene ka), which is different from when the languages and their grammatical structures are intertwined (Don't maskofy me; Chal yaar, aaj bunk maarte hain). The combination of technology, popular culture and the cross-fertilization that is taking place within regional and global cultures is producing a new set of interactions between languages. Formal structures are loosening, and language is not the totalizing force that it once was.

Having said that, even now Hinglish is not bereft of any lingering associations with hierarchy. The truth is that Hinglish is a rung used by the educated elite to descend to a more relaxed engagement with the world than the one used by the emerging classes to ascend into a world of privilege. The Hinglish used by those unfamiliar with the language marks them out as outsiders even today. Hinglish as a medium of communication is employed much more effortlessly by those who know the language and choose to play with it, rather than those who don't.

As a culture, not having one's language has to be a handicap. Of course, in India all cultures do have their own languages, but the absence of a language we take pride in does extract its price. For instance, how does one sing in English in India without using any Western musical form as a point of reference? Singing in English necessitates singing in an alien mode. Attempts to do otherwise stand out as lame and contrived. Of course, we are seeing much less self-conscious interweaving of the Western and Indian forms of music. Bands Like Indian Ocean produce a sound that is unmistakably Indian and do so using means that may or may not be Indian. The fusion takes place inside the musicians rather than in the music. But even this coming together of musical forms stops well short of incorporating English.

Over the generations, this too will perhaps change, but for now, thinking in English privileges certain structures of thought and this happens in a way that seems completely natural. The way out is not to attack English, as some believe, but to celebrate local languages much more. In a small way, the return to respectability of lyrics in Hindi is pointer to an awakening of the potential of our own cultural legacy. The power of English is not going away anywhere soon but without the blooming of other languages, we can potentially limit our own imagination.

HOME TRUTHS

Remember those Hindi films with the climactic 'neelami' scenes where the family izzat gets auctioned off to the evil landlord? What was being sold was not merely a plot of land with a building but the very seat of one's being, the place which was both origin and destination, where you would be born and then die and the next link in the chain would take over. The home was a signifier of perpetuity; generations came and went but the family citadel stood firm, if a little ragged.

It mattered little if the home was big or small, decrepit or blooming. Like a mother who is never ugly or beautiful, but just a mother, a home to most had little to do with beauty. We were a reflection of our home, not the other way round. We saw it as the seat of our identity, of 'where we came from' and the values we held dear. It was our flag that fluttered even among the raging winds of variable circumstance that swirled around us. At festival times, we refurbished our homes, slathering it with a coat of pretend newness. As a fertility sign, it needed to look well looked after, rather than beautiful. The home was never a building, always a feeling. No one really thought too much about how it looked; the important thing was that it felt like home. Rooms sprawled into each other. Our lives were strewn across the living space without too much order. To be sure there was some demarcation of space, but it was common to find refrigerators and even Godrej almirahs in the drawing room.

Today, the home is the site where we play out our more

mobile identities. The idea of home is now the idea of perpetual progress; the home is always in the state of becoming, being never fully realized, never complete. We buy and sell our homes, see them as empty spaces to be filled with our brand of loveliness till it is time to move to a bigger house or one that is closer to town, and start all over again.

As an object of adornment, the home becomes a mirror to our evolving selves. Every element in the home is now a potential site of beauty; even the lowly waste paper basket is no exception. The bathroom, which in our traditional world view was banished from the sanctity of the home, is now its glittering jewel. We imagine our homes as colonial retreats as we move to addresses like Windsor Residencies and Chancellor Estates.

Currently, the modern home is a reflection of our new found mobility. Good taste comes in three shades of marble and affluence is a Jacuzzi-sprinkled bathroom. The room is still a collection of objects, not a unified space. We buy beautiful things to adorn a room with, our joy does not come from the totality of the effect but from the singularities of individual things of beauty. Our homes are often overcrowded with things without concern for whether they mesh together. We are currently living in a time where more is better; only a few discriminate between what is appropriate in an overall sense and what isn't.

As we move forward, the idea of a personal signature will evolve and taste will become a key discriminator. Stuffing a home full of objects will not be enough. But as we distribute our sense of self over multiple homes, the need for some anchor will always remain. Home will always be a place to heave a sigh of relief in when one returns, but its role will go beyond just that.

THE WESTERN TOILET AS SIGN

It is not unusual to find classified ads that seek to let out houses underline the fact that their toilets have Western-style commodes. Like an English-medium school, the charm of the western toilet has less to do with any intrinsic advantage that it offers and more to do with the cultural signals it emits. In a country where a large part of the population does not have access to basic sanitation, having a Western toilet in an 'attached' bathroom is a sign of luxury, albeit of a basic kind.

It is not difficult to see why. The Western toilet is designed to create distance between the purger and the purged. Sitting on the throne, one is allowed to do one's stuff without having to acknowledge the nature of one's pursuit. One could be dreaming about lavender talc or flipping through the latest issue of a film magazine, if one is not up to the more intellectually taxing exercise of solving crossword puzzles. The act of purging becomes a rumble in the distance, an easy by-product of more civilized pastimes. The act itself requires no physical effort with things slipsliding away out of the body more or less noiselessly. One is protected from anything too graphic and the flush banishes all signs of what one was up to. The toilet paper is the only bit that sits uneasily with the Indian adopter of this new technology, and the preference is for water, which does get one's hands dirty but thanks to the innovation of a squirty pointy thing that releases jets of water aimed appropriately, even this inconvenience has been reduced substantially.

Western excretion is thus no longer a product of biological exertion but one of cultural convenience. The body is virtually not involved in what is otherwise an intensely biological act. As human beings, we rise above the waste we create and can more or less avoid acknowledging that we created any in the first place.

This is certainly not the case when it comes to an Indian toilet. Refusing to embellish the act with much technology, the commode is open and bar a gentle slope that enlists the support of gravity, does not enable cleaning too much. The flush, when it works is one's only aid, but given that the final resting place of the purged material too is visible, the overall intent is clearly not to paper over what one is doing. One is allowed full access to all senses whilst engaged in the act, as one sits on one's haunches and grimly goads the stomach muscles to hurry things along. The body is fully involved in the process with the leg, the knees, the stomach, not to mention the nose all being prominent players in the action.

When one finishes doing one's business, there is a tangible sense of satisfaction, for one knows one has earned the lightness one feels in the stomach. No wonder the act of purging figures so prominently in conversation around breakfast tables. To have cleared one's stomach is to look forward to the day with air of cheerful entitlement.

The two devices reveal two different world views. Implicit in the Western design, the body and what comes out of it needs to be tacitly disowned and quickly laid to rest. To be civilized is to put distance between oneself and the products of one's body. In the words of anthropologist C. Shilling, things that come out of body orifices carry the 'presumption of dirt'. The Indian toilet acknowledges that purging is a ritually impure act, but accepts it as a part of one's life. The ritual staus of excretion finds expression in the fact that traditionally, the toilet was placed outside the house and was seldom attended to. It was a dirty place, meant for dirty business, and was, in fact, often referred to as 'Pakistan'. And hence it did not need to be purified. At the same time, there was no attempt made to avoid being thrust up close to signs of excretion.

It is interesting that one of the biggest signs of change in India has been the refurbishment of the bathroom and the toilet. It now belongs to the house and is invested in quite significantly in the more affluent quarters of cities. We see the advent of specialized toilet cleaners, bathroom fragrances and ceramic tiles that are a far cry from what was available in an Indian toilet of earlier days. And while this change is still far from being widespread, it is a sign that we are beginning to see our bodies differently.

CHAPTER 9

CHANGING OUTSIDE IN

Change is the blockbuster playing to packed houses in some new theatres of the self. We are finding the need to express ourselves differently as we encounter a rapidly changing world. New representations, experiences and diversions are helping shape us in intensely new ways. Change is penetrating our lives and we in turn are penetrating change.

THE REMIX REMIXED

The remix rollercoaster rolls on relentlessly. For the last few years, we have been inundated with a barrage of remixes, brought alive by music videos. Women in various modes of slow motion undress and undulate to the tune of old classics, cheapened by percussion. The dominance of this new form is so great that the so-called Indi-Pop wave is drier than the taps in our cities. And this is a new form, make no mistake. There is a common thread that runs across most of these videos – old songs that usually fall short of greatness, an elementary storyline, men as gaping spectators, and, of course, well-ventilated women not afraid of catching an occasional cold in the line of duty.

Why are we so smitten with this new form? What explains our fascination for this curious hybrid form of expression that uses the old as a vehicle for something so new? The remix begs deeper understanding, because it is both idiosyncratic and influential and surely says a lot about how we as a society see the world.

The most noticeable thing about the remix video is that it separates the input it sends to different senses – the ear hears the familiar but the eye is treated to a completely new visual landscape. The familiarity of the sound allows us to focus on the eye candy that unwraps itself on screen. The existing song is also sanitized of any nuance and is bulldozed into pleasantness – the result is that we get a combination of eye and ear candy to gratify both the senses.

The remix video is also busy rewriting the beauty code for Indian women by placing clear emphasis on the body instead of the face. The face is no longer a site of beauty but merely the amplifier of the body's desires – no wonder so many of the remix video models have faces that look like Ila Arun's voice. The pout and the glazed vacantness of the eyes that are feasting on nameless auto-erotic pleasures are the usual expressions on the women's faces.

It is interesting how many videos depict a form of baby doll eroticism – there is an air of adolescent passivity in a lot of the depictions. The use of schoolgirls, marionettes and Barbie doll clones is a pointer to the intent underlying this representation. Sex here is seen as being akin to an oral confection – what we see is almost the child-like discovery of sites of bodily pleasure, to the voyeuristic delight of the spectator. The videos are unabashedly sexual, without there being any actual sex shown. The role of men in the videos is merely to be inert reference points – they fulfil the purpose of being the poles around which the dance takes place. This allows the spectator to locate himself in the video much more effortlessly.

The remix video is a sign of our times. It drains the past of its meaning and replaces it with images of easy pleasure. It is part of the move towards pleasure-seeking from everything around us; pleasure without the attendant complexity. The remix video creates a world where everything is arranged so that it can be easily consumed. It is a passport to infantile bliss – it sees sex as a particularly chewy toffee. No wonder our adolescent sexuality finds the remix so comforting – it sells the new in a familiar way and makes what was dark and complex pink and pretty.

SALMAN KHAN AND THE RISE
OF MALE CLEAVAGE

Blame it on Salman Khan. His chest has changed India. Or perhaps his chest has had to carry the responsibility of a change that was already happening. Either way, there is no more potent symbol of changing ideas about masculinity in India than the said bald piece of muscular real estate belonging to Mr Khan. At one level, the biggest change it has inspired is in the idea that male bodies should have a shape, a recognition that has driven many Killer Bunties towards gyms and work-outs. Our vocabulary now includes words and phrases like pecs, triceps, abs, six packs and power shakes. At another level it has made the male body an object of self-conscious construction that generates viewing pleasure. Today, a John Abraham cannot escape being asked about whether he will go shirtless yet again in his next film, to which he primly replies, 'if the role demands it'. Heroes today can be classified in two broad categories, the Shirted and the Shirtless, with the former needing to act to make up for their lack of beefcake and the latter needing to shave in new places in order to stay streamlined.

In the good old days, men routinely took off their shirts to reveal a banian with holes stretched tightly over the grassy knoll their torso was. Sometimes they even discarded their trousers and lolled around in their striped underwear with long nadas. Even now, in large parts of India, men can be found in nonchalant public undress without attracting any attention.

The male body was a sexually neutral zone. It carried little symbolic meaning; consequently, the sight of a naked male torso was devoid of any erotic significance. The female upper body, on the other hand, was shielded in an elaborate number of ways, and the pallu always kept in place. If there was any meaning attached whatsoever to the male shape, it was at the margins. The excessively scrawny were considered 'weak' and found themselves featured in ads for potency clinics and the excessively muscled labelled 'rough and tough' and cast outside the pale of middle class sobriety. As a result, cinema heroes had little need to worry about their shapes and anyone not grossly obese (think of how long Shammi Kapoor survived, not to speak of Sanjeev Kumar) was acceptable as a hero. Men were shapeless and ageless and could play college students till they could walk without visible support. The tough looking were consigned to B-grade films and the small-town circuit. Dharmendra was the exception, in no small measure due to roles in films like *Satyakam* and *Anupama*, where there is no hint of muscle nestling inside the buttoned-up kurta.

Otherwise cinema heroes were usually chocolate-centred men with chins that quivered frequently with emotion, especially when their mummy was mean to them. They were terrified of their fathers, who looked disapprovingly at them while chewing at their pipes at the top of a two-faced staircase in their generic haveli. Intriguingly, they were still required at the end of every film to go through a test of masculinity in the mandatory fight sequence, where they overwhelmed the bad guy mainly on account of being able to say 'dhishoom' more convincingly. In a society where boys were kept from becoming men till very late, here were some boys pretending to be men through an exaggerated enactment of physical prowess before running back to their mummies, this time with a pallu-ed wife in tow.

However, in all this, their body was still a site of neutrality. As the action sequence moved from being the last ten minutes to being the centre of films, the male body showed signs of hardening. Dharmendra, Vinod Khanna and Amitabh Bachchan represented a new leaner, tougher male look. This was a time for the son to begin to step outside the shadow of the father while continuing to be firmly ensconced in the mother's lap.

Where Salman Khan's chest differs from Vinod Khanna's is in the attention it attracts and the meaning it conveys. Salman Khan's chest is in the market for attention, it is an object on display in a show window. It speaks in the language of beauty, not in that of power. Salman Khan's chest is a self-conscious one, aware of the gaze it attracts and seeking to exploit it. It is a tourist attraction, a disembodied site of pleasure with no relationship to the person residing inside. The masculinity of men has become its own surface, the appearance of masculinity a substitute for the qualities that constitute it.

It is the turn of men to be stared at, checked out, rated and shot in slow motion. As the mating market becomes freer and as the power balance between the genders becomes more even, the male body will need more tending and grooming to become a consumer product that evokes desire. Mothers may love their boy no matter what he looks like, but a prospective girlfriend may not make similar allowances.

In some ways this reflects the changing idea of gender itself, with it becoming less fixed and being under regular negotiation. As women ask more questions of their men and start articulating their needs, the man's role too starts becoming less certain and he too, perhaps for the first time, starts feeling a sense of performance anxiety.

Salman Khan's chest carries the burden of this new masculinity. Far from being a sign of certainty, it is a white flag of doubt. It looks smooth and hard but it needs regular moisturising to keep it looking that way.

SRK – BRAND AMBASSADOR
FOR THE MARKET

There must be a lesson in it somewhere. A young man with average looks and no connections comes to Mumbai to be a film star and succeeds beyond any expectations. Along the way, he marries his childhood sweetheart, stays happily married, dotes on his kids, builds a house where he dreamed he would and still remains the nation's undiminished favourite two decades on. He promotes himself, the brands he endorses, the team he buys and the films he makes relentlessly and no one can still have enough of him. Yes, the poor showing of his cricket team had dimmed the lustre just a wee bit, but on the whole Shah Rukh Khan's ability to fascinate an entire nation continues unabated. He has become better looking with time and actually grew six packs at the age of forty. He speaks with a shrewd combination of arrogance and disarming self-deprecation and never descends to being the caricature some celebrities become. Almost no one calls him a great actor; he plays himself, or more accurately, plays Shah Rukh Khan playing the character in most films and again that is what people seem to want.

Shah Rukh Khan strikes a chord with us in some deep unique way. He captures the spirit of the times effortlessly and plays it back to us in a compelling way. He is the mainstream hero who makes us feel good about ourselves. He makes us want to do more, lead a better life by showing us that it can not only be done, but enjoyed without paying any major price. You can have fame, fortune, success, a happy family; you can have it all. And it is easy.

Shah Rukh Khan is the market. He does not merely use market forces, he embodies them. He represents the market's best foot forward, he exemplifies what the market can do for us. He is a giant shining billboard for the market where glitter coexists with good times and fame sits well with family. He sits so effortlessly with business because he makes it look good. We are seduced by his charm into wanting and buying. The market persona has been constructed, even if unconsciously, out of all elements available to him.

The roles he has played, especially the Raj/Rahul persona that made him a superstar, were evangelists for modernity. In films like *Dilwale Dulhaniya Le Jayenge* (DDLJ), *Dil To Pagal Hai*, *Mohabattein* and, to a lesser extent, *Pardes*, he played the siren song of modernity, showing us how the modern was nothing but a distillation of the traditional. Raj in DDLJ tells us how desire in its purest form can melt all forces of the past. Raj's trick in DDLJ is to extract nobility from tradition by submitting to it. He does not fight for his love; he sells its legitimacy to its sceptical buyers. Who can dislike Raj for he unites all the qualities cherished by the old and the young alike, making him the easiest-to-consume character seen in Hindi cinema for a very long time.

In *Mohabattein*, his character is even more naked in his espousal of individual desire, as he battles the forces of the past as represented by Amitabh Bachchan. As the young music teacher ushering in change in a hidebound school run by its patriarchal principal, Shah Rukh markets the desirability of modernity and it is only fitting that the film ends with his taking over as the principal, signifying that the present has subsumed the past and is its legitimate representative. By dismantling the restrictive confines of the past, the individual is rendered free to seek definition through his desires.

Even in 'offbeat' roles exploring the darker side of desire, it is notable that his characters try for no larger legitimacy than the intensity of desire itself. In *Baazigar* the desire for revenge made him worse than his enemy and in *Darr* and *Anjaam*, the desire has no larger justification whatsoever. The individual in these films is driven because of desire and the audience is recruited to cheer.

The recent roles of Shah Rukh have now evolved into a comfortable representation of the market. *Om Shanti Om* is the celebration of a market where the past is no longer a time, but a look. The individual is sufficiently detached from the past so as to be able to play with it. The past can be 'bought' now as a shirt, then again as a hair style.

If Amitabh Bachchan's Vijay was seething in an effort to become an individual under the crushing weight of failed father figures, Shah Rukh's Rahul has rendered himself free of the past and lives in what someone has called 'an ever present'. Add to this his real life story and persona and you have a compelling portrait of man-as-market. He promotes any and every product that comes his way and has publicly admitted to having no qualms about dancing at private weddings, something his peers are leery of.

Bereft of ideology, lacking a centre or core, brand SRK is the distillation of all that we want to be projected on the 70 mm screen called Shah Rukh Khan. Shah Rukh does not merely advertise brands, he is the best advertisement for where it all comes from – the market.

IN GENTLE PRAISE OF
THE SAAS-BAHU SAGAS

It is now almost a reflexive reaction to sneer at the kind of soaps that dominated the screen for many years. Nothing is easier and more natural than mocking, condemning or fulminating at the kind of 'mindless and regressive trash that is being handed down to the poor viewer'. The implicit mental model is that of the defenceless viewer who has to suffer these abominations, unable as she is to fend off the reptilian charm of these cavernous mesmeric stories. The viewer, according to this view, is seduced into being an accomplice. The fault is not hers but that of the powerful beamers of these serials who have a commercial motive for keeping audiences in passive thrall.

There are good reasons for this view to exist. Most of these serials wear only a thin garb of modernity but otherwise depict the triumph of traditional values. The traditional roles of women are glorified and those attempting to challenge these are cast in stereotypical terms. All conflict resolutions favour the traditional, and reaffirm that we do not really need to change our way of life.

But something doesn't add up. The Indian woman has changed; we can see the change all around us. Why would she suffer these representations if these serials brought her no reward at all? The idea that the audience is a passive mass without an ability to reject the irrelevant is farfetched. It is possible to see how the *Hum Aapke Hain Kaun* view of the bharatiya nari is all but extinct in today's cinema. Are we missing something when we dismiss these serials as being regressive? Are these serials responding to the changing woman and her needs, albeit in a nuanced way?

The one big change that is most striking is in the physical appearance of today's housewife that we see on the screen. Gone is the institutional meekness of the pallu, the careful subordinateness of her gaze and the modulated mildness of her tone. Replacing it is a new invented aesthetic of domesticity, one which is more graphic, strident and assertive. The colours are bright and flat, the fabric is expensive and shiny – this is a homemaker careful never to be homely. But by far the most striking part of her new persona is her face. Women in today's soaps wear painted masks instead of faces – masks that amplify who they are. The sindoor is like a klaxon heralding impending battles, a vijay-pataka fluttering in the stormy gales of Indian households.

The key device used is that of re-scaling. Hitherto ordinary trifling political machinations within the household are presented to us now as epic battles with high moral stakes. The housewife gets transformed from being a dealer in petty manoeuvring to being a high priestess of values, putting everything on the line in order to save our way of life. The war-paint on the faces of the female protagonists, the background score borrowed from epic sagas, the significant pause after every shattering statement all point to the magnification of the once trivial.

How the story gets resolved is not the key – of course, the traditional value and the retrograde role triumphs. What is important is that today's soaps examine new questions that belong to a modern world. Issues like infidelity, working outside the home, dealing with errant husbands, negotiating roles with the in-laws are all part of the ambit of the soap today. It is only by ensuring that the resolution is not threatening that the serials can open up contentious questions. It is also important that in these serials, it is the woman who decides in most cases, the resolution is not thrust upon her by circumstances alone.

Where these serials succeed is in opening up new areas that can legitimately be debated by women constrained by traditional roles. The woman is depicted as being responsible and mindful of the weight of the past and one who has the power to make decisions. These depictions provide legitimate and enhanced significance for the role played by women in all walks of life.

Not everyone can realistically think in terms of throwing off the yoke of a patriarchal system, nor in fact would they necessarily want to. For these women, the saas-bahu soaps allow for their own personal space to be widened without any backlash. It may not be the perfect answer, but it is a move forward, albeit a timid one.

OF GENUINE FAKES AND
FAKE GENUINES

Who is more fake – Aishwarya Rai or Rakhee Sawant? Mallika Sherawat or Simi Garewal? The answer depends on what we call fake. In today's world we are seeing a phenomenon where the fake is not the opposite of the real but a cinematic amplification of its most desirable features. Mallika Sherawat cannot be fake because she owes no allegiance to the real. Aishwarya can because her reference points are real; she wants to liked, admired and thought of as a good bahu. Mallika's entire persona is constructed, having discarded her 'original' identity in its entirety and fabricated a completely new one in full public view. She is a genuine fake for we know the truth about her and are complicit in not caring. Her persona is not about the truth; she takes our notions of a modern sex symbol and plays them back to us for the price of our attention. On the other hand, Aishwarya Rai looks 'artificial' because she cares too much about reality. She asks to be evaluated as a regular human being and therefore sometimes fails the test.

Simi Garewal is another fake genuine; her posturing is pitiful because it is too clear to us that she is trying hard. There is not a trace of irony or self-awareness about the plastic pretentiousness of her faux elegance and hence she offers herself for easy lampooning. Rakhee Sawant, on the other hand, is a walking parody of herself, making any other attempt to ridicule her extremely difficult. She is a flamboyantly genuine fake and we are riveted to the person she is enacting for us.

The streets of many cities across the world are today littered with genuine fakes. These are products that emblazon their lack of genuineness for all to admire. Far from being shifty apologies, these 'fake' Rolexes and Diesels strut their fakeness. We buy them in the full knowledge that they are fake, we giggle at their resemblance to the real thing, we buy these and wear them aglow with the electric proximity we have to the celebrated. We have no problem in announcing to our friends that what we are sporting is a fake and worth only a fraction of what the real thing costs. The genuine fake allows us to play with the real, we bask in its ersatz glow, liberated by the knowledge of its fakeness.

The genuine fake barters away the materiality of reality for the playfulness of the imagined. The real person vacates possession of oneself and leases out the premises for an imagined creation. The genuine fake constructs himself with little bits of mirrors where you, the voyeur-viewer, see what you want to. Everything is made exterior for the viewer's consumption. Think of Paris Hilton and you will see how the question of who the real person 'inside' is so laughably irrelevant. The real person, such as it is, lies only outside. There is no one home.

Fake bodies, orthodontically aligned teeth, digitally enhanced photographs all help create personas that depend less on what one 'originally' had and more on what can be imagined. Who I am depends less on where I came from and more on what I can imagine myself to be. Madonna's success relies on being able to imagine personae that tap into something just emergent and do so time and again.

In a digital world, where the reproduction retains fidelity, we are close to a time when we will escape the classification of the genuine and the fake. The real and the virtual are in any case being welded together every day. We are close to having films with digitally-simulated actors who look utterly real – in the Internet game Second Life, we trade in virtual real estate to make real money which is in any case a virtual idea.

Reality television manufactures reality with a cold-blooded deliberateness. It juxtaposes characters with situations that allow for the production of some very real reality. It is genuinely fake for it amplifies reality rather than mimic it. The real is today increasingly a mode of expression; it is a kind of narrative that we can choose to adopt. Otherwise, we have detached ourselves from its grounded tyranny. We are free to imagine our future, free to construct our persona. Is Paris Hilton and Rakhee Sawant the best we can do?

THE GREAT INDIAN LAUGHTER PHENOMENON

What would Indian television do without Raju Shrivastava? He hops from channel to channel, effortlessly reprising his old acts as well adding some new ones. His appeal cuts across most classes, and he touches a familiar chord in us with his stories about Gajodhar and vignettes from everyday life, which we find funny in part because they ring uncannily true. His special ability seems to be to peep into the nooks and crannies of our everyday lives, and emerge with flavours rich and familiar. He humanizes all he describes, be it a railway bogie or straps in a compartment, and sees the world as a vast orchestra engaged in producing a comic performance. He uses his body to become not just the people he represents but the things he speaks about.

There are others with their own specialities and together, they have brought to the fore a distinctively Indian art form. The stand-up comic is by no means an Indian idea but what Raju Shrivastava and his ilk practise is a version steeped in our oral traditions. The emphasis on mimicry and impersonation, the use of the song and the emphasis on 'parody' – new versions of familiar stories/dialogues (where would we be without Thakur and Gabbar?) point to a comedic culture that is home-grown.

The current explosion in comedy shows points to something new. The comedic element in popular culture has never been very pronounced in spite of talents like Kishore Kumar, Mehmood, Johnie Walker and Asrani, to name a few. The eighties saw the demise of the comedian with either stars like Amitabh Bachchan taking on the comedy track themselves or leaving it to the double entendre-laced pyjama nada-humour of Shakti Kapoor and Kader Khan.

On television, humour has been even more anaemic. Take away the Hasya Kavi Sammelan, which was about as far as Doordarshan's imagination could go with respect to humour, and you have nothing left. Current serials major in the flatulence-as-comedy school of thought with their emphasis on gross distortions. People who look exaggerated either because of their appearance or their facial expressions do excessive things in peculiar accents accompanied by 'comedy' music set to canned laughter.

A lot of Indian humour has tended to focus on sounds rather than words. Mimicry has been the fundamental pillar of comedy, with many acts across time being about a comedian imitating different voices, preferably of famous actors. The pun virtually does not exist in India, except for its creative use by exponents like Dada Kondke.

Much of Indian humour is rooted in what Herbert Spencer termed 'descending incongruity' – that is, humour extracted out of incongruous situations that underlined one's superiority over the type of person who was being made fun of. Be it the south Indian stereotype, the sardarji joke or even the 'nagging wife' jokes made famous by Surendra Sharma, we found humour quite often in emphasizing the difference between us and the other and validating our own position in the world.

Raju Shrivastav's humour points us to a new ability to find humour in the everyday without necessarily distancing ourselves from what we make fun of. It as an embrace of the 'we', rather than a detachment of the 'them'. While the protagonist is clearly a bhaiyya from UP/Bihar, the nature of the comic narrative does not make the humour exclusive to that set. It becomes a gentle comment on the interaction with things modern told through the eyes of the outsider. This kind of humour reminds us of our humanity in some incongruous way. The mode employed is not distortion but a heightened fidelity to reality.

The ability to laugh at ourselves with respect is a new one. It is not without precedent; the work of Sai Paranjpe in cinema comes to mind, with a film like *Chashm-e-Buddoor* being a case in point. But the dominant form of humour in India tended to escape reality. What we are seeing today is a new engagement with the real stuff of our lives. We are also seeing many other strands of comedy begin to emerge – the satire, the political comment and the insult are all becoming more prevalent in popular culture.

It is curious that at one level, we are seeing much greater intolerance when it comes to representing reality, with so many areas being cordoned off by people who claim to 'own' a particular ethnic group, leader or cause. We cannot show a *Billu Barber* or *Jodhaa Akbar* or screen an Aamir Khan film in a state whose 'feelings he has hurt'. What we can do is to make fun of ourselves with a little more freedom. That's a start.

THE CURRENCY OF CELEBRITY

Is there any celebrity here?' asked the anxious party-circuit covering news reporter with breathless directness. Her eyes had scanned the room in which an award ceremony was taking place and had found it wanting of a newsworthy target. The room was full of people who had done enough to win awards but that was clearly not enough. They lacked the alchemic halo that surrounds the modern deity – the celebrity. They were merely achievers; they had not yet found a place in the magical kingdom of the celebrity.

It is perhaps not too difficult to understand why we need celebrities to punctuate our lives. As social hierarchies rooted in birth begin to crumble, new ones must take their place. Yesterday's nobility is today's starlet – both enjoy prominence unmerited by their actions. The celebrity today does what nobility did yesterday – help make our ordinariness bearable by showing us what the human condition is capable of being. Both are stars in very distant galaxies – they beg admiration from very far. But what makes the idea of the celebrity an exciting one is that unlike nobility, it is possible to acquire celebrity-hood in one's lifetime.

Celebrity-hood is an attention bank – it is nothing but the wealth amassed by accumulated public attention. The celebrity basks in the brilliance of the light that we have shone on them; their glitter comes from the light our collective gazes have conferred upon them. The celebrity is a person magnified by our attention, an inflatable doll puffed up by the labours of our collective blowing. Looked at this way, there can be no undeserving celebrity – by definition, one cannot be a celebrity unless one can command public attention. If socialites today are celebrities, it is merely a measure of what as a society we want to turn our gaze towards.

In some ways the idea of celebrity is similar to the idea of money. Money reduces the value of what it measures to a single number. It becomes possible to compare the value provided by things as diverse as a work of art, an apartment, a foundry, and a music system by asking what they cost. The idea of celebrity similarly converts all fame, no matter what its reason, into a single unit of measurement. Just as money makes only that which can be translated into rupees valuable, celebrity confers value on only that greatness which translates into public attention. So writers, especially in Indian languages, academics, teachers have given way to media performers, socialites and wealth creators in the celebrity stakes.

Like money, celebrity erases its mode of acquisition. Just as a hundred rupee note is silent on how it was earned, celebrity-hood makes one immune to the mode of acquiring it. Once you are a celebrity, it does not matter why you became one. Paris Hilton is famous today – the fact that this fame was acquired by having her sexual romps distributed on the World Wide Web is just a footnote in her now impressive CV. Her fame currency is as valid as a gangster's money currency. Once earned, it is irreversible.

Celebrity converts greatness into a consumer product. Like other consumer products, the celebrity is standardized, packaged and advertised. It comes with a handle that allows us to grasp it. We do not need to know anything about the person's area of expertise – what we buy is the brightness emitted by the fame and not the source of the light. So we can celebrate Hussain without knowing anything about art and Yuvraj Singh without following cricket. In the same way as money makes everything potentially acquirable, celebrity makes greatness consumable by all.

The idea of measuring the world by weight rather than value, by glitter rather than preciousness, can be seen all around us. Ratings reduce all television programmes to a single frame of measurement – everyone chases 'eyeballs'. Attention overrides viewing pleasure. From this perspective, no distinction can be drawn between a programme that influences you deeply and one which you watch while teaching your daughter trigonometry. We see lists like The Ten Most Powerful and 50 Most Influential, which again substitute weight for value.

Celebrities represent greatness made pornographic. Earlier, if you were great, you became famous. Now it is, in many ways, the other way round. In a commercial world, money is the measure of success. In a media world, celebrity has become a measure of greatness. Interestingly, we have nothing to complain about – celebrities are merely a 70-mm projection of the stardust in our eyes.

SUBURBAN ESCAPE

On the outskirts of a Delhi, a new imagination called Gurgaon is going through its birth pangs. And Gurgaon is not alone. All across the country, every metropolis is growing a version of itself in and around its outer limbs. These new spaces are dotted with colonies that carry names like Ridgewood, Greenwood, Belvedere, Chancellor, Regency, Presidency, and come suffixed with descriptors like villas, mansions, heights, village, greens and estates. A bulk of the housing options come as apartments, and in spite of the traditional Indian reverence for land, these are often preferred by buyers today.

The suburb today is increasingly placed as a counterpoint to the city from which it has sprung up. It extricates itself from the entwined memories and structure of the traditional city, and attempts to create a new habitat cast in its own likeness, or at least in one's imagined likeness. Free from the invisible designs of the past, and the responsibility to live within its confines, the suburb creates its own arc of progress. It is united not by someone else's past but one's own present. It brings together people of a similar mindset and station in life. If the city arranges its inhabitants in community-based clusters, the suburb organizes them on the basis or their social and economic identity.

The suburban mindset is open to experimentation as it seeks out new cuisines, new modes of entertainment and the latest avenues of consumption. It features shops of a new kind, hospitals that reek expensively of service, educational institutions that flirt with progressiveness, restaurants that dole out more experimental food. Children here learn dancing, karate, take theatre classes, while studying for the IIT, of course, while their mothers can join continental cooking classes, take yoga lessons and learn driving, only in the colony, you see. As an alcove peopled with white-collar, white-money residents, the suburb is an experiment in discontinuous change.

The suburb was born many years ago; in its earliest avatar, it consisted of cooperative housing societies that sprung up within cities but along its rims. These represented the first generation of home builders, and reflected some of the changes that we see in their full-blown form today. Here, the preference was for land, and thus the row house was born. Although this did mark an escape from the city, it was a timid escape. The colony name either reflected the community cluster of which it was a part or was an invocation of some god or the other (Saraswati Vihar, Krishna Nagar). Even when the name connoted newness (Navjeevan Vihar, Model Town), care was taken to keep most benchmarks familiar. Over time, the city grew around it, and as most people from the traditional city started building a base in the new part of town, the suburb reversed into the town and donned its identity.

Today's suburb is not that careful about keeping the benchmarks familiar. On the contrary, it actively seeks to build a new kind of bubble for itself, one that bears little resemblance to the past. The use of steel and glass, the comfort with high rises, the creation of new clubs that provide for a new kind of intermingling, the desire to live near artificial lakes, golf courses and 'forests', the ceaseless reference to idyllic pastoral havens in the kinds of names these concrete structures go by, all point to a desire to create something aggressively new.

Given that the young today earn higher incomes at lower ages, coupled with easy access to financing makes the suburb an abode for a new generation of home creators. This is the first generation that will build their own homes in such large numbers. The suburban home is not inherited but created by oneself. It is now a result of choice rather than circumstance. The colours on the wall, the décor, the choice of furnishings, the kind of wood work, are decisions that need to be made by the couple themselves. The home itself is seen as if it were a gadget for it is evaluated through the filter of the features it offers. The homes of today must have marble floors, wooden floors in some rooms, a family lounge, new types of taps and handles, and for those willing to pay more, terrace gardens, walk-in closets and of course, the much coveted Jacuzzi, which carries with it an aura of delicious sinfulness.

Eventually, of course, the language of these new imaginations may not possess a rich and varied vocabulary. For most of this suburban imagination is painted in the colours of someone else's dreams. The architectural styles adopted point to an absence of any aesthetic urge other than to create a world that is far away from the past. The trouble with manufacturing Eden is that one is limited by one's imagination. So, at one level, the suburbs hum with the energy of those who feel compelled to create a world of their own, even if it is limited by what they can make of it. But then, creating paradise is never easy.

CITY STORIES

Cities tell stories. As sites where dreams play games with reality, where the future finds a way, often unwittingly, from the clammy embrace of the present, where aspirations aggregate and roots wither, cities are the advance troops of civilization. And the stories they tell are, above all, about who we are and want to be. At the same time, every city has a unique story that comes from its own past, its own combination of communities and cultures embedded in its own distinctive geography.

Interestingly, as India arcs upwards towards its desired future, its main cities tell their own stories. At one level all our major metropolitan cities are negotiating visions of their own future by finding ways to usher in the modern. However, the mode employed in each case is quite distinct and revealing.

Delhi is the city whose reach always exceeds its grasp and where today becomes tomorrow even as we speak. A city grounded in the culture of the refugee, it understands that loss towers above everything else and that one can never have enough to truly insulate oneself from it. So the quest for more and the power of now are the twin forces that drive the city. Built circularly, Delhi has no limits set on its growth as it radiates outwards in inexorable heaves.

Mumbai, on the other hand, is a city predicated on motion. Crammed into a small strip of land, the illusion of space is created by constant movement. Mumbai is exposed when it stops. The city of dreams is a pressure cooker that blends everyone in the cauldron of crammed space and time. If Delhi's ambition is horizontal, based on the visible conquest of man's circumstances, Mumbai soars vertically, as human beings learn to rise above themselves, whatever be their pursuit in life. But not everyone gets access to elevators, and half of Mumbai squats in slums, looking upwards in expectation. For them, ceaseless motion and perpetual hope is the only answer the city can give them.

Bangalore is a city blinded by its own light. The only temperate island in India, the city has got overheated by its success. If global warming were a metaphor, Bangalore would be its poster child. The pensioner's paradise is now a traffic junction without lights and no one seems to have a copy of the road map. Bangalore has lost something concrete and found a lot more that doesn't quite add up. Bangalore is in danger of belonging to the world but having no one who belongs to it.

Kolakata is a city haunted by its unrealized potential. Harbouring a sense of destiny denied, Kolkata has made progress in the last few years but not definitively enough. It is no longer doomed to decay but hasn't quite found a viable wellspring of hope. But Kolkata is a city that clasps its residents to its oddly comforting bosom and, to that extent, makes stakeholders of its residents, something a Delhi or a Bangalore are unable to do sufficiently.

Perhaps the city that is the least understood is Chennai. Stereotyped as the conservative bastion where a strange brand of idol worship is practised, Chennai is periodically heralded as 'having woken up'. But of all metros, Chennai is perhaps the closest we have to a realized city. It has its own popular culture, its own brand of politics and its own set of heroes. Having settled caste-based social tensions a few decades ago, it is a self-contained island that simmers with contentment. There are hardly any malls in Chennai, and though that will change, it seems that this is a place whose people do not need consumption to shore up their identities. Chennai is open to change but on its own terms. Chennai points us towards the difference between progress and growth, change and transformation.

While every city is grappling with different sets of issues, seen together we get a good idea of the questions that occupy us today. We can grow but can we retain a sense of who we are? We can prosper but what of the millions tumbling into these magnets of material promise every day? We can use the city but can we truly belong to it? Every city barks some questions and whispers some answers.

CRICKET HYSTERIA

Are we really obsessed with cricket or are we obsessed with being obsessed and is cricket merely a useful outlet for this deeper need? The recurrent hysteria, alternating between adoration and vituperation and directed at whoever the current cricket captain is and his team, has only unyielding intensity in common. The adoration was always present, what is new is our ability to heap venomous abuse at our cricketers, no matter how sacred they may appear to be otherwise.

Fans who give freely take away at will, and if this were merely reflective of our passion for the game, then it would be quite natural. And certainly, at times the performance of the team has been abject enough to merit the ire that comes its way. It is not just the losing, some would argue, but the craven manner of the surrender and the absence of even a hope of winning that most fans respond to.

However, the dimensions of our anger and the way we express it are illuminating. Every time the team does poorly, we start questioning the amount 'we' pay our cricketers. We point fingers at the ads that the cricketers seem more involved in. We start demanding that performance drive payment. Why is money at all important? When we start using money as a measure, we are revealing the implicit deal that we have with our cricketers. In this transaction, we lionize them in return for their making us feel good about ourselves. The game is of little real consequence; victory and defeat have become detached from the game itself and have assumed a distinct life of their own. The money they are paid does not deliver value unless it is deployed in the production of victory. As spectators, we are giving them an advance payment in anticipation of their pleasing us. When they fail, they become contractual defaulters and attract an emotional penalty clause from us.

Everyone then conspires to create a wailing wall of recrimination. The great are dragged through mud; statues in India are nothing but effigies-in-waiting. We revel in this bloodletting; far from ignoring this or underplaying it as we did in earlier times, today defeat is a spectator sport too. Television channels have understood the power of defeat; for it is here that we indulge in some primitive passions as we defile the sacred with barely concealed glee.

That politicians join in is hardly surprising; they have been our patented archetype for a lynch mob. They are the most vocal, most uninhibited and the screechiest when it comes to rabble rousing. They denounce, declaim, filibuster, thunder, boycott and walk out when they are feeling civilized; otherwise, they throw chappals and chairs. So for them to lead this hysterical chorus is entirely to be expected. The only thing to remember is that in this case we too are the parliamentarians we usually laugh at and cringe from.

What is truly revealing is our reaction to our victories. If defeat makes us a lynch mob, victory makes us surgeons who skilfully dissect its viscera with forensic precision to isolate the pathogens. Even here we seek out the 'defaulters', the 'match ke mujrim', as one TV channel calls them. We are never completely happy; someone has always failed to deliver to the implicit contract we have with them. Performers are separated from the failures and are then excessively feted till they fail.

The implicit world view demands an absolute atomization of happiness; we must be gratified not merely by the outcome but by every element in it every single time. We are throwing a perpetual tantrum in which every desire of ours must continue to keep coming true. Not only must we win every time, Sachin must score a century and that too in the dominating style that we expect from him, without slowing down as he nears the magic mark.

It is as if we cannot believe that at a time when everything must turn our way, here we have something in which we have invested so much of our identity turning upon us. We see the cricketers as ingrates, not merely as poor performers. Our reaction to our cricket team is perhaps a harbinger of the anger to come; it is the flip side of the wave of optimism that is sweeping urban middle-class India. It tells us of our coming inability to handle any reversal. Along with a sunny view of the future is a foreboding about the present. Cricket was a vehicle of hope which when it sometimes delivered, gave us untold joy. When it is a carrier of panicked expectation it gives us only varying degrees of sorrow.

CHAPTER 10

CHANGING INSIDE OUT

*A*s *our external circumstances change, so does the mindset employed to deal with the world. Modernity as a state of mind has now begun to uncoil itself from amidst the modernity of outward signs that are put on display. New patterns of thought are emerging and we are reconciling and combining ideas in interesting new ways.*

CHAPTER 10

CHANGING INSIDE OUT

THE JOINT STOCK FAMILY

If Hindi cinema and TV serials are to believed, the family continues to be at the heart of our everyday lives. Bahus are valiantly overcoming scheming relatives and men are dressing like chandeliers at weddings. Conflicts between generations seem to have abated, with a rare alignment of goals appearing between them. Everyone wants to be an MBA and everyone's parents agree. Arranged marriages thrive, albeit in a new, improved, elastic form. Tradition, it would appear, is winning and yet again, India has fought off the insidious influence of modernity.

All this is true, but it is perhaps one of several truths that make us who we are. For behind the apparent continuity of the family structure lie enormous changes that are helping reshape the contours of our everyday relationships. At the most basic level, the role of the family as the primary source of one's identity has changed. In many parts of urban India, it is rare to come across the 'which-family-are-you-from' question anymore. The family is no longer the tree on which the individual is permanently attached as leaf and where detachment equals arid death. Instead, the individual is the tree located in what is still a dense grove of kindred souls. Families are increasingly not fixed in the past, but are formed dynamically in the present. Yesterday's joint family is the Joint Stock Family of today, where everyone is a shareholder building family capital and not an inheritor living off a legacy.

The nuclear family is about the individual being able to

realize her potential in the protective clasp of the collective. The family allows us to expand the surface area of our own selves so that we multiply our positive experiences. At its most desirable, it functions as a raucously supportive audience that feeds our magnified sense of self. The idea of values, or sanskar, continues to shape families but in a less doctrinaire way. It was easy earlier for the abstraction of values to harden themselves into rituals of action – the 'no one from this family will dance in front of strangers' kind of proscription was easy to make and passed for 'family values'. In today's world, such certainty is hard to justify; behaviour codes need to be more fluid as we encounter rapid change that makes such absolute rules seem absurd.

In a larger sense, family 'ties', especially outside the immediate family nucleus, are loosening into discretionary affiliations. Families are used to multiply pleasure, and the other side of families, the carrying out of mechanical duties, is increasingly being given a miss. The family is no longer welcome as a site of aggregated expectations; it is more an arena to show off our successes, both real and imagined. In that sense, we are increasingly not belonging to families as much as it is the families that belong to us. The family has become another possession, and like all possessions, however cherished, needs to be useful to us. The use-value of the family is the key to its current success; it provides us with grounding weak enough to allow us to fly.

Like all emerging tradition in India, the family is becoming a horizontal rather than vertical structure, in that it is rooted in the present rather than the past, and is in the active process of adapting to today's needs rather than imposing its own fixed sets of constraints. For much of middle class India, the family today is a facility that we enjoy rather than a rule book that we follow. It is composed of people rather than roles and we are discovering the joys of connecting with each other as individuals. Correspondingly, we are able to decide which part of the family we value and calibrate our participation accordingly.

The nostalgia that surrounds families comes from a strong need to protect the idea of continuity even as we alter its meaning. The idea of families is stronger than ever but what it means to be part of one has changed significantly. We want to experience our own individuality, but do not want to be alone. We need to perform as a unit of one, but need the appreciation of others. As we move into a better time, we need an audience to root for us. After all, who else will clap for us?

THE LOGIC OF THE ARRANGED MARRIAGE

Why does the institution of the arranged marriage survive in India in this day and age? The India I am talking about in this case includes the educated middle class, where the incidence of arranged marriages continues to be high, and more importantly, is accepted without any difficulty as a legitimate way of finding a mate. Twenty years ago, looking at the future, one would have imagined that by now, the numbers of the 'arranged marriage-types' would have shrunk and the few remaining stragglers would be looked down upon as belonging to a somewhat primitive tribe. But this is far from being so.

The answer lies partly in the elastic nature of this institution (and indeed that of most traditional Indian customs), which allows it to expand its definition to accommodate the needs of modernity. So today's arranged marriage places individual will at the heart of the process; young men and women are rarely forced to marry someone against their wishes. The role of the parents has moved to that of being presiding deities, with one hand raised in blessing and the other hand immersed purposefully in the wallet.

The need for some 'arrangement' when it comes to marriage is a very real one, both here as well as in those cultures where arranged marriages are anathema. The blind date, being set up by friends, online dating, the speed date, reality 'swayamvar'-type shows are all attempts to arrange ways that one can meet a potential spouse. Here the idea of love is being not-so-gently manufactured by contriving a spark that could turn into the cosy fire of domesticity.

The arranged marriage of today is more clearly manufactured but it also offers a more certain outcome. Online matrimonial sites are full of young professionals seeking matches on their own, knowing that what is on the table here is not a date but the promise of marriage. In the West, the curiously antiquated notion that it is the prerogative of the man to propose marriage makes for a situation where the promise of marriage is tantalizingly withheld by one of the concerned parties for an indefinite period of time. Indeed, going by Hollywood movies, it would appear that to mention marriage too early in a relationship is a sure way of scaring off the man. So we have a situation where marriage is a mirage that shimmers on the horizon frequently, but materializes rarely. The mating process becomes a serial hunt with the man doing the pursuing to begin a relationship and the woman taking over the role in trying to convert it into something more lasting.

At a more fundamental level, the idea that romantic love is the most suitable basis for a long-term relationship is not as automatic as it might appear. Marriage is the only significant kinship tie that we enter into by choice. We don't choose our parents, our relatives or our children – these are cards that are dealt out to us. For a long time, in a lot of cultures, and even now in some, marriage too is a relationship we do not personally control. This view of marriage works best in contexts where the idea of the individual is not fully developed. A young Saraswat Brahmin boy, earning in four figures, was sufficient as a description and one such person was broadly substitutable with another.

As the role of the individual increases and as dimensions of individuality get fleshed out in ever newer ways, marriage must account for these changes. The idea of romance makes the coming together of individuals seem like a natural event.

Mutual attraction melts individuals together into a union. In contexts where communities fragment and finding mates as a task devolves to individuals, romance becomes a natural agent of marriage. The trouble is that while the device works very well in bringing people together, it is not intrinsically equipped to handle these individuals over time. For the greater emphasis on the individual has also meant that personal needs and personal growth come to occupy a privileged position in every individual's life. Falling in love becomes infinitely easier than staying in it as individuals are no longer defined primarily by the roles they play in marriage. So we have a situation where people fall in and out of love more often, making the idea of romance as a basis of marriage not as socially productive as it used to be.

Romantic love seeks to extend the present while the arranged marriage aims at securing the future. It keeps the headiness of romance at bay, and recognizes that romance and the sustenance of a socially constructed long-term contract like marriage do not necessarily converge. Of course, the arranged marriage has its own assumptions about what variables make this contract work and these too offer no guarantees.

In a world where our present has become a poor indicator of our future, the idea of 'arranging' marriages continues to hold charm. Whether it is cloaked in tradition, as it is in India, or in modernity, as it is elsewhere, the institution of marriage needs some help. The expanded Indian view of the arranged marriage functions as a facilitated marriage search designed for individuals. Perhaps that is why convented matches from status families will continue to look for decent marriages, caste no bar.

THE WOMAN, EXTERIORIZED

If advertising is some sort of moving map of society, if it shows little vignettes of how we would like to see ourselves in the everyday conduct of our lives, then it seems to suggest that women in India have become freer on the outside by becoming tied to a new set of anxieties. If the earlier protagonist in advertising was the housewife who played the role of fusspot and appeaser-at-large, forever trying to live up to the often cantankerous expectations of her family members, today it seems to be the young teenager constantly worrying about whether the real or imagined spots on her skin, body odour, dandruff or cracked lips will ruin her chances of romance with Rahul. New sites of self-doubt are being manufactured; cracks in the foot being visualized as spaces from which one's self-esteem leaks out.

Anxiety is the common motif that runs across both worlds. The woman is represented as having emerged from the home only to be assailed by doubts of a new kind, all of which serve to exteriorize her. If earlier, her role as homemaker caused her to locate her identity in the smiles of the people she worked so hard to please, today we see her identity residing in how pleasing her external appearance is to the people who matter. The arena has changed, the source of anxiety is new, but the story is an old one.

In earlier advertising, the home was seen as the natural habitat of a woman tied to home, and the working woman was seen as representing a new kind of freedom that was both envied and feared. The idea of a woman outside home was imbued with a sense of opportunity and a desire to make something of her life through the dint of her efforts. With time, we see a gradual reversal of meaning attached to the idea of 'being outside'. No longer is it a sign of a new mindset or of unrealized potential; it is instead an arena where one is evaluated on one's external beauty. Triumph in job interviews, successful marriages, dates with hot hunks, approval of peers all need to be won through slick surfaces.

The desire for freedom is conflated with a desire for great skin and that of personal ambition with no dandruff. The idea of an essentially imperfect body being painstakingly made worthy of approval and eventually, success, is seen all around us. By itself, that is not such a surprise. It is the virtual absence of the other side of the evolution of women's aspirations that is difficult to understand. The woman is imagined either as a repository of traditional values centred around the home or as a vessel emptied of everything but her sexual exterior. Her being is vested in her outwardliness; once we drain out her traditional role, we seem to be left with nothing else but her appearance.

And it is not advertising alone. Cinema has made the heroine someone who wears short skirts and dances to songs sung in a randy husky voice. Modernity gets signified through a cosmetic change in looks; the inner world of the woman is either unchanged or simply deemed unworthy of attention. The idea of depth, of an unfathomable enigma that men needed to penetrate, has been replaced by that of an unattainable body which men desire to possess. The irony is that at a time when women seem to be possessed of a driving energy and an unflinching desire to make something of their lives, all modes of popular representation seem to all but ignore this aspect of the woman and focus purely on the external. Be it the item girl, the self-hating housewife with wrinkles, Jassi or the beatific bahu on television, all archetypal female representations focus on the woman from the outside.

Of course, it is true that in general everything is being exteriorized. Much more of who we are lives on the surface; it is not a phenomenon restricted to women. The difference is that the journey to greater freedom for women is being subverted by the emphasis on the external. Women are being allowed to come out of homes only to be locked up inside the mental cage of external appearance. It is not that the emphasis on appearances is by itself noteworthy; but that the control over one's appearance too, while seeming to lie with the woman, is actually being governed directly by the expectations of others.

Self-hate is a powerful motivation that moves markets. As John Berger said, 'the publicity image steals our love for ourselves and offers to sell it back to us for the price of the product'. That price might turn out to be a bit steep.

THE FEAR OF WOMEN

My mother never called my father by name. As I am sure was true of most middle class Hindu mothers of people from my generation. Women called their husbands by saying Ai-jee (a respectful form of Hey you), Sunte ho (Are you listening) or the more picturesque Mohan ke papa (Father of Mohan). This was a decidedly curious practice; one could understand if the name were used along with a respectful suffix, if that were the intent, but the proscription on using the name is revealing.

And this was not the only distinctive feature that defined the relationship between spouses. They did not sit together in family get-togethers; in fact, the wife rose to move away if the husband accidentally stood or sat too close to her. Public displays of affection were unheard of and most children of my generation would perhaps have never seen their parents display any signs of intimacy whatsoever. In fact, finding time for romance even in the early stages of marriage was a herculean feat. Barring the wedding night ritual, where consummation is culturally legitimate, indeed it is decreed, the new bride was quickly appropriated by the mother-in-law and the husband was left starving for attention, a situation well documented by sundry Indian films.

Reproduction and motherhood were the key goals and questions about the subject could be put in a disconcertingly direct manner if the newly married couple did not quickly put on display the product of their exertions. Fertility in women has been a treasured virtue, one which is the cause of much joy when the woman is married and much anxiety till such time as she is single. To have an unmarried daughter on one's hand was to tempt fate; a whole battery of proverbs in various languages document this fear about women with unregulated sexuality. Parents were expected to stand guard over their unmarried daughters and the sooner they got them 'married off' the better for all concerned. With the advent of education and greater unsupervised contact between the sexes, this task became an onerous one and the films of the sixties and the seventies document in unself-conscious detail the efforts made to keep women from any romantic entanglement. The words used to describe such relationships testify to how these were seen – 'lafda', and 'chakkar' come to mind, both of which are redolent of a sense of the complications implicit in these affairs of the heart.

The idea that marriages were performed between roles draped on individuals, rather than between individuals themselves, is a key feature of the Indian arranged marriage. Women, in particular, were expected to reside in their roles. At any given time, they played one among several roles that came accompanied with their own behaviour templates; she could variously be the Dutiful Daughter-in-Law, Sacrificing Mother, Indulgent Bhabhi, Obedient Daughter, Concerned Wife or Shy Bride, to name a few.

Even after marriage, the anxiety continued to centre around the power of her sexuality. The reason for keeping the relationship between the spouses essentially role-based was to try and limit the power the woman was feared to have over the man. The integrity of joint families was sought to be preserved by keeping the two at sufficient distance. Not allowing a woman to use her husband's name is a brilliant idea when seen in this context. It ensured that access to the most basic signifier of a person's individuality was denied to his wife. It underlined the hierarchy in the marriage as well its essentially impersonal nature. The

Hindi social film is a full-blown treatise on this subject; it documents vividly the nature of the anxiety at work.

Typically, in one version of the Hindi social, the home is visualized as heaven on earth, one where the male siblings adore their parents and sing happy songs in their praise. Enter a new bride, often from a more affluent and modern family, who wears Western clothes and manipulates the husband and leads him astray. Soon there is discord, with the errant couple asking for their share and finding a way to ruin the family financially. Before you know it, the mother is reduced to acting as a servant and just after the interval, gets accused of stealing something and is thrown out of her own home. At this time, the younger son steps in, and with the help of a kindly outsider, decides to teach the elder sibling a lesson. This is generally accomplished quite quickly by way of finding a way to impoverish the arrogant couple, who see the error of their ways and come crawling back to the family, with the woman back in a sari, which sees its former glory restored. In many cases, the turnaround involves the elder son 'coming to his senses', which is signified by his slapping his wife, an act that instantly converts her into a domesticated version of herself.

The sexualized woman, bent on consumption, 'eats up the family' using as a front the husband, who turns on his own family. Another male intervention, made culturally legitimate by the transgressions of the woman, puts her back in her place and she returns to the fold, chastened. Typically, the people chosen to play the errant siblings tended to advertise their wimpishness (Anil Dhawan, Raj Kiran, Monty Premnath, the early Gulshan Grover and such like).

Over the last few decades, we have seen a fundamental change in the way women see themselves. Armed with education, which ironically has been a product not so much of a parental desire to arm their daughters with economically productive knowledge but of a desire to find them better matches, the woman defines her relationship with the outside world in new ways. In many cases, she is no longer financially dependent on her husband; even if she does not work outside the home today, her education makes her potentially financially independent at any time.

Her view of herself is no longer contained in and by how others see her. She is no longer a sum total of the roles she plays. She may choose not to underline this fact by tacitly continuing to play these roles without too much apparent change, but she is increasingly 'playing' at these roles. Her pleasure now comes not only from that of others; she is herself a seeker.

This change has given fuel to the universal fear evoked by women and one that has informed much of how family life has been constructed in India. To top it all, not only is the woman an active and independent participant in her own life, she now looks at the man with an array of reciprocal expectations. For the first time in his life, the Indian man, brought up by his mother to believe that he is the centre of the universe, has someone evaluating him, and finding him wanting.

The outbreak of moral policing we see in the country is only partly political. It arises out of an overarching anxiety about women upturning the cosy social order that we have been comfortably ensconced in. One thing common to most acts of moral policing in India is that they involve the regulation of women. What they should wear or shouldn't, where should they go, how they should behave, how should they be represented, and so on. So whether it is about women drinking in pubs or wearing jeans to college or being seen with their admirers on Valentine's Day or even in public parks, outrage gets sparked off most easily when women are involved.

The distance between different social groups amplifies this anxiety. The 'modernity' of a certain class is seen to be gradually infiltrating everyone in India. And while what is right or wrong is a context-sensitive cultural construction, the fact that when women are involved our fears get multiplied is something we cannot deny. The fear of women is here to stay; one has only to look at our neighbours to see how far it can go.

THE IMAGINED SCARCITY OF OPPORTUNITY

Students with 90 per cent being nowhere. The crushing pressure of competition as the struggle for good education gets more intense. Cut-offs functioning like symbolic guillotines, snapping a child's ambition clean. It's a good story, a compelling tale of how difficult it is to succeed in today's world, where a sliver of extra performance marks out the good from the mediocre.

The only catch is, it is not really true. Of course, there is competition and the really top professional courses and colleges are very difficult to get into. It is also true that cut-offs at the undergraduate level too have risen significantly. But eventually marks are just numbers; all that really matters is one's relative performance. That is as true today as it was yesterday.

One problem is that educational opportunities have not grown in line with the economy. We have far too few good colleges with far too few seats. The private sector has failed so far to make a dent in this area, and it is for the most part because it is too naked in its greed. It is a telling commentary on the private sector that in an area where demand is so palpable and where ability to pay is disproportionate to one's means, it has been unable to make headway against poorly funded, poorly run government institutions simply because it is overly concerned about making money.

But even after accounting for the scarcity in educational opportunities, the current paranoia doesn't make sense. The desire for a particular course or a particular college is, in most cases, an irrational one, based on popular opinion and hearsay, bearing little relationship with the real world. It really makes no difference if one graduates from a Kirori Mal college in Psychology or a Sophia in English from a career perspective. In most cases, it is the post-graduate degree that matters. In a job interview, the college attended makes no difference; in most cases, it is not even noticed.

The trouble is that people who feed this anxiety, that is, parents and most schools, are woefully out of touch with what is happening today. Too much has changed; the wisdom of yore has become the ignorant dogma of today. The naivete of this group would be touching if it did not serve to assail the student with so much self-doubt.

Most importantly, for the first time, India lives in a universe that is expanding. The number of opportunities has exploded; not only has the number of jobs gone up but there is today a bewildering array of new careers that were unheard of yesterday. A lot of these are talent-based and allow for kids to make a career out of something they are good at and enjoy doing. Significantly, what matters increasingly is not where you came from but where you are capable of going. Qualifications matter less; performance much more.

The language of scarcity is rooted in the public sector discourse of the past. It lives on in education because it is still the domain of the government and its apparatus. It lives on in spite of the visibly new world outside our windows because in some strange way, we want it to be so.

The rising cut-offs are seen as yet another sign of progress, yet another marvel of modernity that we shake our heads in disbelief at. The 'children today are so bright' discourse has on its flip side 'compete or die' written on it. We want to believe that our children must do much more than what we did and we exaggerate the threat posed by competition towards this end.

We focus relentlessly on the pinnacle, making IITs and IIMs our superbrands, forgetting that the real story lies elsewhere.

The India story is not about its top achievers; it is about the rise of the middle. The median salaries have gone up; the hitherto 'ordinary' students are the ones who have gained the most. Today, people with all kinds of qualifications are doing well; the BPO industry is all about people with virtually no qualifications doing very well. But we focus on the microscopic top, and allow the achievement of a tiny minority to tyrannize the rest of us. Unlike the US, where the blue-collar worker is the centre of society, India, in spite of the vast majority at the bottom, chooses to look only at the very top. As a result, we are missing the real progress that we are making as a society.

Of course, we need to increase access to quality education. But let us not forget to acknowledge the new freedom that the young have in the India of today. To all those who have missed what they thought was the opportunity of a lifetime, let me assure you that you ain't seen nothing yet.

THE PARANOID PARENT

Ask any parent anywhere on this planet and they will tell you that there is nothing as sinister, nothing as singularly depressing and dispiriting, as Arpita's Copy. This is something that you usually stumble upon at your quarterly school visit, feeling otherwise relieved because your child, in a rare fit of petulance, has done reasonably well at the mid-term exams. Just as you feel that this time you could escape with your self-esteem relatively intact, you come across Arpita's Copy. Now this is not just a copy where a tidy conscientious child writes in copious detail about everything, taking care to label things in boxes and uses eighteen different coloured pencils while describing My Favourite Holiday, this is actually a Sinister Plot hatched to make your parenting skills look bad by rival parents with way too much time, patience and colouring ability on their side. The child is merely an instrument; it is the parents who get graded.

The whole school evaluation process grades parents with a bewilderingly complex classification system that involves stars, smileys, goods, very goods and keep-it-ups. This is a complex system with an intricate hierarchy that your child seems to know perfectly well but which is designed to keep you in a state of permanent guesswork – are two smileys in a week better than a good and a keep-it-up? And what about Arpita? What has she got?

Just as schools find new and diabolical ways of evaluating parents, so do parents use dizzyingly complex ways of rating schools. Schools are never strict enough or lenient enough, they simultaneously pay too much attention to extracurricular activities while being far too caught up in studies. Their teachers are always both too detailed in their assessment of the children while not being attentive enough and so on.

At the heart of all this is our new conception of parenting as an arena of performance rather than as a condition dealt to us by a timeless natural process. The word parenting itself reveals the change of an idea that was a noun into one that is a verb. The pressure today is therefore to be Doing Something Constructive all the time; action substitutes wisdom. The frenetic action is attributed to the rise in competition that the child must today face. In truth, at least part of this competition is the one amongst parents as to who is doing more.

Most of us were brought up without too much deliberate parenting – mothers were unquestioning founts of nurturance while fathers were vaguely dissatisfied taskmasters who tuned into your life every time you brought home a report card. The pressure was undoubtedly on the child to be either the Good Son or the Dutiful Daughter who got into Science and put oil in their hair every Sunday. It was implicitly believed that children were born complete and that with time they merely became an adult version of who they already were. The role of parents was therefore to keep them on the right side of society. Today, the child is seen as an entity that is mouldable and the role of the parent is to build a person out of a child. This puts tremendous responsibility on parents who believe that their actions determine their child's future and hence every small step becomes a Big Project where a minor mistake would make your child a dribbling sociopath tomorrow.

Hence the persistent belief that enough is not being done for the child in spite of the perhaps unfortunate truth that more than enough is being done to him. The fear gets compounded by a nagging sense of insufficiency in dealing with this question, one that parents have not been prepared for. Children need to perform in order to make parents feel good about themselves. In that sense, not much has changed; children still become instruments for the realization of some parental goals. If earlier Getting into Science was enough to make parents proud, now almost nothing is good enough. Ninety per cent is too little and one extra-curricular activity too basic. And yes, there is always an Arpita lurking somewhere with her wretched copy.

RETRIEVING SPACE SLYLY

Every year, come February 14, some shops will inevitably get damaged as will some young couples get roughed up. Valentine's Day inevitably arouses strong feelings and has become a site of contestation between different interest groups in India. Similarly, there have been instances involving women in pubs, college principals banning jeans, ads that are deemed vulgar, and so on. It would appear that as India adopts new cultural practices, it encounters resistance from sections of society who fear the change that has got unleashed as part of the process of economic reform and globalization. This is perhaps inevitable; it would be natural for an ancient civilization like India to resist such dramatic change.

Except that the truth is not that simple. True, there is resistance in a section of society towards change of a kind; at the same time, we are seeing a huge amount of change pass unchallenged, and perhaps even celebrated, by the very sections that are opposing it. The trick perhaps lies in the way change is managed. A pattern common to much of middle class India is to seek additional space for oneself without seeming to go up against tradition. A variety of subtle strategies are being employed to create a larger playing arena for the individual, without posing any overt challenges to existing institutions.

One way is to celebrate tradition while simultaneously hollowing it out. For instance, every locality in Delhi strives to put its own grand version of a Jagrata, the all-night prayer in the honour of Vaishno Devi Mata, but the bhajans that are played here are set to the tune of popular Hindi film songs, some of which were originally controversially raunchy. So it is not uncommon to come across a bhajan set to Choli ke peechche kya hai (Mata ke dil me kya hai) or Kajra re (Mata re). People feel free to get up and dance, men and women, draped in the cover of piety. The parallel narratives run simultaneously, and it must be said, seamlessly.

A version of this strategy is seen also when it comes to celebrating festivals, where the pleasure notes resident in these are heightened and the drearier aspects are edited out. A wonderful example is the relaunch of Karwa Chauth, the north Indian festival in which the wife fasts the entire day for the life of the husband, and can eat only after she sights the moon. It once used to be a ceremony about sacrifice, and was wreathed in much solemnity. Thanks to Hindi cinema, Karwa Chauth is today a festival of excess and joy. The wife continues to fast the whole day, but the focus now is on the celebration to follow once she can eat. She gets gifts from the husband, gets taken out for dinner, and in a few cases, is accompanied in her fast by her sympathetic spouse. In many ways, it is the culturally acceptable version of Valentine's Day, one in which married couples reaffirm their relationship through an act of symbolic sacrifice.

Achievement is another cloak in which change is often smuggled in. This works particularly well in the case of women, who use it to win freedoms that would not be available if they were sought under another label. Beauty pageants are a good example of this strategy. Women from all parts of India change into swimming costumes and sashay down ramps while being scrutinized up close by a large number of people, an experience that is so far removed from their existing realities so as to make the mind boggle. I have heard of parents accompanying their daughters to a contest that went under the name of Item Bomb, wherein a music channel was looking for women to do an 'item song' in a forthcoming film. To accompany your daughter to a contest where she strips to something short and shimmering and wraps herself around a pole and sways suggestively is an experience new to most middle class parents. But couched as it is in the language of achievement, the action is neutered culturally and passes muster.

A variation of this strategy, whereby the new action is attributed to a desirable old value, is seen in the case of housewives who spend increasing amounts of time and money to lavish attention on themselves by way of personal grooming. Visits to beauty parlours, something frowned upon traditionally, are now attributed to 'maintaining myself for my husband', and hence part of one's marital responsibilities. Yesterday's indulgence becomes today's task and is thus a legitimate part of one's to-do list.

This ploy of contravocation, the act of recruiting a desirable value in order to defend a contentious one is a particularly interesting one. It found wonderful expression in a film called *Kya Kehna,* which featured Preity Zinta as a young woman who gets pregnant before marriage and where the boy in question refuses to marry her. In a scene where she is humiliated publicly at a college function, in a way that one can be only in a Hindi film, she gets on the stage to defend herself. Faced with an implacably hostile audience, she offers a unique argument – that it was fine for her to be reviled as a woman, but that she was now a mother-to-be and that her mistake, terrible as it was, should not alter her hallowed status as a mother. She asked for forgiveness as a woman, but asked for understanding as a mother. The device used is interesting for it amplifies a culturally desirable trait while diminishing the significance of an undesirable action.

This argument is taken one step forward when it is contended that the new is, in fact, a purer form of the old since it captures its original intent better than the existing practice. Here, the existing practice is portrayed as being ossified and a distorted reflection of the intended tradition and the new is imagined as a more authentic version of tradition. Rightwing Hindu activists use this particularly powerfully when they contend that their actions represent Hinduism and its original intent better. The new, unfamiliar action gets attributed to what was originally intended but could not be achieved.

The most common way of retrieving space is to expand tradition, while retaining its benevolent canopy. The arranged love marriage makes elastic the idea of mediated matches by accommodating the desires of the individuals involved. The electric diya, which stays lit unlike its traditional counterpart, smuggles in the convenience of technology by being able to offer better ritual performance.

There are other strategies too. The young use the device of loudly setting limits for themselves so that they win parental approval for their actions ('Will not stay out after 10', thereby skirting any arguments about going out at all). Sometimes tradition is worn as a costume that allows for more modern behaviour to pass without demur. Marriages are now celebrated with more apparent tradition, but are routinely full of drinking and dancing to popular music, something not quite kosher earlier.

When change announces itself and wears its intention too nakedly, it can come up against resistance. But change in India is ever present; it lurks about in the shadows, snaking its way silently across significant parts of lives. We want change, without necessarily calling it that.

CHAPTER 11

MEDIA SMOKE AND MIRRORS

No other force has influenced change in India as much as its media. Bursting with chaotic energy, Indian media has in the last decade or so exploded in scale and mutated into a complex phenomenon of sweeping power. It has become an alternative universe while continuing to shape how we see the existing one. It mirrors, magnifies and distorts. It gives us new benchmarks and a reality full of false ceilings and hollow bottoms. No reading of India is meaningful without an examination of the role played by the media.

21-INCH INDIA

Year after year, our Independence Day is marked by what is now a predictable air of celebration. Newspapers are full of opinion polls that focus on what seems to be our current obsession, viz., when we would achieve superpower status as a nation. The television is full of people who usually fill television screens talking about things they usually talk about. There is by now a well-rehearsed ritual that we go through in our effort to congratulate ourselves. Over the last few years, we have managed to create our own version of a country called India, a version we keep perfecting in our covert pact with reality. And this version of India is one that fits inside the 21-inch television screen; all that lies outside it is no longer part of an India we wish to inhabit.

The 21-inch India that we have created is a construct based on a few set issues, and even fewer people who are allowed to represent the various sides of these issues. If Mumbai is to be spoken of, it is in terms of its spirit, the lack of infrastructure and the callousness of politicians, and the people to go to are Messrs Rahul Bose, Prahlad Kakkar and Shobhaa De. If it is politics we are discussing then again, out come some well-worn debates and the screen brims over with the lawyer brigade with Messrs Kapil Sibal, Abhishek Singhvi and Arun Jaitley holding forth. Morality questions become the purview of people like Ashok Singhal and a woman with a big bindi who appears to regard every living being on the planet with barely concealed disgust as scum in an advanced state of moral decay.

It is as if we live in a media-created world with its own artificial sky dotted with manufactured celebrities. In this comfortable bubble, celebrities shroud us in a canopy of forgetfulness; our world and our view of India gets miniaturized to what fits on television. The screen is too small for rural India and hence 70 per cent of India can find no mention unless someone gouges out somebody else's eyes, preferably in front of TV cameras and when the light is good.

It is not that serious questions do not get debated, but that these questions pertain to a small fraction of India. One of the surveys I mentioned at the beginning of the article listed population, corruption and terrorism as the key problems facing us. It is revealing that poverty is not something we regard as a problem any more. One could argue that population is, in fact, a surrogate for poverty, but if that is the case it says a lot about how we see the world. Population is a prism that the affluent and neo-affluent see poverty through for it carries within it the anxiety about there never being enough for everyone. The unarticulated fear is that 'even if we do better it is not going to help because there are so many people to divide the fruits of progress amongst'. Population reveals my anxiety about my wellbeing and what will accrue to me rather than a concern about others who are poor. It also represents a latent sense of threat as the numbers of the marginalized 'others' swell and start beating down the doors of the affluent.

In another sense, 21-inch India has overthrown the larger nation in a media-led coup. The city has displaced the village; the glitter has pushed the grime into the background, the flyover is now the index of progress and not, say, rural electrification. When we talk of a water crisis, we talk of cities, when we talk of crime we bemoan the lack of justice meted out to the families of Ruchika Girhotra, Jessica Lal, Priyadarshini Mattoo and Nitish Katara.

The irony of course is that 21-inch India is utterly irrelevant electorally. The politicians who grace our television screens struggle to win elections and those who do are the ones we fear and demonize. The politician is hated by all, and while this is not a difficult thing to do, at least part of this animus comes from a fear of the other. Politicians represent an India we have successfully shut out. We don't write about that India, we don't include it in our serials and it has certainly been banished from our mainstream films. We are not ready to deal with the very real reality of that India and hence we tar all politicians in a paint of recrimination. The more things go wrong, as in the case of Mumbai after 26/11, the greater the frenzy with which we denounce the political establishment and the greater our frustration at coming to terms with our own insignificance.

21-inch India wants to secede from mainland India; some would argue that it has already done so. But then who are we to hold an opinion; let's ask Rahul Bose what he thinks.

THE LIMITS OF DEBATE

Do you feel an overwhelming sense of hopelessness watching a debate on any political or social issue in India? On any issue, the stand that political parties will take is more or less pre-determined. We know that the BJP spokesperson will spin it in a certain way, overlooking the party's own statements made a few weeks ago. We know the Congress will summon outrage but in the next state where it is faced with a similar situation, do exactly what the BJP did. So what's the point in listening to two paid lackeys from the two sides pretend to shout at each other on national television? Similarly, a sting operation, such as Tehelka's Gujarat expose in 2008, is unlikely to change the mind of even one person since the positions are entrenched and thus all events are seen through the prism of one's chosen side. The public prosecutor seen in the Tehelka sting talking about how he deliberately misleads Muslim plaintiffs, is able to recant his statement saying that he thought he was rehearsing a script, and the only people outraged are those who already were! You either love Narendra Modi or hate him and that is that. Equally, you are a secularist or not, a believer in abortion or not, against big dams or not. Once the side is chosen then all judgement is suspended and we get into debate mode.

Debate is at the heart of the idea of democracy. Contrary world views are allowed to compete for public approval, with the winners being given the opportunity to convert their thoughts into action. We encourage oppositional politics for we believe that through that clash, through that locking of ideological horns, will emerge a blueprint for our tomorrows. We extend the idea of the debate to other public forums; television arrays strong proponents of opposing views against each other, seminars ensure that different voices from across the ideological spectrum are represented.

The trouble exists at two levels. Firstly, in the political space, we have a growing irrelevance of ideology. So people have no belief to defend, merely some recent action. The reason why lawyers end up becoming spokespersons for parties is that apart from being skilled tap-dancers around logic, they are used to building arguments on the basis of who is paying them. They do not require a consistency of world view in order to perform. Point them in the direction of a position and they fill in the details. Television helps them for it is a medium tailor-made for bluster; you cannot rewind in order to reflect and challenge. Confidence and loudness suffice.

The deeper problem has to do with the fact that debates ossify our imagination. We are unable to rise above the same old questions that have always dogged us. Truth becomes a choice between two extremes or, at best, is a point in between the two pre-defined poles. We cannot re-configure solutions in new terms, trapped as we are in the old. Worse, we are unable to acknowledge the grey areas that lie between the extremes.

Take the debate on abortion. The liberal position is stoutly pro-choice without any moral self-doubt. How can we ignore the fact that abortion involves taking a life for the convenience of some individuals? The technical debate on what constitutes a life is surely slippery enough so as to afford some self-doubt? But to be a liberal one cannot ask this question. Nor can we ask why Gujarat supports Modi as strongly as it does. Surely, he must have touched something real among the people who elect him and conspire to believe his version of what happened in 2002?

To condemn Modi or the Left, as the case might be, is easy. To take sides and mindlessly look for evidence that supports one's point of view is even easier. To engage in debate as a way to affirm one's position is to negate the idea of debating. If to debate is merely to loudly expostulate one's chosen stance, then it is mere haranguing.

Perhaps the time has come to move beyond the binary limits to our imagination imposed by the debate. We must look to the third view that is able to imagine the world in terms not thought of before. Otherwise we will be forever locked in a battle where the loudest will appear to have won.

OPINION AS TRUTH

Eighty-six per cent believe Swami Ramdev is right, 57 per cent believe rapists should be hanged and 31 per cent believe kissing is against Indian culture. Pick up any newspaper or watch any channel and you will be subjected to a barrage of information about how people feel about things. Opinions have become news; we are becoming more interested in what we feel about events rather than the events themselves. We are witnessing a frenzy of collective preening; we are obsessively concerned with what we think.

News today is interactive, reality shows are all judged by the public, business today measures our confidence in the business outlook; magazines routinely publish opinion polls on their covers, especially if they have to do with sex. Everywhere we find a heightened interest in what the public thinks and believes about things, big and small.

The popular is more legitimate than it has ever been. At one level, this is easy to understand. We have come from a past where we listened to everyone else's opinions. Our parents determined what we studied, where we worked and who we got married to. We were taught in shut-up-listen-and-mug-up mode of education, which left little room for our opinions. Our life was a litany of rules; we were forever watchful in our compliance. Our politicians lectured us like we were children; the government treated us with the respect reserved for dribbling idiots and the newspaper editors saw us as robotic followers who could be led by the nose to wherever their current intellectual pretension took them. We were made to apologize for enjoying anything that was not lofty; for years AIR did not carry popular film music – we had to practically excavate the 25M band to locate Radio Ceylon for the *Binaca Geet Mala* when we wanted to listen to recent film hits. Popular cinema was routinely crucified; and we were the reluctant recipients of endless eulogies about New Cinema, ignoring the fact that most of it was pretentious juvenile claptrap. It largely involved morose men with intense beards scratching the fuzzy underbelly of our society for olfactory adventure; an activity that does not guarantee Great Works of Art. The sole purpose seemed to be to deny the audience an iota of entertainment, a mission in which they largely succeeded.

Greater purchasing power, combined with commercial television, has freed us from the tyranny of listening to news we don't want to. Everything now revolves much more around what we think and what we want. News channels worry about their ratings; the pressure is to show the news that people want to see. The power has moved from the experts and the intellectual middlemen to the ordinary people. Singing ability is judged by the audience, the 'Indian of the Year' is arrived at as a result of a poll; a recent Miss World too was selected by the people.

It is almost as if public opinion is becoming a substitute for the truth. The popularity of anything is almost its justification. We conduct a public trial of a fact or event and then pronounce judgement on it. Truth becomes a participatory sport; we can all join in and by definition the answer we arrive at becomes the truth. The whole Intelligent Design debate in the US is a great example of where the legitimacy of the popular can take us. Science must accommodate the ludicrous lunacy of Intelligent Design because it is an idea popular among a large number of people.

At a less extreme level, the quest to feed the popular centralizes and homogenizes our actions. Like contestants in a beauty pageant, we parrot our lines because we have been told that this is what people want to hear. The formula flourishes because we start judging things not by their intrinsic value but by how we think the world will see it. We will create those things that we believe people want. The market shifts the location of creation from the creator to the buyer. This, of course, assumes that as buyers, we know what we want. One thing is certain – we will relentlessly get what we deserve.

THE EFFECTS OF LANGUAGE

Why are all Hindi news channels so excitable? Why do they brim over with passion about every subject, be it the marriage blues of some unfortunate couple, Rakhi's stage shows and the hourly performance of the Indian cricket team? In the name of news they rave and rant and go entirely with the flow of events, rather than cast a critical eye on them. The world becomes a spectator sport and news anchors become the commentators whose role is to make us, the viewers, feel the excitement sitting in our homes. There is no need felt to provide perspective for that calls for an ability to detach oneself from the event and examine it dispassionately.

Come to think of it, why are Hindi sports commentators so excitable? The difference in the English and Hindi versions of the commentary is startling. The Hindi commentator sees the game as perpetually exciting and believes in magnifying every moment through the sheer force of lilt. The sound of the commentary communicates more than the meaning of the words it contains, and it is easy to figure out what is happening by listening to the cadence of the radio commentator even if one cannot catch the words. Typically, the Hindi commentator is much more comfortable on radio than television, for he is at his best when he has the full burden of communicating not only what is happening on the ground but the feeling that it generates. On television, he needs to account for the fact that we are privy to what is happening; his role is to underline, analyse, point out and provide perspective, things that do not seem to come with great ease.

Now it cannot be that all people who choose to commentate in Hindi lack the ability to provide all that or that all those who speak in English are cold fish unmoved by the events that unfold around us. Could it be that the two languages, and the culture they represent, see the world in fundamentally different ways? Could there be a Hindi view of the world, which is essentially different from views represented by other languages, in this case, English?

At first glance, this is a preposterous proposition. How can the language one speak change the content of what one is saying? There are great analytical thinkers who express themselves in Hindi just as English has its share of emotionally expressive writers. But while language may not entirely determine the nature of discourse carried out in it, could it play some role in it?

Take, for instance, how in the world of advertising, Hindi slogans have an uncanny need to rhyme. The 'Ek ya do bachche, Ghar mein hote hain acchhe' school of tag lines continues to this day. Given the oral nature of our culture, it is easy to see why rhyme was so important for it was a device to preserve memory. The Hanuman Chalisa, the dohas, the singing/chanting of shlokas in a prescribed lilt, the reciting of the pahadas to learn multiplication, all point to the need to keep memory intact in a world where things were not written down and where few people could read.

The effects of orality might well be behind the natural slant of Hindi news channels and commentary. The spoken word resides in a world that is totally immersed in the present; when we speak we are always in the moment, we cannot but have a ball-by-ball view of the world. When we write, we do so with retrospective detachment, we use logic, we sequence our argument, building it step by step. When we speak we do so with emotion and gesticulations, we repeat ourselves for effect, meander when we think of something else. Logic is not that critical; the emotional force and intent behind what we are saying is.

Comedy in Hindi too is largely involved with voices and sounds. Wit does not come naturally; the pun is extremely rare for both are measured manipulations of the mind. The Hindi comedy serial relies on people speaking funnily rather than being funny; the comedian historically needed to look and speak like one.

So when the Hindi news channels speak in such a distinctive voice compared to their English counterparts, it is not an accident. There might be a natural tendency that comes not from the people running these channels but from the language that they speak in.

THE BIAS FOR EXTREMISM

The easiest way to become somebody in India is to say something very provocative, very loudly, very often. In no time, you are on television, first being covered and then being assailed by sundry critics. Now is the time to be trenchantly unrepentant and add fuel to the fire by broadening your diatribe. Soon you become a regular member of a television panel, and part of the pantheon of influential voices in India.

Rakhi Sawant showed us how a little could a long way by using the most provocative part of her body – her mouth. Raj Thackeray demonstrated the power of homeopathic violence by shrewdly placing it in front of television cameras. In the case of the Shri Ram Sene, the media was given balcony seats and perhaps fed popcorn so that it could report the staged violence without straining itself too much. And Varun Gandhi put his foot in his mouth only to discover that he could run faster this way. Suddenly he was on every screen, and his name popped up in every debate. Had he worked tirelessly for Pilibhit, he would be nothing more than the faintly familiar 'other' Gandhi. Suddenly, he was a bona fide leader, with a point of view that needed to be represented. He had built a base for himself, not just in Pilibhit or among diehard right-wingers, but had also created a visual constituency for himself on national television.

Of course, it is curious how we have managed to invert the meaning of what constitutes offensive speech. Today, private bodies get offended very easily and there is an implicit censorship on many things (we cannot even use the word 'barber' in a film title) while the state is unable to take cognizance of the most flagrant transgressions made by people making deliberately inflammatory statements. People's sentiments are hurt very easily by relatively inconsequential and accidental perceived slights while frontal attacks of the most provocative kind go by without any real deterrence. Akshay Kumar's zip can cause more outrage than Raj Thackeray's lip. The former has to apologize, the latter builds a political fortune.

One could also ask whether the laws of the land also end up conspiring with publicity hounds given the symbolic nature of punishment meted out to motormouth offenders most of the time. Far from deterring provocative speech, it actually helps fan it, given that one can end up looking like a martyr without suffering any actual imprisonment. Of course, in Varun Gandhi's case, Mayawati's action in slapping the National Security Act (NSA), even if it was a deliberately contrived overreaction, made the punishment more real.

In a larger sense, this search for easy impact pushes the discourse towards the extreme side of any argument. Debates get framed by those who take polarized positions, people in the middle are too wishy-washy for our times. Extreme positions seem to have become a surrogate for significance and clarity, and these receive a disproportionate value. Of course, extremism seeks out more extremism; a Varun Gandhi gets a Mayawati in return, and a provocative speech, the NSA. Even on television, it is the extreme cadre that holds our attention. The reason why we are seeing a rise in brutish behaviour on screen, be it in the form of warring judges in a reality show or an expletive-hissing extravaganza in the guise of a youth show, is that television is compelled to create a sense of manufactured spectacle that ensures that we do not take our eyes off the screen.

For that is what eventually matters. Given its flickering transience, television keeps our memory cache permanently empty. We do not remember why somebody became famous, only that we have heard of them. Notoriety is the currency of television, and no matter how many earnest anchors attack what they see as unacceptable, the very act of doing so on television defeats the purpose. That is perhaps television's ultimate paradox – it wields enormous power without being in control of it.

Of course, staying in the news is not easy given that more and more people have figured out how easy it is to become famous. Why, even the redoubtable Ms Rakhi Sawant is not as frequent an inhabitant of our screens as she used to be. But the writing on the wall needs no translation – the visual extremists are here to stay and we will keep watching them.

IT'S THE FORM, STUPID

That television is the most powerful engine of change in India is an assertion that is unlikely to be challenged by most. But what may not get the same acceptance is to argue that what is powerful about television is not so much its content but its form. To put it differently, television, by virtue of the particular combination of extension, intensification and amplification that it offers by way of technology, creates a set of far-reaching effects.

Television is set in relentless continuous time. It makes the world a whirl of ceaseless events that move with alarming speed. The television news screen is a hive of crawlers, information worms slithering along the surface of time, oozing newness. The tone is urgent, the pitch dramatic. News is designed to create impact rather than memory. Did the cash-for-votes scandal really happen not too long ago? And whatever happened to the infamous Doctor Death who traded in human organs? Does Nithari ring a bell? Is it a vast conspiracy of amnesia on the part of all channels acting in concert or is it in the nature of television to wipe its disk clean every so often?

The much lamented absence of depth on television too has its roots here. There is no rewind button on television, no way to flip back to an earlier page for a more leisurely read. There are no past issues to thumb through, no archives for reference unless some kind soul has uploaded what we want to see on youtube. Television cannot support reflection in the way that print can. Of course, some channels will still carry more depth than others, but taken as a whole, television struggles with introspection.

By virtue of being set in continuous time, it tends to narrativize reality into 'stories'. Like a film which takes stills and turns them into an illusion of fluid time, television news converts individual bits of facts into narratives. What does not fit into these neat stories becomes difficult to deal with. So it matters little if the story changes very frequently, but the world must come to us in little capsules of digestible stories.

By far, the most powerful influence of television is its legitimization of individual desire. The impatient individual armed with the remote is increasingly an apt metaphor for the way we, as a people, are beginning to consume our world. Television places the consumer at the centre of its universe. It is obsessively concerned with the popular as manifest in its ratings, and 'this is what people want' becomes an absolute argument that can brook no opposition. It is a democracy of desire, where the individual believes that his desire is a priori, legitimate. Television promotes those instincts that cultures work hard to suppress. At one level, this is vastly liberating for large parts of India, where most of us grew up repressed to some extent or the other. It takes away the pressure of behaving 'like one should' and allows one to act as one feels. In doing so, it also allows those hidden, too-impolitic-to-state urges to come out into the open and get catered to. Crime shows, salacious up-the-skirt shots of cheerleaders, tales of misfortune told with ghoulish glee all become par for the course.

More fundamentally, ideas like secularism, tolerance, and temperate balance start looking like impositions. One can argue that the recent surge in intolerance that one sees from a large section of society is in some way a product of a 'televisionized' India, free from the need to pretend to be politically correct. The pent-up feelings of resentment and entitlement have rushed out and get both tacit and explicit support from television. In a certain sense, television has made Indian democracy more real, in that we are today dealing with issues that come from how people, when not pretending to be someone else, and when not subject to editorial admonitions, really feel about things. The prejudices are out in the open, be they those with a communal tinge or elements of class hatred (will Mayawati really become prime minister?).

Television shapes its content by its form. The same media house which, in its print avatar, can be a model of balanced reporting, becomes a rabid purveyor of half-truth set to a dramatic sound track. On television itself, a channel's English version strives for relative accuracy, but has no qualms in letting its Hindi counterpart run riot with the truth. It is as if the media owners themselves are not able to exercise full control over the content they put out; they are compelled to follow the implicit code of television.

In Marshall McLuhan's words, 'we become what we behold. We shape our tools which, in turn, shape us.' The content, he goes on to argue in his characteristically extreme way, is 'the juicy piece of meat carried by the burglar to distract the watchdog of the mind' and 'it has about as much importance as the stencilling on the casing of an atomic bomb.' The televisionization of India goes way beyond television. We are increasingly what we watch.

SECTION THREE

DILEMMAS OF CHANGE

CHAPTER 12

NOT EVERYONE IS INVITED

The euphoria around the new India that is emerging from within the folds of the old serves to obscure the fact that change has come to India very selectively. More importantly, the idea itself has been appropriated by a small section in a way that does not call attention to itself. Through a process of a change in benchmarks, vocabulary and an apparent universalization of concerns, what benefits a few has often been assumed to benefit all.

BLINDED BY LANGUAGE?

A hospital nurse is a great leveller. To her, it doesn't matter what you do in the world outside, how much money you make, and what your views on some burning subjects of the day are. To her you are just another 'patient', that somewhat pesky breed of whiners who oscillate between sullen neediness and absurd gratitude. The 'patient' needs to be handled with a combination of brisk indifference and occasional solicitude and all is usually well.

Similarly, at a school, one is a parent, to be dealt with as someone infantile struggling to become responsible, having been burdened with progeny who they may or may not be doing enough for. To a shopkeeper one is a 'customer', to an auto driver a 'sawaari', at a hill station one is a 'tourist' and so on.

These aggregations are natural, given the repetitive nature of these interactions; but they also help shape the way in which we choose to see the world we live in. By making every person who is suffering from some ailment a 'patient', the nurse seeks to reduce the staggering diversity and the emotional immediacy of disease into a generic fact of life. The aggregate converts first-person specifics into third-person generalities. Human interactions of an individual kind are replaced with transactions between roles; transactions that help drain the interaction of its emotional significance. We can cope with the world better, if we can become immune to new experiences and can develop the ability to see everything as familiar and known.

In a larger sense, we are helped into selective blindness, numbed into oversight. The word 'slum' converts the condition of the urban poor into a phenomenon – we are able to accommodate a vast amount of human misery under the umbrella of a single word. The aggregate 'slum' in a way legitimizes the presence of this condition and inures us to what lies beneath. We can cast our eye over a vast area of hovels densely packed together in fetid squalor and see only a 'slum'. The 'slum' becomes the natural condition of the urban poor and we are able to talk about razing it or resettling it without feeling any great pangs of guilt. Similarly, the idea of 'the masses', that most generic of generics, allows us to confer qualities of a single primitive being on a very heterogeneous set of individuals.

The eye is indiscriminate in what it sees and hence needs to learn how not to see everything it comes across. Our mind uses a complex set of strategies to see what we feel comfortable with – one of which is to band diverse experience into a single aggregate that shrivels diversity into a hardened stereotype.

Which is why the city is crammed full of the invisible majority. We have stopped seeing the vast multitudes that throng the streets, or those who sleep at odd hours of the day on footpaths; we exclude large parts of the metropolis from our mental map of the city. Which is why electoral results are always counter-intuitive – remember how foxed we all were when the good Dr Manmohan Singh lost in South Delhi? Our conception of South Delhi as an oasis of education and 'good sense' took a knock as the numerical clout of the invisible majority struck back. In a larger sense, this also explains why we are able to exclude rural India from our conception of the New India that we are beginning to become proud of. The 'village' is a shorthand for primitive passions, of people like Lalu Prasad Yadav, who are a distraction from things that excite us, and hence can be ignored.

However, even now, when an international visitor reaches Bangalore, that talismanic destination of New Economy pilgrims, what he sees first is not an economic miracle but the hypnotic dance of poverty that envelopes his senses. We constantly rail against foreign media for focusing on India's poverty and not its many successes, but part of the truth is that they merely report what they see whereas we see what our mind asks us to.

It is natural for us to do so. We need to find a way to cope; having been cursed by the ability to see everything, we need the help of language to help our eye sweep across a vast array of diversity and see nothing at all. Or nothing out of the ordinary.

THE FLYOVER AS METAPHOR

For most of us, flyovers are the primary sign of urban development. Flyovers have the ability to intrude aggressively into our consciousness; they are imposing 'projects' full of the material that builds nations – concrete and steel. They disrupt everyday life for a period of at least a couple of years, and it is clear from that disruption that something significant is afoot. They work as shorthand for progress; cities throw flyover statistics at each other in a bid to prove their own progressiveness.

It is not difficult to see why flyovers are so critical in the urban development project. Flyovers represent the ability of the present to take a leap over all the accumulated messiness of yesterday. Flyovers create space 'over' the past, large vistas of clean uncluttered space magically appears where there was filth and squalor. The past is not destroyed, merely skipped. Flyovers are a kind of fast-forward button in space – don't see yesterday's reality as a constraint, just fly over it.

The underlying neatness of the solution – no demolitions, no rehabilitation, just a use of technology to levitate into the future – is extremely attractive politically. At another level, it allows for the construction of the New Urban Landscape that is aesthetically pleasing, that buries the untidy smelly tumult of the 'old' city. We cannot demolish slums and other inconveniences, but surely we can erase them from our consciousness.

Flyovers dramatically reorder the space they inhabit. Formerly busy markets become forlorn bargain basements reverting to a primitive form of mercantile existence. Hitherto towering buildings appear at eye level, dwarfed into accessibility. Lofty perches through which the world was surveyed now get covered with curtains in a desperate bid to avoid being optically penetrated. The flyover changes the power distribution inherent in the habitat. Everything gives way to this new 'modern' outsider that sits fatly in its conquest.

The past becomes much like the 'empty' space that lies just under a flyover, a space that no amount of beautification has ever managed to redeem. Cut off from the sun, severed from its surroundings, this is the mirror image of modernity, a kind of serrated netherland created by the present. It is revealing that this pidgin space is created directly by the neatness of new technology; the same technology that gives us the wide clean space of the flyover gives us this fuzzy underbelly of dubious utility. In some ways, this space is merely the more extreme form of what happens to the conquered space. The old city becomes the forgotten city, to be accessed for the more menial 'lower' tasks through a thicket of smells and potholed lanes.

Flyovers are part of the new hierarchy of space. Having gone through the uptown/downtown hierarchy, which gave differing valencies to horizontal space, the city today is building a new vertical haven, perched well above the sights, sounds and smells of the teeming multitudes. In some ways, all traditional space hierarchies are in the process of being overturned. If earlier the centre of the city was its source of energy, today it is the margin where the action is taking place.

Take Gurgaon. This is a city built to escape the past. Built on income and not wealth, Gurgaon is a sanctuary for the newly powerful. New winners in a new sport, the residents of Gurgaon have no desire to be part of the city's power structure or be held in the grip of its past. Gurgaon represents the joint invention of a new present, modern, shiny and with 100 per cent power back-up. The most critical difference that exists in Gurgaon is the birth of a new mindset, one that is free from a lot of the baggage of the past, a forward-looking future-oriented view of the world.

The desire to build a new future, away from the grubby fingers of the past, is revealed even more strongly in the new highway projects that we see across the country. These superhighways are essentially nothing but private conversations between two cities, excluding everyone else from what is being said. Travelling down the Bombay-Pune highway, my brother remarked to me that this didn't look like India and he was right, in one way. Our conception of India after all comes really from the people of India, from the way Indian villages look when we pass by. New highways bypass this India and cut a swathe through the India that is made of land and not of people.

The highway is in many ways a virtual entity, a kind of dotted line that hovers mythically around the areas it touches. The only two definite real entities are the two destinations it connects. Unlike its less exalted predecessors, which included everyone they touched, the superhighway is meant for the powerful and the rich for the purpose of continuing to be powerful and rich.

There is a new India that is emerging. We are finally at the threshold of a real leap forward. Which is why it is critical that we ask what kind of progress do we want. To believe that if one section of people makes giant strides forward, somehow others too will move forward a little, is a fallacy as has been repeatedly proven in the past.

In a democracy, we can fly over the past for some time, but can we outrun it for ever?

THE REVENGE OF THE
SPEEDBREAKER

What's with our obsession with speedbreakers? We may or may not build great roads but we sure know how to build great speedbreakers – a lot of them. They are such a regular part of our landscape that we barely think about them except when our intestines crash into our kidneys as we encounter an unmarked one lying in our wait while grinning fiendishly in the dark. We manufacture our speedbreakers with care and evilness in equal measure, and have, over a period of time, developed a full range of options.

The gentlest one is the Rolling Hill speedbreaker, which allows us to hug its curves as we pass smoothly across, with not much loss of speed. Then there is the Humped Whale, the size of a minor hillock, that the undercarriage of our vehicle must scrape across. A variation is its two-humped cousin, which lives up to its name, and er... nails us twice. And finally, you have the most evil of them all, the Stutter Bump, against which slowing down is of no use. It is a punishment delivered for the temerity of travelling faster than we can walk and is like six of the best delivered on the seat of our pants.

The speedbreaker exists to defeat the purpose of the road. Motorized transport became possible because of the macadamization of the roads and the speedbreaker is the tarmac's revenge on itself. By freezing speed momentarily, the speedbreaker slows down the entire traffic by creating a deliberate bottleneck.

It exists for a good reason – given the kind of driving that goes around, we need to be protected from our own speed. Since our traffic police rarely enforces any law unless it happens to be its appointed week (a la Lane Changing Week or Zero Tolerance Week), the only check that citizens can hope for is the speedbreaker, which, apart from being a surefire method, has the additional advantage of being impossible to bribe.

But there is a larger need that drives us to put up so many of these. At some level, we are afraid of speed and the distance that gets created between those speeding and the rest of us. The speedbreaker is the political front, the battle line that marks the tussle between those with the means to speed and the others. The speedbreaker attempts to tame the world of the fast; to force it to slow down and acknowledge the other world. This is most apparent on highways, where every village and small town puts up speedbreakers that convert the highway into the property of the community. The speedbreaker localizes the road by bringing its pace in line with that of the community. It is an instrument of conquest, an attempt to blend the outsider into the local.

How we see the speedbreaker depends on where we stand; to the fast the speedbreaker is an anachronism that refuses to acknowledge progress, while to the others the speedbreaker is an admission that progress is an abstraction whose reality affects different classes differently.

The unmarked speedbreaker is as much a sign of civic inefficiency as it is as a somewhat twisted restorer of natural justice. It is the vigilante of the road – the Robin Hood that robs the fast of their speed for the protection of the slow. The unconscious intent seems to be to foster uncertainty among those speeding. For speed needs certainty; embedded in speed is an expectation about the future continuing to be predictable. We make a commitment that is equal to the braking distance of our vehicle but the unmarked speedbreaker subverts that certainty. It creates an artificial pothole, one that faces north this time.

Speed needs certainty because most forms of mass transport operate in realms of relative certainty. Air space is relatively uncluttered and it is a testimony to the need for certainty that even small birds flying around the airport can disrupt the safe passage of aircraft. The railway is a similar attempt to provide certainty by demarcating its path sharply and with certainty. This certainty too gets challenged at a level crossing, where some idiot always decides to play chicken with the speeding monster. The new highways, therefore, try and emulate this certainty by being constructed in 'empty' space; they steer clear of inhabitation as much as they can. They are the new corridors of certainty in a landscape that otherwise thrives on chaos.

For it is when speed has to acknowledge others that it gets unstuck. Speed becomes its own justification; the faster always believe that the road 'rightfully' belongs to them. It allows trucks to contemptuously wave aside the gnats that are cars, and cars to curse those on scooters, and the scooters to bemoan the cyclists. To the bigger and the faster, the slower and smaller is an obstacle; a clumsy primitive barrier that must be broken down, brushed aside or, at the very least, overtaken. We tailgate, honk incessantly and manoeuvre persistently till we get our way past these.

The speedbreaker is the natural ally of the slow. Like the seasoned pedestrian who will deliberately stroll in front of your speeding car, knowing that you have to stop, the speedbreaker lies secure in its power. It forces all to kneel before it; our undercarriages genuflect as they bow and scrape in front of these deities of divine come-uppance. If they are irritating, it is because they are meant to be so. In a world that is becoming too cocky and certain, speedbreakers are strewing it with a minefield of questions.

Speed will always both seduce and defeat human beings. Balraj Sahni's famous attempt in *Do Bigha Zamin* tells us that men will try to move at speeds that are beyond them, and that they will fail. Speed will put distance between some of us and the others, and this distance will only grow. The speedbreaker is a lame attempt to reverse this truth; if you can't stop progress, at least give it a sore back.

THE POWER OF INFLATION

It appears that you cannot win an election for sure even if the economy grows in double digits; you can, however, lose one when inflation rises even fractionally. That is the hypothesis on which the anxiety about galloping inflation rates seem to be based. The idea is paradoxical – one would expect that in a poor country like ours, where so many promises of prosperity have turned out to be hollow, actual delivered growth would be a guaranteed vote catcher. After years of marginal growth, we are accelerating into something approaching speed. Shouldn't this be a good time for us to live with a little inflation?

The problem is that progress as a statistical measure is very different from the one that is experienced in everyday life. The economy is in any case an imagined idea. Shape has been given to very abstract ideas by a barrage of measurement indices. The nation 'becomes' the economy and in turn the economy 'becomes' us. We infer progress from the numbers that are thrown at us; without these most of us would be unable to state experientially as to how fast we are growing.

In actual fact, we infer progress not from abstract numbers but from our lived reality. Malls, highways, souped-up petrol pumps and flyovers are our indices of progress. We experience progress when our airports improve and the power goes out less frequently. When these signs of progress are within grasp, they serve as powerful drivers of aspiration. But inflation reverses this sense of access for those who were close to these and for the poor, communicate the opposite; they advertise with neon glee the widening distance between themselves and the others. Inflation is the economic index that is experienced more vividly by more people more often than any other. It is the most democratic of all economic indices and thus has the greatest power.

Psychologically, inflation defeats the sense of progress for those on the margins of consumption. It changes the rules of the game even as it is in progress. It induces an exhausting sense of having to forever accelerate in order to merely keep up. It negates the notion of a better tomorrow by changing its definition. Doing better is now not necessarily good enough. One is defeated by time; money becomes a chimerical idea that can, without warning, evaporate or shrink. A context of overall growth serves merely to underline the cruelty of inflation. Growth is what happens to others, inflation is what happens to me, is the feeling. In some perverse way, the poor end up paying for someone else's progress.

Nothing is worse than having something at last and then having to forego it. Consumption is the sand that slips away from the tight fists of the those emerging from penury. We are all the more risk averse when we put something we already have at stake than when we gamble on a future event. We can afford to not get what we don't have but to lose what we own induces extreme anxiety. Growth is a vague future promise, inflation an all-too-tangible reality. Inflation is a dying bird in hand, growth is a rustle of feathers in the bushes.

Inflation does not merely dampen our outlook towards the future, it subverts the very idea of a future. It reinforces the traditional notion of the future as something inherently treacherous and binds us to a today that needs to be coped with. It is a vote against hope and a warning against its futility. At a time when India is stirring itself into action after decades of torpid lethargy, it serves to undermine the gathering energy of the emerging class.

In a larger sense, prices evoke eras. Remember when petrol was Rs 5 a litre (I do) and Rs 50 bought you a whole bagful of groceries? Lower prices evoke simpler times when the pressures of coping were less insistent. Prices are the pitch at which we lead our lives. As they rise, our lives become shriller. For the affluent, the feeling is tangible but can be seen as an acceptable part of progress. For those without this luxury it is the sound of the ground disappearing from under their feet.

WHAT WE DON'T WANT
TO KNOW

Do we, out of an intense desire to see the world the way it should be, deliberately misread the way it is? The debate around Raj Thackeray's pronouncements about North Indian outsiders in Mumbai is centred around the inappropriateness of his remarks and the transparent nature of the political game he is playing in inciting the local Maharashtrian population. It is also argued that the Mumbai of today is unlikely to be amenable to such crude prodding and that the tactics that brought the Shiv Sena into prominence forty years ago are unlikely to work in today's context.

Fair enough. But how much of that view is analysis and how much is hope? For instance, in a poll carried out by one of the channels, as many as 76 per cent of people in Mumbai disagreed with Raj Thackeray's views. Among Maharashtrians the number was around 59 per cent, still a healthy majority. Looked at another way, as many as 41 per cent of the locals agreed with Thackeray! The same number goes up to 61 per cent when asked whether his outburst was genuine. For two out of five Maharashtrians to feel this way is a fact that needs to be taken note of and not brushed under the statistical carpet.

The fear that we don't want to know the truth gets further validated by the kind of coverage we see on television. While the title of these discussions is open-ended and provocative, the way it is set up reveals the intent quite clearly. For instance, on one such show, the studio guests were people of a type – Dipankar

Gupta, the sociologist, Vandana Shiva, the eco-feminist, Mahesh Dattani, the playwright, and other such luminaries with impeccable liberal credentials. The other side was represented by the sole MNS spokesperson, who was roundly assailed by all and who, in typical politician style, seemed remarkably unperturbed about the whole thing. In another show, the host Rajdeep Sardesai mounted a frontal attack on the same gentleman, trying to get him to apologize for the violence. It almost seems as if the truth, if revealed, would be too ugly to handle; the effort is instead to heckle reality till it confesses.

The same pattern was seen in Gujarat, where for years, we refused to believe that Narendra Modi had the enthusiastic support of middle class Gujaratis. The desire to believe in our own ideals about democracy made it very difficult for us to digest Modi's undeniable popularity. We can see the same story repeated in the deep conviction that a section of society has about the stupidity and regressivenes of the saas-bahu serials; a conviction that has been decisively exposed as being ridiculous by their continued popularity for years now. In fact, more often than not, when major social issues are polled, the results tend to confound our cosy assumptions about what people want.

Because something is incomprehensible and offensive to one section, because it militates against a particular world view, it is deemed to be an aberration. We then look for ways to deny the significance of that occurrence, hiding behind all possible ways of interpreting information that justifies our world view. This wilful blindness is an effort to keep the illusion of stability and order intact. It is also an imposition of one point of view on the rest of us.

At the heart of the problem lies a fundamental contradiction about democracy. It depends on the wisdom of people but can in no way guarantee it. If the country were to be run on the basis of opinion polls, chances are that India would be a very different kind of place. Conditioned as we are to blindly trumpet the power of democracy, we get stumped when see it turn upon the ideals we hold dear. We try and deal with this by denying what we see. We argue with reality, we try and browbeat it into some kind of submission. But reality festers in the shadow of neglect and it is only a matter of time till we are forced to acknowledge it.

The real question is, do we really want to know the truth?

THE VANISHING VILLAGE

Channel surf through the eighty-odd channels you get on television today and try finding a single image of rural India. If 70 per cent of India lives in the villages, we certainly do our best to keep it a secret. Especially when it comes to Bollywood and the advertising that we see on TV. Gone are the days of the village potboiler with belles sashaying near wells before being almost married off to lecherous moneylenders. The village is no longer a prominent site of action; everything seems to happen only in the city.

Representations of rural India follow one of three distinct discourses. The first is of the village as the headquarters of primitive passions; a place where politicians run kingdoms and policemen gouge out eyes. The village is no longer a location but an indictment; it is today a projection of urban fears about a powerful but thankfully distant other. In other words, in our minds all of rural India has become equal to Bihar. A place where people in rustic accents create muscled mayhem only to have their eyes gouged out occasionally by policemen in idealistic rage.

The second discourse is that of the village seen through the nostalgia-tinted lenses of the NRI. This is the village of the zamindars with photogenic mustard fields swaying in synchronized grandeur. The village becomes the seat of hallowed memory and is aggrandized in retrospect. Films like *Dilwale Dulhaniya Le Jayenge, Pardes, Pyaar To Hona Hi Tha* all celebrated the notion of families wrapped up in abundant fertility that overcame the potentially disruptive forces of modernity. The NRI village reeks of desi ghee, not cow dung, and prefers havelis to hovels.

A third and emergent view of the village is as a project that needs urgent attention. Shah Rukh Khan in *Swades* typifies this new sense of the village that can be saved by the objective forces of technology. It marks a new depiction of rural India as seen from the eyes of the city. The village is made to value all that the city does. Technology is seen as the change agent that can transform the village into a version of the city. This theme is echoed in the highly innovative e-choupal initiative launched by ITC; the advertising shows a farmer leapfrogging into an entirely new world, leaving all the problems of the village well and truly behind.

In some crucial ways, the very idea of rural India has undergone a change. From being seen as the heart of India, we now see it as a remote outpost that is the opposite of the India we call our own. The village today has no voice of its own – all three discourses outlined above are all perspectives that are urban in origin. The village is an image that we consume in our cities. Our reactions differ depending on the meaning we want to extract from the idea of the village – be it fear, nostalgia or interventionist zeal.

Otherwise, traditionally, advertising has always ignored rural India. Except for fertilizers and saria, one is hard put to find rural images in the advertising we see. And here too, the stereotype dominates – men with large moustaches talk loudly while Dhanno sings about khushhali in a countrified frock. Things are changing, though – Coke has used stories located unselfconsciously in rural settings and depicted rural protagonists as archetypal New Indians full of confidence and self-belief. The advertising for Shell lubricants has a truck fleet owner explain the benefits to us in a rational and reasoned manner that steers clear of caricatures. Advertising in regional languages is taking this further with the advertising for brands like Coke and Sprite resonating with rural characters oozing personality. However, in spite of some changes at the margin, the truth is that rural India is barely represented in our advertising.

Overall then, this is the Age of the City. Our reference point is Chicago and not Chikmagalur. From this vantage point, rural India is another planet with which we have, at best, a dim affinity. Bollywood has little patience with rural India; it no longer provides any material for fantasy. Advertising, on the other hand, is slowly waking up to the rural market. As the rural consumer becomes more assertive, this is a space we should watch closely.

CHAPTER 13

THE POLITICS OF A NEW INDIA

Nothing in India is as resoundingly Indian as its political system. A national election sees 400 million individual acts of democracy being executed towards a single end. As with everything else, we have taken a modern progressive idea and made it our own. It is only politics in India that is truly democratic and it is only when we think about India in political terms that we have no choice but to include all of India in our calculations.

MEDIEVAL DEMOCRACY

It is interesting how in an election when a coalition finds itself shy of a majority by a few seats, we all assume that the requisite numbers will be cobbled together. Of course, this will mean that some independents will be given inducements to lend their support and some opposition members lured away from their own parties, actions that we classify under the technical term 'horsetrading', a practice that is now a legitimate part of our electoral calculations.

We might be occasionally upset as we were when some parliamentarians displayed a crore of rupees on the floor of the House, but we have otherwise grown used to the fact that a bulk of our politicians are corrupt, and in politics largely for personal gain.

How could this state of affairs have come to pass? How can we allow Parliament to become populated with the kind of people it has? Why is it that in spite of the nakedness of the horsetrading seen time and again, we re-elect the same people the next time around too? More importantly, and intriguingly, how do we reconcile this with the state of the nation, which, while going through a temporary slump, is not doing too badly? By all accounts, given our politicians, India should have been a banana republic. The levels of open corruption, given the obvious venality of a large majority of those in politics, should have resulted in an ungovernable mess.

Could it be that there is another way of characterizing the nature of our democracy, one that explains, even if it does not justify, what seems to be happening on the political stage? While it is clear that India is some distance away from its intended polity, there is a logic of another kind that drives its unintended polity. As long as we measure our current reality against what we had intended to achieve, outrage and incomprehension will continue to be our dominant modes of response. It is only if we are able to construct a mental model of what is in fact happening, can we hope to achieve a measure of understanding and hopefully, drive a realistic agenda for change, as deemed necessary.

What if the feeling that most of the electorate shares, viz., the politicians are not here to serve us but to exercise mastery over us, is not a critique but an objective description of reality? Instead of seeing ourselves as a democracy, what if we really are a distorted form of elective and distributive monarchy? It can be successfully argued that India is an election-o-cracy more than it is a democracy, in that the primary quest of the democratic process is to allocate power. The exercise of that power, once gained, is subject to much looser standards of performance. The key idea of elections in India revolves around power and not mandate, patronage not policy.

Our politicians are nothing but regional satraps, chiefs of small territories, warlords and leaders of small principalities who barter their influence for power. Like their medieval counterparts, their allegiance is to the people who are loyal to them and the use of all means, fair or foul, is legitimate in the pursuit of their interests. Criminality is not a big problem, since the line between legitimate strength and illegitimate muscle becomes academic in such a scenario. It is as if each of these 'states' has its own private army, and eventually the only legitimacy that armies possess is that they represent the institutional power of a designated state. The kind of tactics seen in Parliament in the cash-for-vote scandal in 2008 go back a long way; Indian history is full of examples of inspired duplicity that we celebrate as a sign of a warrior's canniness.

What we call corruption is, in this model, nothing but a form of tribute paid in negotiation for power. Money moves from those who need something to those who have a momentary advantage. The powerful extract their share of wealth from the system, having been conferred with a right to rule.

By reducing the idea of democracy almost exclusively to elections, we have converted those who should have been our representatives into our rulers. We tolerate their whimsicalities, bow and scrape at their every pronouncement and give every politician, however lowly, the right to put on a red siren on their cars and hold us up for hours. The idea of political dynasties and our comfort with it is a sign of that the political system in India is a monarchy-like institution in disguise.

Why have we allowed this to happen? We installed a political system that had no roots in the Indian ethos and like in many other walks of life, Indian reality has reconfigured the intended system into a hybridized extension of its past. Democracy in India was conceived as a twentieth-century project but functions as a modified version of a medieval idea. We were not ready for democracy and did not see the point in it in its pure form, so we created our own version. It is an idea that works within its own frame of reference.

That doesn't make it right or desirable, but it does provoke questions about the kind of political system that has a realistic chance in India. If we were to be more democratic about the idea of democracy, what would it look like?

SYMPATHY FOR THE HAVES

Every time the government makes noises about the inequalities of income and the need to do something about it, a storm of protest is immediately visible in mainstream media. There is much to be said for all the editorial concern but what is interesting is not the opinion of the mainstream press but the fact that this opinion is the mainstream one. The press, which was a bastion of the left-leaning intellectual, has decisively moved the other way. In a larger sense, today there are few places in the mainstream media, barring a very few exceptions, where the concerns of the well-off do not find prominent play. Belief in reform has become an article of faith. As has the legitimacy of the wealthy.

Television is full of the weddings of the rich, talk shows gush over the rich, their progeny and their wives who are all without exception 'women of substance'. We see journalists schmoozing with the corporate elite at expensive restaurants and golf courses, when not being taken for a conducted tour through their magnificent homes. The excess display of wealth by the rich is appropriated as a 'sign of India's progress', the Mittal mansion and the Chatwal wedding being cases in point. From a time when we carried our poverty, and the presumed cleansing power of the trenchant frugality that accompanied it, on our sleeve, today we seem more inclined to sidle up to those with wealth and curl up in their corner.

Perhaps we were tired of being poor and spent by having to watch every rupee that we spent. As we catch a whiff of ease, as we wheel the wheels of our life lubricated by the little grease of affluence that has come our way, we look to those ahead of us with approval rather than resentment, aspiration rather than sullen despair.

Of course, the truth is that the 'we' in question, the middle class educated, were never poor. We donned the mantle of poverty quite convincingly, but while we lived in constrained circumstances, we were never denied the essentials of life. What has happened is that in effect the middle class has defected en masse to the other side. In our own self-image we are no longer poor and its romance, questionable in the first place, is now totally lost on us. We are now on Vijay Mallya's side as we gaze yearningly at his lifestyle, willingly overlooking the fact that economic reform has merely turned his silver spoon into gold. For there is a belief that the spoon is up for grabs and that anyone can get their mouths in its vicinity.

But all is not well. While much has been done in terms of creating a sense of optimism and access to social and economic mobility, so much more remains to be done. As the media becomes a mirror to its own consumer base and as the Left becomes even more irrelevant as it huddles into its own constituency, a vast number of Indians will lie in no one's constituency for they will be consumers for none. The part of India that has not been included in this new alignment of interest is making itself heard. The gunshots echo in the distance, but their noise is growing louder.

LATHIS IN UNIFORM?

The year 2008 was a bad one for the police in India. The Noida double murders underlined what we suspected all along – that our police force is transparently inept when it comes to solving crimes. The usual argument against the police force is that it is corrupt and is a willing tool in the hands of its political masters. This continues to be how the force is perceived but now we also believe that along with this cravenness lies an inability to even comprehend the ecosystem in which crime operates in India today.

What makes this a particularly serious matter is that as we saw in this particular case, police ineptness ended up being a licence – to theorize wildly, besmirch reputations, including that of a young girl, on national television, and go against every principle of justice, including that of the presumption of innocence. The problem, apart from a lack of ability, lies also, as many have pointed out, in a disconnect the force has with emerging urban mindsets and modes of living.

Cultural distance produces a distorted ability to draw fanciful conclusions from what others, more attuned to urban middle class mores, would see as routine everyday actions. The police uses the frames of perception it has to make sense of what they see. To imagine that parents would be comfortable with a young girl having friends of the other sex is something that is not easy to accept. To understand that it is possible for adult men and women to be friends without a sexual motive is again something that lies outside the collective experience of the police force. There has always been in India a salacious thrill about imagining the perverse sexual actions of the 'other' class. Who hasn't heard the 'wife swapping through car keychain' story; one has heard countless versions, all told with the same breathless certainty.

But there is an even more fundamental reason why the police finds itself unable to deal with demands of this kind. The police in India has never been about action, but always about a show of institutional strength. We want 'police protection', 'police presence' and 'police bandobast'; in other words we use the police in its static collective sense, to signify the power of the state. The most nuanced action that the police is capable of is to lathicharge a group of people, and its greatest technological innovation is the tear gas shell. The preferred mode of investigation is to round up suspects and beat the living daylights out of them till someone confesses. It depends on institutional force to break down the criminal. It has no conception of crime, only of criminals, and hence is helpless when no easy suspects are available. At its best, the police acts as an enforcer of rules. It can, if it so desires, be good at controlling riots, challaning offenders and deterring offenders by their 'presence'. It cannot, however, be trusted with anything that requires analysis.

The police in India is best summed up by the lathi, or 'danda' as we know it. The police force is nothing but a lathi in uniform for it expresses all that the force can represent, comprehend and achieve. Its power is as blunt as this sturdy, if basic, implement. Backed by the legitimacy that comes from being representatives of the state, police action in India is about overwhelming the other rather than separating the good from the bad. Discernment, the ability to filter out the truth from the lies, the piecing together of an event from the fragments visible later – these are all skills that the Indian police force has not been designed to deliver. If it fails today in its task, it is entirely understandable, for the police in India is not about crime detection at all.

Of course, the problem stems from the abysmal conditions in which the police force operates. Rock-bottom wages, terrible working hours and an oppressively political environment make this an utterly thankless job. The state is happy to use the police for its own political ends. Unfortunately, as India pulls away from its past, it will need a police force that reflects its new concerns and conflicts. We cannot have one that has only the crudest and the 'thickest' mode of intervention at its disposal – the danda.

THE YOUTH QUOTA

What's with our obsession with the young? Whether it is cricket or politics, youth has become the new rallying cry. We want a younger cricket team and will go to any lengths, including sending back in-form players used to overseas conditions and replacing them with rank newcomers. We lament the unrealized potential of our young politicians freely and frequently. Why, there was even talk of a cabinet reshuffle to accommodate young blood after Rahul Gandhi apparently said something to that effect.

As a reaction to the stranglehold that the old have had on Indian public life, with doddering octogenarians holding positions that require energy and stamina, it is understandable that youth should hold some allure. The promise of youth is that of vital new energy, a desire to leave the past behind and an ability untainted with self-doubt. The reason why our triumph in T-20 World Cup was so important to us was that it confirmed our belief in what was coming. It told us that we could create a bold new future by pointedly ignoring the past and choosing to back what lies ahead. Looking to the future is a rational act, for India is finally a country that believes not merely in its allegedly glorious past, but in its increasingly certain glorious future.

But not all youth offers us the same kind of hope. The much vaunted youth brigade in politics is a case in point. Most of the so-called young politicians are nothing but those in whose mouths silver spoons have been thrust by circumstances. We know them not because of their actions or their new ideas but because of their surnames and their fresh photogenic faces. They carry their age as a halo around themselves while the rest of their persona follows. In some ways, they offer the illusion of youth because far from representing newness they are merely a version of the past. They represent spurious change and spurious continuity; they are progeny of some better-known people. To see them as a sign of hope is to thrust our need for change on what, for the most part, may be undeserving shoulders. They exist because of television for they offer a simulated consumer generated image of what politicians should look like. In the alternative universe created by television, plausibility is good enough.

What we are really in love with is the idea of youth. The desire to look to the young is in part an indictment of the old as it is a sign of our impatience to get ahead quickly. In our hurry, we can confuse the sign for the real thing. For youth by itself has no value. Converted into a token 'quota' it becomes bereft of all meaning.

It is in what youth can represent that hope truly lies. When a Dhoni bats with no acknowledgement of the possibility of failure, when he displays an eerie calm in spite of having nothing in his past that can explain it, then we see what the young can do for us. But eventually it is his ability that will bring about change. Being twenty-six is something that will pass.

BETWEEN TOKENISM AND SYMBOLISM

Sending pink chaddis to the perpetrators of the Mangalore incident marks an interesting transition in the battle against the enforcers of morality. From the standard response that vacillated between fuming and foaming, we are now seeing a new kind of reaction, one that uses symbols instead of words. Given the fact that the Mangalore attacks were themselves of a symbolic nature, in that they used a single action to create a larger debate about an issue of concern to the attackers, it is interesting that we are beginning to see more creative responses that recognize the power of symbols. Now, a symbol is really a device that collapses a larger meaning into a representative action, so the question that naturally arises is: what exactly are pink chaddis a symbol of?

Of course, they do signify irreverence and help keep the discourse silly. This is an important thing to do, for the moral crusaders win when they force others to debate the questions that they are raising. The chaddis seek to make the other side look inconsequential rather than threatening, and thus to trivialize the righteousness with which they otherwise brim over. But for symbols to work, their meaning must be equally accessible to both sides. In this case, I am not sure if that is the case. Besides, the symbol of pink carries with it troubling undertones of gender, and begins to tread on the territory of another common symbol in Hindi cinema, the bangle, used to taunt a man about the lack of manhood. Choodiyan pehan lo etc.

The distance between powerful symbolism and tired tokenism is a very small one. Lighting candles in protest might be a powerful sign of a bigger intent in some cultures, but in India it is a culturally bankrupt symbol. Signing petitions and forwarding them to a minister may work in some countries, but do we really believe that an action like that carries any meaning in India? At a seminar I attended recently, a senior person from a media house that had carried out a similar campaign took pains to explain to us how they ensured that the petition was designed to be a size so that 'it would not fit into a wastepaper basket'. So much for our faith in ministerial mediation.

And yet, there is no denying that imaginative and resonant symbols are a powerful weapon in unequal battles. For they make a small action go a long way. Currently, the best exponents of symbolic action are the terrorists, who use violence in small concentrated doses to produce a disproportionate effect. Some political parties understand symbols better than others. The Babri Masjid is a case in point, where a disused mosque became a sign of something much larger. The reason why this symbol worked and another one, like the Ram Setu, didn't, lies perhaps in the fact that the former collapsed within it a larger historical angst about perceived subjugation while the latter was, at best, indicative of governmental indifference about the veracity of our mythological epics. The 'Mandir wahin banayenge' chant points to the importance of the act of destruction of the existing masjid, for only then is historical retribution symbolically achieved.

Using symbols powerfully is an art that comes naturally to a few. Gandhi mastered it, using it in several imaginative ways to point to a larger, deeper truth. Be it the use of an obscure salt tax in a protest or in the insistence on cleaning toilets, the symbol simultaneously compressed a truth and amplified its significance. A single photograph showing a bejewelled King George V and a half-naked fakir spoke about the injustice done to colonies more graphically than anything else.

Of course, precisely because symbols can be so powerful, they tend to be overused and cynically exploited, and thus rendered ineffective. Continuous symbolic action unaccompanied by any real one makes the symbol transparently empty. Today, the Gandhian symbol of the charkha, the spinning wheel or khadi has been exhausted of any meaning by its repeated and empty use by the political class. Equally, symbolic actions detached from a larger purpose are easily revealed to be petty acts of tokenism. Appointing Pratibha Patil as president without any accompanying desire to rethink gender equations in India takes the cause of gender back rather than forward. Attacking Sania Mirza for disrespecting the national flag because her foot appears to be resting in its general direction is to use a symbol cynically.

We live in a world where it is easy to confuse the token act with the symbol and the symbol with the action. In a world where media amplifies the smallest action by filling its frame with it, it is easy to mistake the symbol for the real thing. Deeper understanding of symbols, their use and their exchange, as well as clarity about their limits, is desirable. In the meantime, pink chaddis is a start.

THE MIND OF THE TERRORIST

We are angry. The terrorist strikes in Mumbai have stirred us into an outpouring of frustrated anger. We feel we are being too weak, too willing to be taken advantage of. We hate the terrorists but hate ourselves even more for allowing this to be done to us. Talks of retaliation, pro-active forays into Pakistan and hot pursuits fill our newspapers, magazines and TV channels. The fact that the latest victims were 'people like us' living in Mumbai makes things worse.

The randomness of terrorism is what makes it so potent. Any random strike may kill only a few but it kills something inside every one of us. The kernel of fear is planted among millions even if the actual victims are a fraction of that number. Terrorists exert power over our belief in our own lives; we know life and death is not in our hands, but in this case it comes into the hands of someone who can randomly exercise that power over us and blow our well-ordered life into smithereens.

Fear makes us angry; we feel the need to hit back. Only there is nowhere to really hit back. Terrorism as an idea rests not on the terrorist action but on our response to it. The action is symbolic; our reaction is what makes terror real. We are compelled to hit back; and we do so at those who are visible to us and who we can somehow link to the terrorists. Terrorists plant fear and direct the resultant anger towards a group which, in time, becomes the fountainhead of terrorism. By creating a false enemy and by forcing us to attack it, in time we manufacture a very real one.

In any case, there can be no counter to terrorism. Of course, we can tighten security, chase down and apprehend those responsible and see that they are brought to justice, but none of this can crush terrorism. Our responses all operate within the bounds of civilization, where the highest value is the respect for other people's lives. This respect comes from our own obsessive concern with our own; to be civilized is to respect other people's right to live as much as we do our own. The terrorist frees himself from civilization by rejecting this concern for his own life. The suicide bomber confounds us because he renounces his attachment to his own life; and there is simply no answer that we can possibly have to that renunciation within our notions of civilization. In Jean Baudrillard's words, terrorism is a gift that cannot be returned. Every 'gift' carries within it a possibility of reciprocation; in this case there is simply no way to reciprocate. Killing the terrorists in question is empty retaliation; for what they planted was not a bomb but an idea; an idea that is not going to die in a hurry.

Terrorism forces us to turn our attention away from the real problem and focus instead on the 'terrorist' problem. In doing so, we have no choice but to adopt the ways of the terrorists, for conventional methods all operate within the limits of civilization. The US sets up a gulag, we create draconian anti-terrorist laws, some of us justify what happened in Gujarat.

There is an elegance then to the concept of terrorism, however horrific its practice might be. Terrorism is self-generative; it ensures a response from us which, in turn, ensures that more terrorists are born. The illusion of retaliation is very difficult to resist. Our notions of 'strength' and 'toughness' push us into violence; we convert a symbolic war into a real one. We can end up sending our soldiers to their death as a result of this need to do something, in the belief that this is somehow a deterrent for terrorists. Iraq tells us that far from being a deterrent, war against a people mass-manufactures terrorism.

So we are left with a problem that is truly frustrating. There are enough ways of believing that we are doing something to counter it, but none that can make us believe that we are solving it. We are locked into a belief system from where there are no roads to peace; and that is the ultimate victory of the terrorists.

READING THE POLITICAL
POSTER

A common sight on Indian roads is that of a bunch of oily looking netas grinning ingratiatingly while being jammed together on a political hoarding. Any self-respecting hoarding has at least a dozen-odd aspirants 'felicitating' some other leader, who is invariably shown pointing upwards in what is no doubt a goosepimple-raising call to take to space travel. Every party has its own version, with the possible exception of the Left, and there is little to choose between any of them.

The size of the grinning faces tells us about the size of their stature but the common message is clear. Here are a bunch of people imposing themselves on the electorate with a clear warning of their intention to make the size of their faces larger in times to come. The excuse for appearing on hoardings can be anything from Sonia Gandhi's visit to the announcement of the emergence of yet another neta-son on the political firmament or even a great desire to wish people on the pious occasion of Gudi Parva.

What is interesting about this phenomenon is the nakedness with which it reveals the true nature of politics in India today. Unlike the political poster of earlier days, where the message was the key (be it on the lines of 'The Revolution is Coming!' Or 'Garva Se Kaho Hum Hindu Hain'), here no mention appears of a message of any kind. The party is nothing but the sum total of the ambition of its greasy leaders-to-be. And the ambition is not framed in terms of what the politician can do for the people but what the party can do for the politician in order for him to do something for himself. The political poster is an internal communication that signals to the party the clout that each person enjoys.

In some ways, the politicians are presenting themselves like products do. Any concern for the consumer is a device to get them to buy the product. When a brand congratulates people on a festival or 'associates' with any event, it is purely to insinuate itself in the consumer's life. The politician is today doing exactly that, except his prime target is his own party leadership. The absence of intra-party democracy means that the voters have no role to play in his pursuit of power, at least to begin with.

Also, unlike the past, where it was important to pay homage to the pantheon of leaders in the party, now the key is to pay homage to oneself. If, in earlier times, it was mandatory to operate under the benign blessings of the holy trinities of Gandhi-Nehru-Patel or Marx-Lenin-Stalin, today the leaders are respected so that they can be used. The photograph of an Advani or a Sonia Gandhi is now used as an excuse to put up one's own mug shot, and the relative size of the pictures leaves one in no doubt as to who is the real hero of the day.

The location of these hoardings is revealing too; usually roads near airports are most favoured so that all incoming and outgoing deities are reminded of the 'good work' being done by the advertisers. Of course, no specific claims are made; there is no room in the hoarding for that. Mere presence is deemed to be sufficient; one can no doubt imagine Sonia Gandhi taking furious notes of the names while zipping past these monuments.

The truth is that politics is now an extremely lucrative profession but unlike others, there are no clear road maps to getting ahead. As it becomes liberated from the task of doing things for others and becomes one where one gets to focus on oneself, it begins to operate pretty much like other businesses.

You join a company to get ahead or else you seek better prospects elsewhere. You try to get noticed by senior management using every trick available and unlike the corporate world, where such opportunities are institutionalized, in politics these have to be created.

So, here's to the grinning faces on the political poster. May you be noticed, may the party give you the ticket you covet, and if you really make it big, may your progeny grace the same poster ten years from now.

THE CITY NAME AS CULTURAL
PROPERTY

So another one bites the dust. Only New Delhi now stands alone, untouched by the renaming frenzy that has been doing the rounds. It is customary for a certain section of society to rave and rant every time this happens and it is easy to see why. It seems transparently clear that the motivations of the politicians behind these rechristening attempts are merely to exploit sentiments and garner votes. What a great way of mobilizing popular support without actually doing any work!

That being said, the question still remains – why is this act a popular vote-catching device at all? What needs does the mere act of renaming a city fulfil? The question boils down to one of ownership. To whom does a city belong? As a magnet of opportunity, it attracts people from far and wide; in Bangalore's case the catchment area is global today. As a city gets overrun with new inhabitants, it slowly becomes unrecognizable to the older sections. It is easy to empathize with U.R. Ananthmurthy's characterization of the existence of two cities, Bangalore and Bengaluru, belonging to two entirely different groups of people. The residents of this metaphorical Bengaluru find it increasingly difficult to locate themselves in the mental model of their city. In a curious inversion, the insiders become the outsiders, they become the 'problem' that the new infrastructure must solve. The original city becomes the embarrassing eyesore, the bottleneck in the grand plan of making it 'world class'. The city becomes a virtual and potential existence, and is experienced only in terms of what it could be but is not. The city is defined by all that it lacks, by those who consider it their natural prerogative to own not just the city but the very idea of a city. By defining the city as a cosmopolitan hub, we privilege the newest arrival, rather than the oldest member. The natural spokesperson for the city becomes the one who has the least allegiance to it; all arguments are made by this group or by others on its behalf.

The real fault lines lie not so much between the 'outsiders' and the 'insiders', for one could argue that most city dwellers are in some senses 'outsiders' of different vintages, but between the visible and vocal minority and the silent invisible majority. Cities condemn the latter to a kind of mental exile that occurs in public glare. We experience them as a 'crowd' but otherwise simply do not see them. So Bangalore is for us the city of laidback people who drink copiously at pubs when not working at some cutting-edge IT major. Everyone and anything that does not further this 'brand' of Bangalore is automatically considered to be a roadblock to progress.

By far the most interesting argument advanced against Bangalore's name change is that it will come in the way of our international standing. Here we are slowly making progress in impressing the world and back we go into the past with a funny sounding name. Bengaluru defies the phonetic tyranny of the hardwalled Anglicized sound; it infuses the city with a singsong sense of the primitive. What will the West think? How will they pronounce this oh-so-Indian name? Will people shift their R&D headquarters to Tbilisi or to Reykjavik in tongue-tripped disgust? The desire to perform for the West, to constantly crave their approval, is perhaps the worst reason to oppose the name change. We don't change our names so that Americans can pronounce it, at least not yet. Beijing is doing fine as are Kolkata, Chennai and Mumbai.

The other argument, that there are far more important things for us to do than get embroiled in trivial meaningless pursuits, is a fair one. The question, of course, is: trivial for whom? Demands like these abound, but gain momentum usually when there are grounds for a large section to feel powerless and insignificant. The riots that broke out after Dr Rajkumar's passing make it clear that disquiet simmers malevolently under Bangalore's placid surface. If, along with catering to the needs of 'world class' Bangalore, we were equally seized of the urgent need to make 'old' Bangalore more livable, then it is likely that the demand for a name that marked 'local' ownership would never become widespread.

So does this argument mean that we should change the names of all our cities in order to appease its 'original' residents? No, what it does mean is that we show greater sensitivity to the motivations that drive this demand, when such motivations in fact exist. The solution of changing names may appear to be populist and even silly, but there are times, like in the case of Bangalore, when the problem may well be a significant one and recognizing that may be an act of wisdom. Perhaps a good answer in cases like these is a referendum – if it is indeed the will of the people then let not the liberal bigotry of the visible few come in the way.

THE DEATH OF VULGARITY

Is anything vulgar anymore? This word, once used to describe a whole host of actions, from ostentatious displays to salacious representations, is seldom used nowadays, except by those who use it as a moral stick to beat others into submission. The idea of vulgarity has been appropriated as an epithet to be used by groups with extreme views on how others should behave.

I grew up in a time that was mortally afraid of anything that remotely reeked of vulgarity. The word itself was an ugly reminder of the import it carried, with the indecorous bulge of consonants that stumbled out of its trousers. To pronounce something vulgar was to banish it from the ranks of the civilized, by deeming things to be inappropriate rather than illicit. The idea enabled a society like ours to mark its boundaries as well as to defend its implicit belief system.

We have come a long way since then, baby. Watching the IPL auctions and the media interviews thereafter, I was struck by the absence of that word from our active vocabulary today. Here we had a spectacle where the richest and the most glamorous body shopped the purest and the most talented by bidding on them. The sums of money were staggering, the owners' pride at having filled their stables with thoroughbreds, obvious, and the media attention that preyed on this event, fawning. Afterwards there was a television interview, with the 'owners' all resplendent in designer glasses, talking about their acquisitions. In the entire interaction, there wasn't a trace of self-consciousness about what was happening. After all, they were rich and beautiful and they had already bought Ferraris so why not sports stars now? Teams are bought and sold everywhere but what we are revelling in now is the spectacle of acquisitions. The market in India is not content to be an invisible mechanism but wants to strut around dressed in gaudy finery. Wealth becomes real only when displayed. Money seems to create a vicarious thrall as we tingle in electric empathy when we hear tales of the Ambani or Mallya billions.

In a larger sense, the tendency to fragment the world into hierarchical sectors, each with different social valencies, has given way to a more uniform social field governed by the common currency of money. The legitimacy of money, and its ability to speak in a uniform voice, has blunted the sharp differences that existed earlier. The security once derived from one's social class, which made money secondary, is no longer as much in evidence. The club, with its focus on exclusivity based on where you came from, has given way to the five star hotel with its focus on how much you can pay.

At one level, we are seeing a welcome democratization taking place. Old hierarchies are collapsing and mobility is a more transparent affair and is accessible to many more. Barriers of birth are being replaced by those of money and achievement. On the other hand, we seem to have actively abandoned the desire to qualitatively discriminate between things and are content to accept what is thrown our way uncritically.

Of course, in a world full of diverse people, there can be no uniform standard of good taste. One person's aspiration can so easily be another person's vulgarity. The question is whether the idea of using any standard is being applied at all. By not actively discriminating between things, by being open to everything that the world throws at us in a passive way, do we help create a world where we will be ruled by people with the loudest voices, fattest wallets and biggest sticks?

THE PUB AS SIGN OF FREEDOM

If what happened in Mangalore, where an extreme group attacked young women in a pub, was disturbing, what happened in its wake was even more so. The first enquiry launched by the National Commission of Women, after making many agitated noises, shifted the blame on to the pub and set about checking its licence, before a new enquiry was launched. Politicians, from both sides of the aisle, made deep rumbling sounds about halting the rise of the 'pub culture'. Media got into overdrive, hyperventilating about freedom and celebrating the woman's right to drink. The pub became the new battleground for freedom, democracy and Indian values. In a country where there is still one state where no man or woman is allowed to drink at home, far less at a pub, it was an interesting paradox.

It is clear that what happened in Mangalore was terrible and the perpetrators of the crime need be punished. Our problem increasingly is not that we are becoming more intolerant as a society (a favourite question for TV panel discussions) but that we are becoming more tolerant of symbolic intolerance. We tolerate publicity-seeking non-entities too much, giving them far too much leeway in mounting these symbolic assaults on basic freedoms. We are afraid of giving them salutary punishment and end up creating monsters, who gradually turn real.

But it is important to put the Mangalore incident in perspective. Here was a fringe group that carried out a one-off symbolic attack, purely to garner attention. It was not indicative of a mass movement, nor was it accompanied by a larger attempt to curtail individual freedom. The fact that media cameras were on hand to record what happened, as indeed they always are in events of this kind, gave the intent away.

And then, there is the larger question. It is one thing to uphold the principle that every individual has the right to exercise his or her freedom to do whatever is legal, including having a drink at a pub without being questioned, molested or beaten up. Drinking as a sign of freedom is one thing, but to literally promote the cause of drinking is quite another. No one can be prevented from drinking, but that doesn't quite translate into everyone being encouraged to do so. The principle needs vigorous upholding, the practice not necessarily so. Just as banning depiction of smoking on screen can be opposed as a violation of a basic freedom, but that cannot mean that we should promote the act of smoking – we cannot confuse the principle with the practice.

From the looks of it, we live in a time when it is important to celebrate things like bar girls, drinking, sexual openness as marks of freedom. The same fervour does not extend to issues like the right to dissent or the right to free information (the RTI is the result of action by committed groups and not any mainstream media action). The idea of freedom seems to have gone through an interesting transformation. In popular imagination, it no longer exists as an idea in its capitalized, lofty avatar and is instead pursued as a set of pleasurable activities in our everyday lives. Freedom has implicitly become synonymous with the freedom to have fun without hindrances or challenges.

This is understandable, for we have grown up in an environment where individualistic pleasure of any kind was circumscribed. We experience freedom most not when we cast a vote, but have a drink. But for the same reason, we should be able to understand why a large part of India will have reservations about the 'pub culture'. Forget the hooligans who manipulated the media and focus on the other voices that are coming out asking questions. To dismiss these by labelling them as right-wing reactionaries who are coming in the way of India's progress could well be an act of self-deception.

Just as there are people who see drinking as a sign of freedom, there are others who see it as a sign of a life immersed in shallow pleasure seeking. The 'pub culture' does not refer to the act of drinking in isolation, but to what is seen as the larger world of easy gratification and sensory self-indulgence that builds up around this institution. One may not agree with this characterization, but surely this view should avail of the same freedom that the other one enjoys. And who can challenge the fact that what we called the middle class Indian way of life till a few years ago, looked upon drinking as an undesirable social evil. It is not unnatural for a large part of India to be uncomfortable with a change that they are neither prepared nor comfortable with. That doesn't give them a right to beat up people, but surely they have a right to hold that view and pursue all legitimate means of promoting their beliefs.

The fear of change and the indiscriminate love for it are not too far apart in the distortions they can bring. It is all right to ask if we want to be a country where we define our identities through acts of consumption and self-gratification. Freedom comes from being independent-minded, and that means liberation from biases of all kinds and the ability to genuinely appreciate all sides of an argument.

$

CHAPTER 14

DREAMS OF GRANDEUR

For a section of India, our biggest and most critical audience is now the developed world. Tired of being the world's poster child for poverty, middle class India of today wants payback, and wants it quickly. We want recognition, and we are not that fussy about where it comes from or how genuine it is. We are not that particular even about whether it truly belongs to India. We will celebrate Bobby Jindal and appropriate Slumdog Millionaire; after all their India connections are plausible, if not real, or even, as in the case of Jindal, desired.

$

RACISM AND BRAND INDIA

Our fascination with 'Brand' India continues. Now it's the time to fret about being done in by racism. Is the Orient Express racist because it thinks being acquired by an Indian company will not sit well with its luxury image? Is the Indian tag tacky in a category like this? What is this if not a residue of a racist labelling of Third World countries as interlopers in a world of genteel refinement. The world is happy to let us manufacture shoe uppers and man call centres but start getting into areas that are earmarked for 'them' and the civilized veneer slips away. What do the natives know about luxury? We could point to Rajasthan, the fact that the Oberois have two of the world's best hotels in the top five, we could point to what is most pertinent in this, the track record of Taj across the world for an answer. We could point to the sterling record of the Tatas as one of the most transparent and progressive companies in the world.

Granted that there are stereotypes about India and granted that the West can be extremely racist when it comes to business. But is this really about racism? Are we guilty of celebrating when the West gives us certificates and whining when they say something hurtful? We are happy to receive compliments we do not fully deserve; for instance, there is a perception in some parts of the world that everyone in India is a code writing software genius and we are absolutely fine with that. So what's wrong if occasionally we experience the flip side of being an emergent global player?

Because the truth is that given the nature of market forces, what Orient Express believes is not unreasonable, if not perfectly true. It is not arguing that the Tatas are, in fact, incapable of running the business but that in the eyes of the world the India label is not associated with the qualities expected from a top-end luxury brand. A brand is essentially what people give credit to a product or service for; and in the general perception of the world, top-end luxury is not an immediate association with India. That doesn't mean that there are no instances of Indian brands doing well in this space but merely that the dominant association with India is not yet of that nature. It is reasonable for the Tatas to get upset about this, but is it really an unreasonable perception about Brand India?

Would we in India be thrilled if the Oberois were taken over by a Nigerian company? In having doubts about the ability of that company to do justice to the standards set by the Oberois, would we be displaying racist tendencies? We would merely be reflecting the popular sentiment that Nigeria, while being a fine country in many respects, was not known worldwide for knowing its wines. The truth is that development is asymmetrical; we are making progress in some areas but clearly have a long way to go in some others.

Also, the market is not an instrument that relies on perfect knowledge. It bases its reactions on sentiment and shallow perception. A brand is what others believe of it. We go hoarse talking about Brand India without acknowledging what it means to be a brand.

In fact, the really interesting question is who the racist is here. Our reaction to this development speaks more about our need to win approval from the West than about the Western response to India. We obsess so much about what the West thinks of us that we celebrate every trivial compliment, appropriate anyone vaguely Indian (Bobby Jindal) and hanker after international recognition (The Great Oscar Question). We are hurt because the West is being mean to us. Otherwise, what does it matter what one isolated voice in the West thinks of us?

The 'India as superpower' chant is in danger of becoming a shrill parody of itself. In our impatience to 'dominate' the world, we are in serious danger of skewing our priorities. It is we who are speaking in the language of conquest; we want to shake off our colonial past by becoming our erstwhile rulers. Which is why we uncritically celebrate the half-truths told in our praise and hysterically bemoan the half-lies told against us. In our desire to be admired, we forget that we need to focus on doing things that are admirable first. Eventually, India will overcome its Third World tag. But there is some way to go yet. And if we continue to dream in the language of conquest and domination, then what right do we have to call someone else names?

$
AN ABSTRACT SALUTE TO THE INDIAN SOLDIER

It was a touching moment. In an award ceremony held by NDTV in 2008, the Indian of the Year turned out to be the ordinary soldier. Beating a host of politicians and film and sports stars, the unsung jawan got his place in the sun. Everyone in the audience felt the tug of emotion as some jawans and a widow of one the brave accepted the award from the prime minister.

In some ways, it reversed the general tenor of the night as well as of award shows in general, where the overwhelming interest lies in celebrating the celebrated. An award show is measured not by who gets the award but who attends the function. The bigger the stars who receive the awards (hopefully personally), the more prestigious the awards. So in the midst of all this glitter, it was refreshing that thought was spared for someone at the margins of our consciousness, toiling tirelessly to keep us secure. The vote verged on the unanimous; people of this country tired of posturing pretenders and reel life heroes cast their vote for the genuine article.

But there is something going on here that needs deeper probing. For starters, why was the soldier worthy of recognition in 2008? We had no major incursions; Pakistan was pre-occupied with its own problems for the most part and while keeping the country safe is a continuous exercise, 2007 did not make more demands on the jawan than was the case in the past. The award was more a general recognition than one located in that time period. Arguably, the jawan could win this award every year if nominated.

Why would a country going through the throes of development feel the need to acknowledge its soldiers as most worthy of acclaim? Why not the businessman or the software professional or any other foot soldier of the economic revolution? What does it say about a country when it chooses its martial face as its most representative dimension? That the soldier deserves this consideration is by itself incontrovertible but why now and why with such intensity of feeling?

At a certain level, one could argue that this is a guilty search for some purity in a world turning rotten. The soldier can have no room for personal desire, has no control over his own actions and risks his life for the rest of us unquestioningly. What is most valuable is within least control; his life is deployed at our behest. There is undeniable truth in this but again this is not the whole truth.

Our interest in the soldier is a cozy abstraction. We have no real interest in his hardships; news reports about corruption in the armed forces are met with a yawn. Few want to join the army and a large number in it want to leave for a more comfortable life. We do not agitate for better facilities for the jawans; our interest in not in the reality of the soldier but in the idea he represents. We have mythologized something very real into something safely abstract. Eulogy is a convoluted form of erasure; we can get on with our lives having given tearful token acknowledgement to someone whom we have turned into an abstraction.

We use the idea of the Indian soldier to bolster our desire to make India a powerful force. Everything is war for us right now; our standing with other countries, the Oscars, cricket, to name but a few fronts. In cricket we routinely compare our cricketers unfavourably with 'our jawans toiling tirelessly on the border'. We celebrate our jawans because they represent the combined forces of strength, discipline and ordinariness. We feel noble acknowledging them and they in turn make us feel strong. They are the ultimate possessions of an assertive consumerist society for they can ask for nothing in return. They, of course, get nothing out of this except a trophy, which will most probably rest on a general's mantelpiece.

Many years ago, we adopted the slogan of Jai Jawan Jai Kisan. It is instructive that while we retain our interest in the former, the condition of the latter is no concern to us. Would the same award have gone to the Unsung Indian or the Ordinary Farmer? Unlike the soldier who gives us so much psychologically, the other symbols of tireless ordinariness provide no value to us and hence do not merit much consideration.

Of course, there is a silver lining to all this. Given the mood of the times, we should be thankful that the award went to the real soldiers and not the actors who played them on screen or a scriptwriter who coined a clever slogan!

$

OF WEALTH AND WANT

Four out of ten ain't bad. Who would have thought it? A few years ago, the idea that four of the ten richest people in the world would be Indian would have been a thought in the realms of fantasy. Clearly, we are doing something right. Some invisible barrier has been lifted, some boundary erased, some fence dismantled for this transformation to occur. Of course, a lot of credit does go to economic reform but the real change is in the mind. For today we are looking outwards with confidence rather than curling up inwards in self-deprecatory fear. The wealth of these few individuals is a larger sign; of a country where enterprise is no longer focused on coping with constraints but imagining new possibilities.

And yet, how can this fact be good news alone? Surely, the fact that India corners a lion's share of the really wealthy is a pointer to something a little wrong. Of course, we are growing rapidly and are an emerging force, but that is all about tomorrow. Even the oft-quoted BRIC report puts us among the top three economies of the world only by 2050! For a country that is 126th on the Human Development Index, to have such concentration of wealth in such few hands, must surely cause some disquiet.

And yet, the overall feeling generated by this news is celebratory in nature. There is a feeling of collective pride in this 'achievement' by India. In fact, when it was rumoured that Mukesh Ambani (or was it Anil?) might have become the world's richest man, there was a palpable sense of pride among a lot of middle class Indians. It is interesting that we have begun to embrace the riches of a few as our own while shunning the penury of many as belonging to 'them'. The poor today are an electoral fabrication, vestiges of an India we are eager to leave behind.

The 60,000-crore loan waiver by the government in 2008 is very often seen through the lens of an electoral gimmick, a regrettable leakage from the economic system in order to accommodate the desire to pander to those who vote. The language used to describe these two worlds is telling – sops for the affluent are 'concessions', 'relief', and 'duty drawbacks' while being couched in a larger vocabulary of 'reform'. To reduce taxes for the consuming class is not an act of pandering to those with means but a farsighted move to 'unshackle the energies' of consumption. Sops for the poor are met with much tongue clucking – these are subsidies that are unsustainable, populist measures aimed at garnering votes. It is as if the economy is imagined as that productive part of the financial system that caters to those who consume. Looking after the others is an act of leakage.

Of course, even this critique is couched in the language of the market. Waiving loans is tantamount to punishing those who played by the rules of the market. The underlying and unstated assumption is, of course, that the market behaves democratically, and that all those touched by it have the same opportunities, something patently untrue.

At a function organized by a leading financial daily in 2008, the finance minister laid out his vision for the economy going forward. It was telling that when the audience, comprising of business leaders was asked to pose questions, every single question was about trying to get some advantage for themselves. The business sector is terminally self-serving and that perhaps is its dharma; the trouble occurs when we arrogate to it the mantle of representing the entire country's financial system.

The real question then is not whether we should curb the riches of a few. It is possible to take the view that in an economy where new sectors are opening up, those who build these new categories will gain abnormally. One can see the wealth of these entrepreneurs is a kind of 'pioneer's bounty', which they perhaps deserve. With time, it is likely that we see a more even spread of this super-wealth as we have many more billionaires without necessarily having so many Indians in the top ten list. The real question is also not whether the loan waiver is a good or bad idea.

The question boils down to our implicit view of who makes up the abstract idea that goes by the label 'Indian economy' in our minds. This is by no means an objective idea, for in the way we speak of it we reveal our own biases about what constitutes it. When we talk about the 'economy' we are, for the most part, speaking of one component of it that we are concerned with. A more inclusive notion of the economy would allow us to balance our need for wealth with our responsibility towards want.

$

GLOBAL DREAMING

Some time back, I was at a meeting attended by alumni of all IIMs on how to build the IIMs as a global brand. As a subject it is broadly indicative of the mood of the country, for the very next day I was at another seminar where 'Marketing India to the World' was the topic being debated. Usually these discussions follow a typical India-is-ready-to-take-on-the-world-in-everything-except-cricket pattern and can be safely avoided or slept through.

The interesting thing about the IIM discussion was that the enthusiasm of the alumni for the subject was not shared by the directors and senior professors of the IIMs at all. Their consensus was that the IIMs, however well regarded in India, had a very long way to go before being considered world class. They pointed out the abysmal salaries that the faculty drew in India, spoke frankly about the absence of any research emanating out of these elite institutions and the inability to attract any meaningful number of foreign students, given the absence of infrastructure. Add to this the distortions caused by constant governmental interference, and the picture looked anything but promising.

There are two aspects of this debate that have larger ramifications. The first is that we discussed this subject at all. Given the pitiful number of seats that elite educational institutions in India account for and the pressure on these from reservations for the socially backward, one could argue that globalizing the IIMs should be the last thing on our minds. And as the professors pointed out , if not in so many words, if one looked at the ground realities, this question walked the thin line between fantasy and insanity. The need for a globally respected IIM brand came from its alumni, to bolster their credentials retrospectively, and not from the institutions themselves.

This is symptomatic of the current trend towards a sense of drunken euphoria that borders on megalomania. As a nation, we seem to have interpreted an ability to walk as a sign of an impending Olympic sprint medal. Our ambition has catapulted from being a participant in the world order to leading it with fanfare blaring. We want Bollywood to cross over, we want Mumbai to metamorphose into Shanghai, we want to become a superpower and 'regain our rightful place' in the world, we want everything that we do to be acknowledged by an adoring world, by which, of course, we mean the West. We adore our cricket team when they win a few tournaments and abhor it when they lose and make our desires look silly. And we can mount our fantasies on flimsy foundations – the fact that IIM students get salaries that we cannot comprehend is evidence enough of their global credentials.

The 'we' in question is, of course, a small minority that has appropriated for itself the mantle of India. Which brings me to the second larger dimension of the IIM debate. The divergence in the view of those running these institutions with the exuberance of its alumni is a graphic reminder of the divide we see in India today between the residents of a New India and others. This becomes almost poignant in the case of the IIMs because the divide is between the teachers and the taught, between those who equip students with the means to succeed and those who apply this knowledge. The IIM graduates today have a good chance of starting at salaries higher than what their teachers can hope to make. Indeed, often they can in a couple of years offer their teachers jobs at salaries that would make their heads spin.

Like luxury liners, these students cast off from their dilapidated docks into the New World.

The irony is that the air of excellence that surrounds our elite institutions has less to do with their intrinsic quality and much more to do with their scarcity. In a country of India's size, the access to quality education is so limited that anyone who 'gets through' is assured of a passport to New India. This is not a sign of our coming of age globally but of the distance we have to travel in making opportunities accessible to all.

And if teachers of India's most elite institutions can be thought of as citizens of the lesser India, then the divide between the two Indias is without doubt a deep and very real one. The desire to become instantly respected globally will only intensify this division; we will invest too much effort in the concerns of an affluent and vocal minority.

Our priority is to do well by our citizens and fulfil their aspirations. This does not rule out global ambitions, but calls for a hard-headed realistic look at where these ambitions are legitimate. With our limited resources, we cannot fritter away our energy on endeavours that are designed to inflate the ego of a few. The focus of our efforts cannot be outer-directed; we cannot care so much about what the world thinks of us. What matters is the nature of the new reality we are able to create for ourselves. For all of us, not merely a few.

$

SHAME WITHOUT GUILT

Nobody complained when Vikas Swaroop wrote it, nobody batted an eyelid when the film was shot and released internationally. After all, so many films, both features and documentaries, have been made around the subject of poverty in India. The protests started only when *Slumdog Millionaire* started winning international awards. The unkind way of looking at this is to argue that there is no value in complaining about the obscure – only protests about the famous can become famous. But then, it is equally true that only popular films actually do impact the way people see things and hence *Slumdog Millionaire* was worth complaining about only after it was nominated for an Oscar.

Does the West have a vested interest in pinning India to its poverty by refusing to acknowledge the progress it has undoubtedly made in the last few years? Is India interesting only because it is poor? Is the gratuitous use of poverty nothing but an exploitative use of someone else's misery for one's diversion?

Of course, India is stereotyped by the West. Take away spirituality and poverty, and India, to the outside eye, is just a large country with an unnervingly diverse topography and poor sanitation. India's progress is in some ways an act of poor sportsmanship; it was always believed that India would be timeless and enigmatic in a deep, spiritual kind of way. The new India story is thus disruptive and disturbing for it changes the accepted order of the world.

But if cinematic representations about India are stereotyped so are those for all countries. Popular cinema uses the currency of stereotypes because it is accessible to all, most particularly to the American audience, whose capacity for cultural nuance is limited. So you cannot show Brazil without the carnival (or its slums), Russia without the KGB and/or the mafia and England without Hugh Grant. Equally, when an Indian film shows New York, it does not focus on the homeless there, for our dominant perception about the city does not include poverty, however real it might be.

The question to ask is if our dominant perception about this New India is, in fact, the reality. Does the Westerner have to dig out poverty and then amplify it for audiences abroad? In the India of today, any mention of poverty is seen as being faintly treacherous; there exists a tacit conspiracy of silence about the state of the urban majority. By shrivelling the misery of millions into a single word, we banish the slum by giving it a name. We don't make movies about it anymore unless as a prop in a crime thriller. We don't cover it on TV; airport delays attract breathless outrage while nobody would look twice at a story about water scarcity in the slums. More importantly, it is as if we have stopped noticing the vast numbers of the urban poor who surround us. We genuinely believe that Mumbai can be summed up by the Taj. So when someone from outside smells Mumbai in all its fetid rottenness, we are appalled. So what if the story told is one of a New Indian, corkscrewing his way out of his circumstances, as it was in the case of this film.

It was perhaps more understandable why we were touchy about the representation of Indian poverty twenty years ago. At that time, we feared that to be our unchanging reality and it made us deeply ashamed. Today, when we believe that India is on its way up, why do we still respond negatively?

Perhaps it is time to take all the blathering we do about Brand India more seriously. India is unique because it can potentially show the world a new way. In the slums of Dharavi, we find ambition that doesn't lose its way and joy that comes from knowing what is truly precious about life. We can see more clearly why material growth is not the same as progress and how meaning in life is independent of one's means. India will not become valuable to the world by becoming a pale shadow of someone else's ideas but by asserting the power of its own distinctive take on the world.

The slum is not the 'other' India and Dharavi is not an aberration. It is both a condemnation and a celebration of who we are. We need to own it, change it, admire it and hate it. We don't need to ignore it. And if some Western director makes a film about it, we don't need to fear it.

$

A MILLION MATCHSTICKS NOW

How does a country measure itself? What real life indices does it take pride in? How do we experience the progress India is making? Going by current practice, it would seem that we celebrate what we see as the best that India has to offer. As has been pointed out earlier, we pine for Oscar recognition for our films, we cheer when an Indian company takes over a multinational, we root for Indian professionals to take over the reins of large multinational companies, we celebrate our IITs and IIMs which turn out world-class professionals, and we exult when we see more and more Indians appearing on the list of the world's richest people. In short, as is natural perhaps anywhere in the world, we look towards the top when we think of good news about India.

But are these really the best indices of progress we are making as a country? After all, Indians doing well abroad has nothing really to do with India, except in a symbolic and emotional way. And for all their alleged world-class stature, both the IITs and IIMs do not feature in the top ten list of educational institutions and are hardly the fount of cutting-edge research and thinking. We have never won an Oscar for a film made in India by an Indian, and it is anybody's guess as to whether the companies taken over by Indian corporations will turn out to be stepping stones to global dominance or millstones around Indian necks. And even if one were to accept that there are reasons to cheer the progress made at the top, our obsession with the top needs further examination.

Why do we follow with such breathless delight the starting salaries that IIM graduates get every year? We churn out only about 1000 people from the IIMs and only a fraction of this number gets starts of Rs 1 crore plus. IIM students are routinely asked for opinions on subjects of grave national importance, ignoring the fact that the ability to quickly solve multiple choice questions in logic may not entitle one to also solve the pressing problems of the nation. Similarly, to believe that the wealth of the richest few is an indication of the progress that we are making as a country is potentially a dangerous form of self-delusion given the fact that income distributions are highly skewed and that one's person's wealth does not translate into prosperity for others.

The good news perhaps is that the India story is real but that it is about the middle, not the top. What has really changed and changed dramatically is the rise of the mediocre. Middle-level colleges in towns of middling size full of ambitious young men and women from the middle of the middle class are where the change is most visible. Drive out of any metropolis and you will see a staggering number of new educational institutions dotting the landscape. The private sector is creating enormous capacities in higher education; one sees dental colleges, medical schools, engineering colleges, management institutes that have sprung up in the last few years. Similarly, there is an entirely new breed of schools that have emerged in small town India that are determined to deliver more effective education. More tellingly, all across India, and increasingly in the larger villages, one can see computer institutes, English-speaking academies and tuition and coaching schools that promise its students better performance in competitive exams. Clearly, the quality of education imparted is patchy, but for the first time, access to the idea of higher professional education has been democratized.

Even when it comes to business, there has been an unleashing of energy of the small entrepreneur. In rural India, the continuous rise of the share of non-agricultural income, coming as a result of people doing an extra job on the side along with farming, is testimony to this trend. The mobile phone has played a key role in freeing business from location, and it is now possible for the enterprising to dream of creating businesses of a scale that are infrastructure independent.

One reason why the economic downturn has not hit India as badly as it could have has to do with the resilience of the middle. Eventually, India's promise lies in its numbers. As a country of more than a billion people, progress for us must be defined in terms that include a majority. The strides made by a privileged minority need to be acknowledged but surely the real story lies elsewhere. In fact it is only when progress moves down one more notch and includes those who are today at the fringes of subsistence, that real progress can be said to have been made. Unlike China, where the engine for growth is driven from the top downwards, growth in India is the result of an upward push by a large fragmented majority that his propelled its way up in spite of massive constraints. In India, we are not basking in a blazing beacon of glory that comes from the top but the light that we see today is the product of a million matchsticks that are flickering in unison. And that is good news.

POSTSCRIPT

When I look back on the journey that this book describes, I am struck by the implicit paradox in the story of a changing India. Underneath the India of yesterday, full as it was of economic stagnation, stifling hierarchy, chaotic disorder and barefaced hypocrisy, lay an elegant mechanism that shaped the way it managed change. For while the idea of India sidesteps a crystallized centre, the internal mechanism of India works through diversity and fragmentation in subtle and complex ways, as it reveals its intent through an intricate network of thoughts and actions revealed over a period of time.

India's speciality has been in the way it manages change, finding ways to simultaneously harness its energy and contain its disruptive influence even when seemingly accommodating it. This untidy and decidedly non-linear process, which has unfolded over a period of time, has been difficult to pin down. But it has helped middle class India find a way of life that it could sustain and find meaning and purpose in.

Now, when India is appearing to embrace change and freeing up its energy in many diverse ways, and as it moves towards becoming a more modern, economically successful and politically assertive society, new questions are emerging. Will change help India transform itself into a more realized version of itself or will the process of being more affluent and powerful make it a version of a globalized market economy? In what way will the structural forces of media, market and democracy reshape India in the times to come? Are these forces of change too strong even for an idea as tested by time and circumstances as India? In seeking growth and prosperity, is the Indian ability to offer new reconciliations and nuanced answers in the danger of being compromised?

Or will we be able to use the growing democracy of the Indian spirit to find our answers in our own way? Will we co-opt the new economic, social and political structures that we are interacting with and align them with our own distinctive view of the world? Will India frame its goals in terms of an economy or a nation-state, or will do it so in civilizational terms?